UPLIFT AND EMPOWER

UPLIFT AND EMPOWER

A GUIDE TO UNDERSTANDING EXTREME POVERTY AND POVERTY ALLEVIATION

DANIELLE HAWA TARIGHA

NEW DEGREE PRESS

UPLIFT AND EMPOWER

A Guide to Understanding Extreme Poverty and Poverty Alleviation

ISBN   978-1-64137-924-3 *Paperback*

          978-1-64137-707-2 *Kindle Ebook*

          978-1-64137-709-6 *Ebook*

To my mom, Grandma Rebecca, and Grandma Hawa
for your unwavering love and support.
To Fellize, for reminding me every day of life is a gift.

CONTENTS

———

INTRODUCTION

Life isn't fair. This is especially true for the world's poorest. But why isn't life fair and what, specifically, contributes to it being so unfair when you are living in extreme poverty?

When I first considered trying to tackle the topic of poverty, I was overwhelmed by the amount of information already available. Decades of research, millions of organizations dedicated to the cause, and people with more advanced degrees than mine who were senior advisers for governments, nonprofits, or think tanks already existed. When I typed "poverty" into my university's library catalog, over sixty thousand results popped up.

At first, my business-focused brain believed my curiosity was new, but as I reflected on my shifting interests over the years, I realized conducting a self-guided deep dive into poverty alleviation was not as random as it seemed. From the third grade, when I developed far-fetched aspirations of becoming the governor of my state, I had an interest in understanding individuals' problems and finding solutions.

However, I knew I could not possibly be the only student curious about wealth inequality. I knew as a low-income student at an elite university, I felt uncomfortably aware of the stark disparities between income levels every time I walked around my historic campus grounds. I knew extreme poverty in a world with over two thousand billionaires just didn't add up.[1]

As I continued to research and interview experts at non-profits, I gained both clarity about the topic and hope for the future. Humanity is closer than it has ever been before to eradicating extreme poverty. From 1990 to today, over one billion people have escaped extreme poverty. Unfortunately, today's dominating poverty framework utilizes policies with serious side effects:

- Giving money for relief becomes crushing debt.
- Inserting outsiders with donor government interests at heart into local communities is morally complex.
- Promoting short-term volunteer projects doesn't provide long-term sustainability.
- Supporting unequal concentrations of power in government and business has become more harmful than good.

These flawed policies are part of the reason why we haven't seen the "solution" to poverty; because as thousands of people escape extreme poverty every day, thousands of others fall into it as well.

A STORY OF HOPE

In May 2017, Davis Nguyen shared a TED Talk called "Solving Poverty Without a Big Wallet" about a backpacking trip he took after graduating university. He traveled around some of the world's poorest villages, which led him to Sapa, a mountain region between China and Vietnam. There he met a woman named Zer-Zer who had lived in Sapa her entire

---

1   Forbes, "Forbes Billionaires 2020," Forbes Magazine, n.d.

life and sold homemade goods to make a living. Without ever entering a classroom, she managed to teach herself four languages. Davis described her as a woman who "loved people, culture, and language."[2]

Both she and her children woke up at 5 a.m. every single day to sell their homemade goods to tourists in the city center. The journey from their home to the city center was three hours long. When they sold goods successfully, they managed to afford food to eat. When they didn't, they had to depend on the leftovers—if there were any at all—from their successful sales days. Davis wanted to help Zer-Zer, but he knew just giving her money would not be the kind of long-term help she deserved. When the money ran out, so too would his impact.

While he lived in Sapa, Davis and his friends noticed one of the most lucrative ways to make a living is by giving tours. They knew Zer-Zer's language skills, coupled with her local knowledge, would make her an incredible tour guide. The major problem she faced was being unable to read and write in English, despite speaking it fluently. To help her support her family, they made flyers for her to promote what would develop into a small tour business. Within one day, Zer-Zer made more than the average Mung family makes in two months.

What Davis and his friends did for Zer-Zer is an excellent example of how new poverty alleviation systems should be built: through partnerships. Partnerships *uplift and empower* rather than refuse or discourage. Partnerships put knowledge in the hands of those who need a chance to help themselves.

---

2   Davis Nguyen, "Solving Poverty without a Big Wallet," Filmed May 2017 at UC Davis, TED video, 9:43.

MORE THAN MONEY

There are over six hundred million people living in extreme poverty globally—the World Bank defines extreme poverty as living on less than US$1.90 per day.[3,4] To end extreme poverty in twenty years, economist Jeffrey Sachs estimates the total cost per year would be about US$175 billion, which happens to be less than 1 percent of the combined income of the richest countries in the world.[5] While most well-intentioned people believe giving away more money, advocating for handouts, sharing hashtags, or writing lengthy posts for popular social movements are the best ways to address poverty, these methods are not enough.

In fact, as of 2017, the US State Department and USAID provided a total of US$50.1 billion in foreign aid around the world, and yet poverty in Sub-Saharan Africa has *increased* since 2016.[6,7]

Throwing money at poverty isn't working because money is one solution to this complex, global problem. In the short run, money pays bills, covers the cost of necessities, and relieves financial pressure. In the long run, money doesn't address structural oppression built into society, teach people how to advocate for themselves, or empower anyone through skills and knowledge. Using only money to eradicate poverty

---

3   World Poverty Clock, "World Poverty Clock."

4   Dean Jolliffe and Espen Beer Prydzp, "Societal Poverty: A Global Measure of Relative Poverty," WDI—Societal Poverty: A global measure of relative poverty, The World Bank, September 11, 2019.

5   United Nations, "Goal 1: End Poverty in All Its Forms Everywhere— United Nations Sustainable Development." United Nations, United Nations, n.d.

6   Ann Simmons, "US Foreign Aid: A Waste of Money or a Boost to World Stability? Here Are the Facts." *Los Angeles Times*, May 10, 2017.

7   World Bank, "Accelerating Poverty Reduction in Africa: In Five Charts," October 9, 2019.

is like putting a band-aid over a protruding, broken bone. The blood isn't the only problem.

To eradicate extreme poverty, we need to advocate for "Money Plus" solutions. These solutions not only provide money to low-income communities, but also address core dimensions of life and help lift people out of poverty, such as:

- Supporting agriculture and providing access to nutritious foods
- Decreasing child mortality rates
- Increasing school attendance for all genders
- Fighting for the rights and ownership of assets like homes and land
- Improving living standards by providing regular and dependable access to necessities like water, electricity, and healthcare

To support this effort, we also need to challenge the current state of society, specifically related to social, political, and economic factors determining the kinds of opportunities made available to people living in poverty.

Over six hundred million people globally are being excluded from opportunities provided to middle- and upper-class populations, consistently denied representation in governance and policymaking, disproportionately affected by human rights violations, and discriminated against without major defense because they can't pay for expensive lawyers.

The US$175 billion per year won't end poverty instantaneously, which means we have time to approach this from a new, well-informed angle. Choosing to take the longer, harder route means we will be able to address and understand the root causes and complex dynamics of extreme poverty.

WHAT WILL YOU LEARN?

If you are a young, ambitious individual looking for a cause to rally behind, a high achiever searching for a way to make an impact, or simply a curious and compassionate world citizen seeking to understand one of humanity's oldest problems, this is the book for you. Really, it's for everyone.

In this work, I will explore the history of poverty alleviation strategies, like foreign aid and welfare, followed by an explanation of poverty alleviation as it stands. I will address the Industrial Revolution's role in global modernization efforts and the creation of an even wider gap between socioeconomic levels that lasts to this day.

I will dive into the psychological impact of poverty and dispel some ill-informed myths around people living in extreme poverty. I will be providing some context for global poverty with a particular focus on those living in extreme poverty and share some stories about approaches to poverty alleviation that have worked or are working and ones that haven't.

I will also address the link between gender equality and poverty alleviation, highlighting case studies of two countries with different relationships to poverty: China and Liberia. Further, I will touch on overpopulation and the relationship between poverty and family planning.

Lastly, I will address modern strategies and technological advancements in poverty alleviation work along with a discussion about the role of wealthy people in poverty alleviation and suggestions for how you and others can get involved in the fight.

What comes next in the world of poverty alleviation comes down to us.

What are we willing to do to eradicate extreme poverty on a global scale?

PART 1

HISTORY AND CONTEXT

WHERE WE ARE

———

In 2015, I was a senior in high school more focused on getting into a good university than solving global issues or even joining my high school's Model United Nations chapter.

Like a lot of high school students, I was awkward all of the time, confused most of the time, and likely spent more time on social media than I should have some of the time. My days were filled with AP, IB, and online classes, cross country or soccer practice depending on the season, student government responsibilities, and a smorgasbord of clubs I felt would make me look well-rounded and interesting to committees of university admissions boards.

Born in London, England and raised in Ocala, Florida, I was a third-culture kid with dreams of spending my university years at a top-tier institution that would be my ticket to ... something great. What that consisted of changed over the years.

In the summer after third grade, I seemed to have it all figured out. Through a combination of free time, boredom, and curiosity, I mapped out the major goal posts of my entire life plan from my bachelor's degree to my career. I decided I would attend Dartmouth College and spend my days studying political science and economics. Why Dartmouth? They have one of the top programs in the United States for studying political science, and my third-grade self would settle for no less than the best. Also, it was because my mother's favorite color is green, which happens to be the school's official color. I was in the third grade, remember? After, I planned on becoming Florida's first female African American governor. Seriously, I did.

Looking back, I think something about reading Sarah Palin's autobiography in the fifth grade sealed the deal. *If a woman could be governor of Alaska,* I thought in my nine-year-old mind, *why couldn't a woman be governor of Florida?* I was a few years ahead of phrases like "feminism" and "women's rights" becoming a part of my vocabulary, but my ambitions were planting seeds in my mind, pushing me to think big and be unafraid of challenges.

My dreams were driven off-course during the 2008 presidential election. Watching and listening as people in my hometown, everywhere from my church to my after-school activities, derided the United States' first Black president throughout his campaign and his two terms in office made me rethink my goals.

Nothing was off limits, not even his family. It became harder to pretend the attacks were not related to his race as time wore on. In the locker room, I once overheard a classmate saying she wanted to "keep the white in the White House." We made eye contact after she spoke. I didn't say anything. Ultimately, I didn't want to subject myself to the malicious attacks that seemed to go hand in hand with running for office. I knew facing backlash for both my race and my gender would be a lot to take on, so I tried my best to pivot.

In middle and high school, I focused on business after noticing the close relationship between political ideas and the money that made things happen. If I couldn't sit behind the desk, I could at least sign the checks.

In high school, I was president of Future Business Leaders of America during my senior year, read business-centric books in my free time, and tried to understand the nuances of building personal wealth. In university, I took my interest to the next level by trying internships within exciting, high-paying industries like finance and technology both in the United States and abroad.

Fast forward to 2020: as a senior in university, I am still not involved in Model United Nations, but my priorities have begun to shift. My perspective began to change again while working in the business world and gaining a first-hand perspective of how and where large sums of money ended up after changing hands every day. It made me realize things are not adding up fairly, at least not for the poorest of the poor.

WHY SHOULD YOU CARE ABOUT EQUALITY?

Your most pressing bills are probably paid. You likely have some sort of shelter to call "home" every night. Assuming you didn't find an illegal download of this book, you had enough spare cash to buy a copy (thank you). So, why should you care?

Well, I would like to hope if all of us care—even just a little bit—about addressing this issue, then we will all be better off for it. A world without people living in extreme poverty, lacking access to basic, fundamental necessities like food, clean drinking water, healthcare, and education, can improve living standards for everyone.

And I don't think this is an "idealistic" point of view.

Is it idealistic to believe everyone can, and should, be millionaires? Yes. Modern, successful economic and political systems are not currently in place to make that a reality. However, it should *not* be considered idealistic for people to fulfill their basic needs regardless of factors outside of their control, like the country they were born in or the amount of rainfall in their town every year—which are real factors contributing to whether a country ends up being rich or poor and, subsequently, contributes to whether or not an individual ends up being rich or poor.

As Anand Giridharadas once said, "There are self-preservationist ways to change the world and there are ways that actually interrogate your own complicity and your own privilege and put it at risk."[8]

I am choosing the latter, and I hope you do too.

SUSTAINABLE DEVELOPMENT GOALS

Let's return to 2015. While I was pondering my future, the actual United Nations was developing the 2030 Agenda for Sustainable Development. First on the list: end poverty in all its forms.

Now, we can shift away from my personal story and shift toward some of the key facts and data necessary to understand extreme poverty.

There are over six hundred million people living in extreme poverty globally and the number of those in extreme poverty in sub-Saharan Africa has *increased* since 2016.[9,10]

---

8 Ezra Klein, "Anand Giridharadas on the elite charade of changing the world," The Ezra Klein Show, Podcast audio, 59:39–59:47, September 4, 2018.

9 "World Poverty Clock," World Poverty Clock.

10 World Bank, "Accelerating Poverty Reduction in Africa: In Five Charts," October 9, 2019.

As we know, Jeffrey Sachs estimates the total cost per year to end extreme poverty would be about US$175 billion, which, as a reminder, is less than 1 percent of the combined income of the richest countries in the world.[11]

I am not advocating for a "quick" transfer of wealth from the rich to the poor or sending more aid to low-income countries.[12] There is historical evidence to support why that *doesn't* work—more on this later. Without governments contributing, there are plenty of organizations focused on addressing the issue. In fact, there are 1.8 million IRS-recognized nonprofit organizations in the US alone and 111,177 of them exist to alleviate poverty.[13]

The natural next question is if non-profit organizations make trillions of dollars a year, how are millions of people still suffering? [14,15] How is it after decades of research, billions in aid dollars, and countless hours of volunteering, there is no clear solution or guide to addressing poverty

---

11   United Nations, "Goal 1: End Poverty in All Its Forms Everywhere—United Nations Sustainable Development," United Nations, n.d.

12   The World Bank classifies the world's economies into four income groups—high, upper-middle, lower-middle, and low based on Gross National Income (GNI) per capita in USD. The classification threshold is updated annually. As of 2019, the thresholds are as follows: Low-income countries have GNI per capita of at or less than 1,026 USD. Lower-middle income countries have GNI per capita between 1,026–3,995 USD. Upper-middle income countries have GNI per capita between 3,996–12,375 USD. High-income countries have GNI per capita of greater than 12,375.

13   Guidestar.org, Directory of Charities and Nonprofit Organizations, Candid.

14   The following value is based on a diverse range of organizations being considered registered nonprofits including universities, labor unions, some hospitals, business and professional organizations, booster clubs, schools, and more. For more information, visit the National Center for Charitable Statistics Website.

15   Brice McKeever, National Center for Charitable Statistics, December 13, 2018.

now? Why, in 2020, are there still so many people who need help affording basic necessities like food, water, housing, and clothing?

Like any curious student, I began to research and try to find answers to these questions and more. I scoured web pages, read books, watched TED Talks, listened to podcasts, and interviewed experts in academia, fashion, social work, and international development around the world attempting to understand this problem and its myriad of potential solutions. The result was this book.

Extreme poverty is defined as living on less than US$1.90 per day.[16] Why US$1.90? The amount is an average of national poverty lines from fifteen poor countries; the general idea being if US$1.90 is equivalent to the cost of basic needs in some of the world's poorest countries, then someone living on less than that per day would be considered poor regardless of their location.[17,18]

In addition to a discussion about extreme poverty, I will share some unique solutions and perspectives on addressing poverty as well.

---

16 World Bank, 2018, Poverty and Shared Prosperity 2018: Piecing Together the Poverty Puzzle, Washington, DC: World Bank. License: Creative Commons Attribution CC BY 3.0 IGO

17 There are higher poverty thresholds depending on the income level and cost of living in different countries. For lower middle-income countries, the poverty line is $3.20 per day. For upper middle-income countries, the poverty line is $5.50 per day. For simplicity's sake, this book focuses solely on the lowest level.

18 Dean Jolliffe and Espen Beer Prydz, "Societal Poverty: A Global Measure of Relative Poverty," WDI—Societal Poverty: A global measure of relative poverty, The World Bank, September 11, 2019.

SO, WHAT CAUSES POVERTY?

The unfortunate truth is oftentimes people assume poor people are fundamentally flawed and deserving of their economic status. This mindset is both harmful and inaccurate.

There is nothing wrong with poor people. They didn't create poverty.

The majority of people living in extreme poverty didn't purposefully put themselves into that position, and if anyone could find evidence of an individual living in poverty wanting to stay poor and struggle, I would be shocked. Poverty is the product of societal systems, concepts, and ideologies both man-made and too detailed to be summarized in this book. Poverty is an external factor of human life, not a reflection of intrinsic characteristics. To be more concise, poverty is multidimensional, complex, and not poor people's fault.

According to World Vision, the root causes of poverty are a lack of access to basic necessities, gender or ethnic discrimination, poor governance, conflict, exploitation, domestic violence, and fragile contexts.[19,20]

That is a lot to unpack, and it's hard to balance when trying to match those factors to the impoverished faces we see in charity advertisements. Nevertheless, discounting one particular element in favor of a focus on another doesn't create an accurate picture either.

In 2018, the United Nations Development Program and the Oxford Poverty and Human Development Initiative

---

19 Andrea Peer, "Global Poverty: Facts, FAQs, and How to Help," World Vision, February 27, 2020.

20 Fragile contexts are areas with higher rates of poverty due to political upheaval, past or present conflict, corrupt leaders, and poor infrastructure that limits access to education, clean water, healthcare, and other necessities. Source: Sevil Omer. "Fragile States: Helping Children in the Worst of All Worlds," World Vision, August 30, 2017.

developed a global multidimensional poverty index.[21] The index is an update on older human poverty indices from the 1990s and early 2000s created to break down factors contributing to poverty.

The three dimensions of poverty they highlight are:
- Health
- Education
- Living standards

Factors like nutrition, years of schooling, and housing make up the ten subsections. These dimensions will be explored with more depth later in the first section of this book.

For now, it is important to know that poverty is caused by a lot of interconnected factors that feed into each other, and more often than not, cause a nearly inescapable cycle for those suffering.

HOW HAS NO ONE FOUND A SOLUTION YET?

If people seem to understand what causes poverty, then why can't it be addressed? I asked this question at first as well, but I think asking it attempts to oversimplify a global issue and discredits the work of governments, nonprofits, volunteers, and generous individuals around the world. Just focusing on one dimension or cause will not be enough to help the over six hundred million people who are suffering.

What *is* working so far is creating and providing opportunities for people, customizing aid solutions to the pain points of communities, and combating corruption. A holistic approach to tackling poverty would address areas like

---

21   Oxford Poverty & Human Development Initiative (OPHI). "Global Multidimensional Poverty Index," UN Development Program (UNDP).

infrastructure and business development, agriculture and environment, education and gender equality, as well as health and nutrition.

There is no one-size fits all solution *yet* because it doesn't exist. Poverty's solutions are as multidimensional and complex as its many causes.

IS THERE ANY REASON TO HAVE HOPE?

I would like to think so.

Before the Sustainable Development Goals, there were the Millennium Development goals. Reducing extreme poverty by 2015 was a central goal for millennium development.[22] Since 1990, more than one billion people have been lifted out of extreme poverty and child mortality has dropped by more than half.[23] In fact, the target for reducing extreme poverty rates by half was met five years before the 2015 deadline.[24] In the general context of human improvement, global poverty has decreased substantially since the 1700s and overall health has improved.

These major strides give me hope we are headed in the right direction and the solutions are not too far out of reach.

---

22 World Health Organization, "Millennium Development Goals (MDGs)," June 25, 2015.

23 "United Nations Millennium Development Goals," United Nations, n.d.

24 Ibid.

"The first thing I would say to those who say that we must come and give, otherwise, these people are incapable of improving their situation and getting out of their poverty is to ask them why. Why do you think that? Why are these people uniquely unable to get out of their poverty? Are you actually saying that they are, in some sense, inferior beings? Are they different from us? Can they not think for themselves? Is there not evidence, in fact, that when given the opportunity, they do, in fact, get out of poverty themselves?"

— THEODORE DALRYMPLE, AUTHOR AND JOURNALIST[25]

25   Kris Mauren, James F. Fitzgerald, Michael Matheson Miller, Jonathan
      Witt, Simon Scionka, Tom Small, Magatte Wade, et al. 2015, Poverty, Inc.

A WAR, A PLAN, AND A NOT-SO-SILVER BULLET

—

In chapter one, I mentioned the trillion-dollar nonprofit industry and made reference to the vast amounts of foreign aid donated between countries over the years. What is foreign aid? To put it simply, it is the money, services, or physical goods one country sends to another to help it in some way.[26]

It is a natural response to the question of how to address poverty: *Can't we just give the poor more money?*

Understanding why the answer is "no" requires taking a step back in time to the mid-1900s when the current concept of international development was born. Specifically, we need to focus on the sensitive period of time after the World Wars when most of Europe was in ruins and needed support to recover.

In this chapter, I will:

---

26 "A Brief History of US Foreign Aid," Council on Foreign Relations, Council on Foreign Relations, World101, n.d.

- share some of the historical context behind foreign aid with a primary focus on the motivations, results, and criticisms of the Marshall Plan
- explore modern attitudes toward foreign aid
- describe how corruption and greed influence foreign aid
- review the debate on the efficacy of foreign aid today

RED, WHITE, AND BLUE

Before I dive in too deep, it's important to clarify my perspective on these issues. Though I was born in England, I was raised in the United States. I studied predominantly US history throughout my entire education because US history was the most popular option available. I watch American TV shows, listen to American music, and celebrate American holidays. Everything I learn and attempt to understand is looked at through an American lens.

Though I have tried my best to work beyond the scope of my limited point of view by reaching out to industry leaders and obtaining information from a wide variety of resources, my process of synthesizing and sharing information will be influenced by my American slant.

Every story has more than one side, which is especially true when considering a topic like history that is rooted in the retelling of past events. The vast majority of the content contained in my work is simply that—factual information and data. Beyond that, when I enter the realm of opinion and my perspective perhaps comes across as too "Americentric," that is likely because it is.

Now, back to the wars.

THE WORLD WARS

World War I brought to an abrupt halt a period of history previously marked by European-led globalization, technological advancement, and the innovations of the Industrial Revolution. After the war, humanitarian relief efforts started up in the states such as the Committee for Relief in Belgium, which received over US$52 million to support war-torn Belgium, and the American Relief Administration, which was a broader effort from the US government to help countries around the world recover from the effects of the war by providing assistance like food, medical aid, relocation services, and more.[27,28]

After World War II, many countries in Europe were in ruins, and some regions of the continent were on the brink of famine. In addition to this hardship, transportation infrastructure like roads, bridges, and railways were also in a dire state. The development efforts after World War I inspired the efforts made after World War II by an army chief of staff: George C. Marshall.

Marshall was one of the key figures behind the Allied victory during World War II and was valued and respected by President Truman. As a result, Truman made George Marshall secretary of state in 1947. Soon after his appointment, Marshall developed the European Recovery Program, better known as the Marshall Plan, which was announced in June of that year.

---

27 "Commission for Relief in Belgium Raises Millions," History of Giving, n.d.

28 Encyclopedia of Russian History Online, s.v. "American Relief Administration," April 16, 2020.

THE MARSHALL PLAN

The goal and purpose of the plan was to:

- inspire cooperation among European nations
- stimulate economic growth in Europe
- diminish the appeal of communism among Europeans

Over the course of four years, Marshall planned to reconstruct cities, industries, and infrastructures impacted during the war. From April 1948 to December 1951, the United States gave US$13 billion, which is approximately US$155 billion in 2020, in aid to struggling European nations. [29, 30]

At the time, the aid sent over was about 5 percent of the US gross domestic product.[31,32] The US shipped food, fuel, machinery, and money to help seventeen countries get back on their feet after the devastation of the war.[33]

The Marshall Plan has been described by USAID as a core component of the modern-day concept of international development assistance and is noted as a form of "good deed foreign policy," but what motivated the United States' leaders to support a plan to give money away to struggling countries? Or rather, why would the United States give away billions of dollars to European countries?

As the designer of the plan, George C. Marshall himself said, "Our policy is not directed against any country, but

---

29 "History of the Marshall Plan," George C. Marshall Foundation, n.d.

30 "Calculate the Value of $13 in 1947," Calculate the value of $13 in 1947, How much is it worth today? n.d.

31 History.com Editors. "Marshall Plan," HISTORY, A&E Television Networks, December 16, 2009.

32 GDP: the total value of goods produced and services provided in a country for one year.

33 The seventeen countries were Austria, Belgium, Denmark, France, Greece, Iceland, Ireland, Italy, Luxembourg, the Netherlands, Norway, Portugal, Sweden, Switzerland, Turkey, the UK, and West Germany.

against hunger, poverty, desperation and chaos."[34] The core motivations were to:

- Bring peace after World War II
- Create new trade partners for the US
- Encourage economic development
- Isolate the Soviet Union and keep it from expanding its sphere of influence beyond Eastern Europe

Establishing peace quickly after the war was crucial because the last time the world left a conquered nation in ruins, Nazi Germany rose to power. So, the United States was able to help avoid a similar situation and try to curtail the start of World War III. When the United States helped those European countries by investing in their economies, it was able to create new markets for its exports as well. This created a win-win situation where the struggling European economies were given the support they needed, and the United States was able to establish strong trading relationships.

The aid helped to spread the image of the United States as a world power. This "new kid on the block" of major global influencers, less than two hundred years after gaining its independence, was able to give billions of dollars in aid to well-established European countries.

The plan helped ensure the US would be able to shine as an economic and military world power long after the war.

DID IT WORK?

Regardless of the motivations behind the plan, the important part is it worked very well. The gross national product of the

---

34 History.com Editors, "George C. Marshall," History.com, A&E Television Networks, October 29, 2009.

Marshall Plan countries grew as much as 25 after the influx of aid.[35,36] It is for this reason it has been used as a guide for how to distribute international aid ever since.

By granting billions of dollars of aid across war torn countries, the United States made capitalism look appealing to countries that did not already have that economic system in place, which also helped to decrease the Soviet Union's influence. The US government went as far as strategically choosing what countries got the most aid based on their relationships to Soviet power.

Nations like Italy that fought with the Axis powers alongside Nazi Germany, and any neutral countries like Switzerland, received less aid per capita than countries that fought with the United States and other Allied countries. A notable exception to this was West Germany. Though all of Germany was impacted by the consequences of World War II, aiding in making West Germany look revitalized after the war was another way to make communism look bad in comparison to capitalism.

In response to the Marshall Plan, the Soviet Union developed its own recovery aid plan called the Molotov Plan that benefited its satellite countries after blocking those countries from receiving aid via the Marshall Plan.

Why? Stalin was wary of the US government's intentions with their plan and thought it was a ploy to infiltrate European countries, not that he was too far off base with his suspicions. In fact, implementation of the Marshall Plan has been

---

35   GNP: a measure of the total monetary value of the output produced by a country's residents.

36   Encyclopedia Britannica, Inc., The Editors of Encyclopedia Britannica, s.v. "Marshall Plan," January 27, 2020.

cited as the beginning of the Cold War between the United States, its European allies, and the Soviet Union.[37]

WHY THIS MATTERS

But wait, what does all of this have to do with poverty alleviation today? A lot.

Because of the success of the Marshall Plan, it became the United States' main approach to all development aid and formed a key component of how high-income countries involve themselves with low-income countries today. The basic idea was by building up infrastructure, electricity, and education, a country could improve its economic status and make a giant leap into industrialism and modernity.

This sounds great on the surface, but the reasoning behind these investments is not always as altruistic as it seems. Oftentimes, the consultants for foreign aid organizations entering the recipient countries end up negatively impacting the relationship between the government and its people by, in some respects, taking its power away or providing an excuse for the donor countries to maintain their strategic geopolitical holds in a region.

While the government is working in service of its citizens, the foreign aid consultants work in service of their home countries, which stifles the local government's ability to strategize, especially in the long run. Beyond this, it is also important to consider the cultural contexts of the countries receiving aid. What seems modern and beneficial from the perspective of someone living in a middle- or high-income country could end up harming community members.

---

37 History.com Editors, "Marshall Plan," HISTORY, A&E Television Networks, December 16, 2009.

The documentary *Poverty, Inc.* provides two helpful examples of how different approaches to helping Haitians after the catastrophic 2010 earthquake had quite different outcomes. The US government sent rice abroad to help provide food to struggling families. At first, the rice was an important resource but over time, as the local Haitian farmers began to recover, the cheap rice from the United States began to compete and suppress the prices of the local rice.

In contrast, an American couple started a business called the Apparent Project to provide Haitians with the opportunity to help themselves. The Apparent Project provided jobs for the locals to make jewelry. The work lets them earn money they can spend as they see fit. One of their jewelry makers was able to make enough necklaces at her job to save up and buy a two-bedroom home for herself and her family. It took her making two hundred necklaces to buy the land and build a home, but everything associated with the property is now hers. A job—an opportunity to pick oneself up—can be more helpful in the long run than foreign aid.

Another major facet of the Marshall Plan to keep in mind is it was a program used to help impoverished countries—that were once high-functioning democracies with strong institutions and infrastructures—get back on their feet. Though it was successful, it had a definitive endpoint due to the Korean War. In contrast, current foreign aid contributions are provided indefinitely (much of Africa has received aid for at least fifty years) which, among other effects, creates a dependency mentality among receiving countries and a superiority complex among donor countries, further dividing them by their income levels.

AN AGENDA HIDDEN IN PLAIN SIGHT

To understand both the significance of the relationships between donor and recipient countries and the US government's strategic choice to use the aftermath of the war to strengthen its influence, it's important to talk about the Truman Doctrine, which was the first of many ways the US government was able to keep communism from spreading. Ultimately, the Truman Doctrine was a form of containment. The strategy was suggested by US diplomat and State Department Advisor George Keenan, who suggested the United States should try to stifle communist influence in Eastern Europe and Asia.

The doctrine originated in 1947 during a speech delivered by President Truman before a joint session of Congress. It said the United States would provide economic assistance to all democratic nations under threat from external or internal authoritarian forces. At the time, the decision led to two outcomes. First, Greece and Turkey received both economic and military aid in response to the Greek Civil War. Second, the United States began to fear a communist victory would lead to political instability in the Middle East.

The doctrine was significant because it changed the approach the United States took toward foreign policy. In the past, the United States stayed out of regional conflicts not directly involving them. The Truman Doctrine established a reason for why the United States would get involved in foreign conflict and intervene in conflict to spread its personal influence. Long story short: money talks, especially when trying to influence and spread ideologies on a global scale.

Is this fair? Is it right to use war, or recovery from war, as a tool to further a government's personal aims or approaches to governance? While that question is a lot to unpack and dives into more international politics than I need to make my point, it does highlight the complexity of the role of foreign aid in foreign policy.

The reality is foreign aid isn't as simple as it may seem. On the surface, foreign aid can be perceived as a tool to give back and look like a good and caring neighbor country. Is that enough to justify the large sums of aid sent abroad year after year?

Usually, the answer is "no." It's more about the influence you gain and the idea that it can be thought of as a sort of IOU between governments. If the United States provides aid now and let's say, hypothetically, years from now a war were to break out and the roles were reversed leaving the United States as a country in desperate need of aid, it would not be surprising if the United States expected military or economic support from its recipient countries.

How did the United States justify all of this? Aside from the US government's fears about communist influence leading to political instability in the Middle East, Truman took a moral high ground by arguing the United States was compelled to assist "free peoples" in their struggles against "totalitarian regimes" because the spread of authoritarianism would "undermine the foundations of international peace and hence the security of the United States."[38,39,40] From Truman's point of view, the United States was protecting individual freedom and capitalist ideals while also attempting to keep them safe from armed minority powers and outside pressure.

---

38 "The Truman Doctrine, 1947," US Department of State, n.d.
39 Ibid.
40 Ibid.

So, what happened after the Marshall Plan took effect and the aid was distributed? To provide a brief, broad summary:

- Western European economies were stabilized.
- The American export economy boomed because they created more trade partners for themselves.
- The Soviet influence of communism ended up being contained to Eastern Europe.

Essentially, all of the goals the plan had at its outset were attained, which is why the Marshall Plan is viewed in such a positive light.

Aid strategies implemented presently aren't as straightforward.

A MILLION-DOLLAR CREDIT LIMIT

The current approach to foreign aid is to give it in perpetuity. However, a major factor contributing to the success of the Marshall Plan was it was a short-term aid project focused on supporting *reconstruction* rather than *economic development.*

When you're given a timeframe for when aid will be allotted, you're able to make plans and create short-term solutions to problems that tie into long-term spending goals *without* the aid.

Think about how you spend your own money. When you expect income, like a salary, to increase your discretionary income, you are able to budget and plan based on expected income. Let's say you hit a rough patch and can no longer afford necessities, but you get short-term help in the form of a loan from a bank. For the next few weeks (or months), you know you will have a bit of help, *but* two important facts are in the back of your mind:

1. After that time frame, you will need to be able to support yourself or apply for another loan.
2. You need to pay the money back.

Alternatively, what if you were in a situation where you received loans over the course of years? Would you start to treat your loans like an income stream in your budget too? It's a tempting trap akin to a credit card with a credit limit in the millions. Overtime, recipient governments begin to expect foreign aid and develop a dependency on the additional income. *This* is where the true problem lies.

Rather than being a short-term solution to help people get back on their feet, foreign aid has become the silver bullet approach to addressing poverty. And the bullet isn't even silver because the solution isn't actually working. While recipient governments receive aid funding that keeps them from becoming self-sufficient, donor governments have been able to impact the futures of their donor countries and sustain their unhealthy levels of influence.

Without the threat of a cutoff point or some sort of indication there will be a time without aid, governments of low-income countries can continue to treat aid as an income source. And why shouldn't they?

Do you remember this old proverb? "Give a man a fish, and you feed him for a day. Teach a man to fish, and you feed him for a lifetime." While the origins of the phrase are contested, the sentiment still stands. Initially, foreign aid was meant to be a form of "teaching," providing stop-gap funding to struggling countries in a way that is beneficial for both sides. Now, foreign aid has become "giving," but nothing in life is free.

These struggling countries need to pay this aid back—with the exception of the free grant money provided to certain governments—which puts pressure on governments and often places countries in debt traps that, in many cases, leave them worse off than before.[41]

QUICK ILLUSTRATION

As an example of the impact foreign aid has on low-income countries and how governments aim to manage its consequences, consider the West African nation Liberia. My family originates from Liberia, which makes it especially important to me. Because of my family history and because it's one of the poorest countries in the world, it will be covered with more depth later in the book.

When former Liberian president Ellen Johnson Sirleaf started her term, one of her main goals was to decrease the amount of debt the Liberian government had. As of 2006, the country was US$4.9 billion in debt.[42] Over the course of her tenure from 2006 to 2018, Sirleaf worked with foreign governments to reduce Liberia's debt. For example:

- The United States waived US$391 million owed to it by Liberia in early 2007.
- German Chancellor Angela Merkel gave Liberia US$324.5 million to help pay off 60 percent of Liberia's debt to the International Monetary Fund (IMF).

---

41 In that context, grant money is viewed as a substitute for domestic revenues. A lot of the countries that received funds under the Marshall Plan didn't end up needing to pay the US back because the money was given in the form of grants, with a slight caveat being that roughly 5 percent of the money was returned from recipient countries to cover the administrative costs of the plan's implementation.

42 Sue Pleming, "US Plans to Cancel $391 Million in Liberia Debt," Reuters, Thomson Reuters, February 13, 2007.

- Liberia qualified for a program by the IMF and the World Bank called the Heavily Indebted Poor Countries (HIPC) Initiative.

HIPCI provides special assistance for low-income countries with high levels of poverty and debt in an effort to ensure poor countries don't face a debt burden they can't manage.

Despite these efforts, Liberia is still very fragile and, as of 2018, its public debt was US$1.2 billion or about 40 percent of its national GDP that year. While the support of foreign aid can be helpful in some contexts, such as recovery from civil war, long-term dependence can have negative consequences.[43] As Dambisa Moyo recognized in chapter three of her book *Dead Aid,* a shocking trend was identified: "Between 1970 and 1998, when aid flows to Africa were at their peak, the poverty rate in Africa rose from 1 percent to a staggering 66 percent."[44]

Are things beginning to get a bit clearer? The most obvious answer to addressing poverty is to give the poor and needy more money, but money does not address structural issues in society; it doesn't directly provide tools and resources to help people uplift themselves, and it should not be considered the only solution or step in the fight against poverty.

A FADING LIGHT

Let's reconsider the Marshall Plan, the guiding light for modern foreign aid, because the plan did receive a fair bit of criticism.

---

43 "Liberia National Debt 2018," countryeconomy.com, October 16, 2019.

44 Dambisa Moyo, Dead Aid: Why Aid Is Not Working and How There Is a Better Way for Africa. 1st American ed. New York: Farrar, Straus and Giroux, 2009.

In particular, critics argued the economic benefit of the plan was not as great as it was perceived to be. As it was mentioned earlier, the GNP for Marshall Plan countries grew up to 25 percent higher than they were before they were given the aid money.[45] Reports from the time period suggested by the time the plan was in effect, Western Europe was already on its way toward recovery and their governments were already starting to improve.

Basically, the plan may have been implemented at a time corresponding with improved economic conditions.

Furthermore, despite the significant investment from the United States to show its economic fortitude, the funds provided were less than 3 percent of the combined national incomes of all of the countries that received aid.[46] That growth of GNP in the countries during the four-year plan could not just have been the result of aid from the Marshall Plan because it represented such a small amount in the context of their national economies. By the last year of the plan, economic growth in the countries surpassed pre-war levels. Even if the plan was not the only contributing factor to economic improvement, it did have an impact.

WHAT ABOUT FOREIGN AID TODAY?

Polls in 2017 showed Americans believe the United States spends 25 percent to 27 percent on foreign aid, but the true

---

45 Encyclopedia Britannica. Encyclopedia Britannica, Inc., The Editors of Encyclopedia Britannica. s.v. "Marshall Plan," January 27, 2020.

46 Ruediger Dornbusch, Nölling Wilhelm, and P.R.G. Layard. Postwar Economic Reconstruction and Lessons for the East Today. (Cambridge, MA: The MIT Press), 1993.

amount is closer to 1 percent.[47,48]Helping those in need is not hurting the United States financially either and "would do very little to reduce the [federal] deficit."[49]

Data from 2016 shows the majority of US foreign aid spending is spent on conflict, peace, and security (such as conflict resolution in war-torn countries). This also has to do with the relationship between foreign aid and US troop deployments—Iraq and Afghanistan receive the most foreign aid from the United States, and there are plenty of US troops on the ground in those countries.[50]

Aside from conflict resolution, recipient countries have different focus areas such as:

- agriculture
- education
- health
- food aid
- emergency response
- energy
- government
- general budget support
- social infrastructure
- reproductive health

Of the top ten recipient countries of US foreign aid, six spent the majority of their funds on conflict resolution.[51] The

---

47 Ann Simmons, "US Foreign Aid: A Waste of Money or a Boost to World Stability? Here Are the Facts," *Los Angeles Times,* November 20, 2017.

48 Ibid.

49 Ibid.

50 There were around twelve thousand US troops in Afghanistan as of October 2019 and around five thousand US troops in Iraq as of March 2019.

51 Raul Amoros, "Tracking Billions of Dollars in Foreign Aid in One Map," HowMuch, December 5, 2017.

others spent the money on reproductive health and emergencies, typically natural disasters like earthquakes and floods.

CORRUPTION AND GREED, OH MY!

But what about corrupt governments stealing the money who are the true villains in the foreign aid narrative?

Throughout the post-screenings of *Poverty, Inc*, the documentary's producers described corruption as a constant.[52] Throughout history, rulers have changed, laws have changed, and citizens themselves have changed. Corruption has remained. Greed and self-interest have always been around and will continue to play a role in human interactions.

For the sake of this book, I am going to consider corruption a constant too. Corruption is assuredly part of the problems keeping poor countries and, more specifically poor people, poor. I will take more time later in the first section of this book to describe the types of institutions primarily maintaining wealthy elites (exclusive institutions) and institutions providing opportunities for the majority (inclusive institutions).

Outside of that, I am going to assume this: given corruption has remained a consistent factor of global development over time, there must be **other**, more specific issues causing problems and sustaining poverty beyond the corruption. Solely blaming corruption focuses on governments, institutions, corporations, and large influences while ignoring the other dimensions of poverty impacting people's lives as well.

Also, while it is important people are vigilant and hold their governments accountable for the kinds of leadership

---

52 "Filmmaker Q&A," Poverty, Inc.

supported abroad, the majority of US economic assistance isn't given to governments.

The Brookings Institution, an American research group, dispelled this myth in a 2018 article about foreign aid when it noted foreign aid allocation could be broken down as follows:[53]

- 20 percent to nonprofit organizations
- 34 percent to multilateral organizations
- 21 percent to governments
- 25 percent elsewhere

Unfortunately, Brookings didn't specify the "elsewhere" category.

CONCLUSION: THE DEBATE CONTINUES

Whether or not foreign aid does more harm than good is still a fiercely debated topic.

Supporters call attention to the impact foreign aid has had on helping to:[54]

- reduce maternal and child mortality
- reduce world hunger
- improve education
- increase access to healthcare
- stabilize nations

Critics call attention to the:[55]

- corrupt leaders and governments supported through foreign aid
- lack of accountability when funds are abused

---

53 George Ingram, "What Every American Should Know about US Foreign Aid," Brookings, October 3, 2019.

54 Ann Simmons, "US Foreign Aid: A Waste of Money or a Boost to World Stability? Here Are the Facts," *Los Angeles Times*, November 20, 2017.

55 Ibid.

- dependency aid creates
- suppression of local food markets
- fact that any money sent abroad could be spent domestically instead

Regardless of what side of the debate people find themselves on, donor government leaders find it easier to sign a check and maintain the current foreign aid system than make any major changes to how or why foreign aid is donated.

Ultimately, if someone needs money, giving them money can be helpful in the short-term, but it is important to remember money alone cannot be the only answer. Foreign aid is one piece of the solution to alleviate global poverty and eradicate extreme poverty. Addressing poverty's root causes, empowering those in need with tools and knowledge to solve their problems, and creating sustainable, long-term support systems are pressing elements of an effective solution as well. Complex problems often have complex solutions that can't be compartmentalized.

At the beginning of this section, I began with a quote from Theodore Dalrymple who questioned why people feel compelled to give and whether or not the compulsion is rooted in a superiority complex. He asks, "Are *they* different from *us*?"

Questioning why donor countries give as much as questioning why recipient countries are in need will help to clarify why we think in terms of "us" versus "them" in the first place.

"You can't pull yourself up by your bootstraps if you have no boots."

—JOSEPH HANLON, ECONOMIST AND JOURNALIST [56]

---

56   Joseph Hanlon, Armando Barrientos, and David Hulme, *Just Give Money to the Poor.* (Boulder: Kumarian Press, 2010), 4.

WHAT IS POVERTY?

When I interned in Hong Kong in 2018, I lived in a small apartment half the size of my current bedroom and shared the space with two other students.

I could wash my hands in the sink while standing in the shower. Our kitchen was a small countertop with a stove that was really just a single, plug-in burner. We stored it away for extra room. There was no closet, so we lived out of our suitcases. When we bought fresh produce, the heat in the room during the day was so strong all of our food would spoil by the time we returned from work in the evenings. To me, that felt like living in poverty.

For hundreds of thousands of people around the world, the fact I had an apartment, a sink, a plug-in burner, enough clothes to fill a suitcase, and enough money to buy fresh produce would feel like living in luxury.

Poverty is relative and incredibly complex. To form any solutions, we must first understand the problem.

In this chapter, I will:

- introduce a new model for describing the world's income levels

- describe some of the core causes of poverty and the different types of poverty that exist today
- provide brief summaries of the poverty theories guiding poverty alleviation work
- and break down the current poverty alleviation system in the United States

A GLOBAL SNAPSHOT: ROBIN, DREW, TAYLOR, AND CAMERON

Eradicating extreme poverty will require a fundamental shift in paradigms and a reconsideration of the way we view and interact with low-income countries, communities, and individuals. In fact, calling people living in poverty "the poor" is an example of this which is why, for the rest of my work, I will be referring to "the poor" with names: Robin, Drew, Taylor, and Cameron.

My intention with the names is to humanize poverty and provide a sense of similarity. I purposefully chose gender neutral names popular in the United States in the hopes you may even know someone or recognize a prominent figure with the same name.

Rather than thinking of low-income individuals in the abstract sense as a distant part of human life, with names people can begin to consider the roles these people play in their communities. A Robin is as much of a family relative, community member, leader, role model, and friend as a Drew, Taylor, or Cameron.

Instead of pitting the "developed" world against the "developing" world, these names represent the four income levels used to describe the world. This practice of dividing the world into four income levels was introduced by Hans Rosling, a Swedish physician and academic who co-authored the award-winning book *Factfulness*. Now, not only does Rosling use this model, but so do Bill Gates and the World Bank.

The reasoning behind the idea is to move away from the outdated and nebulous titles of "developing" and "developed." A planet with over seven billion people in it living at various levels of income and comfort shouldn't be described by two vague categories.

Instead, the world is categorized by income level. This gives a more accurate picture than simply saying "rich" or "poor." With levels, every dollar counts. In particular, the four income levels divide the world based on gross national income per capita because GNI measures all of the money businesses and people in a country earn as income.

Business Insider created a helpful summary of the system I will use to describe the levels, in addition to their corresponding names, along with information shared by Gapminder, an organization focused on fighting misconceptions about global development founded by Hans Rosling and his children.[57,58] Any time I use the phrase "the poor" from now on, it will be in quotes to indicate I am using it in reference to someone else's ideas and wording.

Level 1 is the income level most relevant to this work. This is the segment of the world's population living on less than US$2 a day.[59] Level 1 individuals will now be referred to by the name **Robin**.

The Robins of the world:

- primarily walk as their form of transportation

---

57 Cambridge English Dictionary, Cambridge University Press, s.v. "Paternalism: Definition in the Cambridge English Dictionary."

58 "About Gapminder," Gapminder.

59 "Four Income Levels," Gapminder.

- cook over open fires
- fetch water via buckets
- sleep on the ground

Robins have more children than the global average of two per household because they need their children for labor; they have less access to contraceptives and sex education, and having more children helps to defend against the high child mortality rate among people living in extreme poverty.[60]

Level 2 individuals make between two to eight dollars a day.[61] These individuals will fall under the name **Drew**.

The Drews of the world:
- ride bikes instead of walking everywhere
- have a gas canister for cooking instead of open fire
- fetch water via tap
- own mattresses rather than sleeping on the floor

One major illness or extreme weather event could push the Drews of the world back into extreme poverty with the Robins.

Level 3 individuals will be represented by the name **Taylor**. The Taylors of the world live on anywhere from eight to thirty-two dollars a day.[62]

The Taylors of the world:
- ride motorbikes or mopeds
- cook their meals on stoves
- fetch water via tap
- sleep in homes with multiple rooms

Taylors can afford to go on vacation occasionally, and their kids have likely finished high school.

---

60 "Income Level 1," Gapminder.
61 "Income Level 2," Gapminder.
62 "Income Level 3," Gapminder.

The majority of the world's population lives in either level 2 or level 3.

Level 4 individuals are the richest of the group and will be represented by the name **Cameron.** The world's Camerons make US$32 a day or more.[63]

The Camerons of the world:

- ride cars—sometimes multiple in the same household
- cook their meals on stoves or in microwaves or eat in restaurants to save time
- have running water, both hot and cold, at home for baths, showers, and cooking
- sleep in homes with multiple rooms and may even have multiple homes

RELATIVE POVERTY VERSUS ABSOLUTE POVERTY

The four major income levels are a helpful way to contextualize the differences between relative and absolute poverty.

Relative poverty, in this context, would be represented by the difference between Drews, Taylors, and Camerons. Though their income levels differ, their basic needs are met for the most part. Maybe Drews and Taylors, depending on where you are from, would not be considered middle class, but they are not as low-income as Robins. Their children can attend schools and receive vaccinations and they can travel abroad for vacation.

Relative poverty explains why a person living at the poverty line in the United States is considered to be part of the richest 14 percent of the world's population and explains why, from a Cameron's perspective, Robins, Drews, and Taylors

---

63   "Income Level 4," Gapminder.

look equally poor.[64] It also explains why it matters there are millionaires while people are living in abject poverty—especially in the context of a world where people are easily able to compare their ways of living to others.

In contrast, the world's Robins live in absolute poverty. Each day is a struggle for survival met with vast uncertainty regarding whether or not they, or their children, will be able to eat, find drinking water, or have a good night's rest. Robins live in a state of economic and emotional distress.

Why is this distinction so important? Because our general sense of well-being is tied to both our absolute wealth *and* our relative wealth. Further, as the Roslings mentioned in *Factfulness*, "Often it takes several generations for a family to move from Level 1 to Level 4."[65]

HUMAN CAPITAL

Poverty is essentially a lack of human capital, but what is human capital and why is it so important in our lives?

Human capital is not just an HR term tossed around in corporate work environments. In economics, human capital is the skills people have. It is an individual's intangible assets if things like their job, money, or home were taken away.[66] Think things like specialized training or higher education. These all contribute to a person's human capital.

---

64 "Information on Developing Countries—Population, Distribution, Growth and Change—National 5 Geography Revision—BBC Bitesize," BBC News.

65 Hans Rosling, Ola Rosling, and Rönnlund Anna Rosling, *Factfulness: Ten Reasons Were Wrong about the World—and Why Things Are Better Than You Think.* (London: Scepter, 2019), 46.

66 Charles J. Wheelan, *Naked Economics: Undressing the Dismal Science: Fully Revised and Updated*, (New York: W.W. Norton & Company, 2019.)

This form of capital is especially important because it sometimes makes the difference between whether a person can or cannot travel for work opportunities. Today, point-based immigration systems are in place in countries like Canada, Australia, the United Kingdom, and New Zealand. Those systems factor in points based on educational level, wealth, language fluency, and more.

Human capital doesn't just include education, training, and work experience, it also relates to characteristics like perseverance, honesty, and creativity—important elements when trying to find and keep a job.[67]

Human capital is what contributes to the creation of new opportunities and innovation. It makes people richer and healthier. This form of capital is shared generationally as well. Parents with high levels of human capital invest in the human capital of their children and the cycle continues down the family lines. When low-skilled jobs can't be automated, young people typically take them on to build up their human capital. Building and investing in human capital is what leads to growth and improvement in societies. Now, more than ever before, human capital has become a crucial factor for the advancement of individuals and, more broadly, for nations.

"Human capital is the primary form of wealth in a modern economy."[68] As automation takes over the simple elements of our lives, our capacity to handle the complexity in our lives—our human capital—will be in high demand. What makes human capital more important for the world's Robins is it can't be taken away. Machines can take over low-skilled jobs and financial capital can be destroyed during rough

---

67   Ibid.
68   Ibid.

economic cycles, but education, training, skills, and innate abilities can never be separated from who you are.

In the third section, I will spend more time discussing the increasing industry demands for human capital and describe how jobs and careers will change in the twenty-first century.

Earlier, I mentioned the word wealth. It's important to make a distinction between money and wealth in the context of poverty alleviation before I continue because money alone is not the catch-all solution to addressing extreme poverty in the world.

In fact, to economists, money and wealth are distinct concepts. Money is considered a subset of wealth, a medium of exchange to buy things.[69] Almost every currency in the world has no intrinsic value aside from its purchasing power. The entire system is based on our confidence we will be able to use our money to buy things we need. In contrast, wealth consists of objects that have value—things like houses, cars, commodities, and *human capital*.[70] Our level of wealth is what contributes to our standard of living and quality of life.

The end goal of poverty alleviation should be to make the world's Robins wealthier, not just give them more money.

WHAT CAUSES POVERTY?

Let's return now to what factors contribute to and perpetuate poverty. Once the root causes are understood, identifying solutions will be easier.

As I mentioned in the first chapter, in 2018 the United Nations Development Program and the Oxford Poverty and Human Development Initiative developed a global

---

69   Ibid.

70   Ibid.

multidimensional poverty index in an attempt to outline how the various dimensions of poverty were divided. Now that we have more background information, I can explain the index in more depth.

The first dimension is health, which includes:[71]

- nutrition
- child mortality rate

The second dimension is education, which includes:[72]

- years of schooling
- school attendance

The third dimension is living standards, which includes access to:[73]

- cooking fuel
- sanitation
- safe drinking water
- electricity
- flooring
- asset ownership

These dimensions are a helpful framework for understanding where problems for Robins begin. For example, because living standards impact quality of life, you can imagine a Robin having inconsistent access to electricity and lacking safe drinking water would lead to them feeling more impoverished than their neighbor who may make enough money to afford bottled water.

The poverty population is much more diverse than many people imagine. It's an elaborate mix of people of different ages, races, sexes, geographic locations, and family structures.

71 Oxford Poverty & Human Development Initiative (OPHI), "Global Multidimensional Poverty Index," UN Development Program (UNDP).

72 Ibid.

73 Ibid.

However, at each level of income, regardless of location, people's lives look quite similar.

To prove this point, Gapminder put together a project they termed Dollar Street to create a visual guide of what life at various levels looks like. The Robins, Drews, Taylors, and Camerons of the world can find common ground between their lives and the lives of those in other countries, not based on religion or culture or country, but through income.

Within these similarities, populations are still large and diverse. This is crucial because it helps to explain why it is hard to say with certainty what the generalized **causes** of poverty are. What can cause one person's economic downfall can simply be a blip in the road for another. We have indices and research and data on our side, but more often than not, every nuance isn't covered.

This is the first complication to poverty policy: it's hard to create generalized solutions to problems when dealing with so many different individuals.

MULTIPLE FACTORS, CAUSES, AND CHALLENGES

Each individual living in poverty also faces many challenges. For example, living in resource-poor communities leads to low-income students attending subpar schools, developing restricted social networks, and lacking access to sanitation. Poverty is also related to increased bouts of terrorism because terrorists hide in areas of extreme poverty.[74]

In areas of extreme poverty, it is common to discover populations have restricted property rights, leading to issues in building wealth in the long term. As discussed earlier, the

---

74   Hans Rosling, Ola Rosling, and Rönnlund Anna Rosling, *Factfulness: Ten Reasons Were Wrong about the World—and Why Things Are Better Than You Think*, (London: Scepter, 2019).

misuse of foreign aid funds also relates to poverty. The poverty-stricken in low-income countries hardly see the aid flows enter their countries. In fact, the Organization for Economic Co-operation and Development (OECD) "has estimated that developing countries lose an estimated 3 times more to tax havens than they receive in foreign aid each year."[75,76]

Lastly, psychological factors also impact the lives of people living in extreme poverty because living in poverty develops a scarcity mindset, making it harder for individuals to make rational decisions. The idea of a scarcity mindset will be discussed in more depth in the second part of this book.

These factors only skim the surface of the tangential impacts of life in poverty.

A major challenge to understanding the root causes of poverty is there are a lot of different ways to measure poverty based on both absolute and relative standards. These measures are not without their flaws though.

NUMBERS IN MOTION

Official standards of poverty don't differentiate between families only a few dollars below the poverty line and families with incomes substantially below the poverty line. This line is critical because ignoring it leads to the static fallacy. The static fallacy is the idea that the number of Robins in the world is fixed, so reallocating wealth to them will instantaneously bring an end to poverty.[77] The reality is that the over

---

75 The OECD is a forum of countries working together to stimulate economic progress and world trade.

76 Ike and Robert Guthrie, "Tax Evasion: The Main Cause of Global Poverty," Africa at LSE, March 3, 2014.

77 James L. Payne, *Overcoming Welfare: Expecting More from the Poor—and from Ourselves*, (New York, NY: Basic Books), 1998.

six hundred million people living in extreme poverty are not a static population. As people escape extreme poverty, more fall into it as well for a wide variety of reasons.

I mentioned earlier from the 1990s until now nearly one billion people had escaped poverty in the world.[78] That is a statistic worth rejoicing over. That amount of improvement in poverty reduction, so quickly, has no historical precedent. However, the truth behind it is the majority of that number—around four hundred million—came from poverty alleviation efforts that took place specifically in China.[79]

In contrast, from the 1970s to the 2000s in the United States progress against poverty slowed.[80] What led the change?

A few key reasons:

1. An increased amount of families with children were headed by single women.[81]
2. Wages for workers stagnated during that time period, primarily for low-skilled workers with limited education.[82]
   a. The workers benefitting from income gains were the college educated who were better prepared for the United States' shift from a manufacturing economy to a global economy based on the transfer of information.[83]

---

78 "United Nations Millennium Development Goals," United Nations, n.d.

79 Kris Mauren, James F. Fitzgerald, Michael Matheson Miller, Jonathan Witt, Simon Scionka, Tom Small, Magatte Wade, et al. 2015. Poverty, Inc.

80 Harrell R. Rodgers, *American Poverty in a New Era of Reform*, (London; New York: Routledge, Taylor et Francis Group, 2015).

81 Ibid.

82 Ibid.

83 Ibid.

3. Welfare spending during the time period could not keep up with the increased number of individuals receiving welfare.[84]

   a. In China's case, researchers have come to a general consensus its shift from a centrally planned to a market-based economy in the 1970s is a major reason for the improvement, not foreign aid. I will go more in-depth into China's miraculous poverty turn around in the second part of this book.[85]

I made this distinction between two global powers to show how, though things are improving, we have a long way to go to eradicate poverty *globally*.

WHO "DESERVES" HELP?

The flawed standard we use to define poverty also influences our perception of what poverty looks like.

These perceptions then shape our thoughts on whether or not the Robins and Drews of the world should be helped. Rutger Bregman, author of the book *Utopia for Realists,* explains this as the separation between "deserving poor" and "undeserving poor," which he describes as a major obstacle to a world without poverty. The distinction is rooted in the idea life without poverty is a privilege people should work for rather than a human right. The undeserving poor are considered the "underclass."

Some scholars define the underclass as low-income individuals in struggling inner-city neighborhoods. Others consider people who live in poverty long-term as the true

---

84 Ibid.

85 Kris Mauren, James F. Fitzgerald, Michael Matheson Miller, Jonathan Witt, Simon Scionka, Tom Small, Magatte Wade, et al. 2015, Poverty, Inc.

"underclass." With long-term poverty also follows other issues like chronic unemployment, drug use, and crime.[86]

For those who care, we have a choice. We can continue to debate who "deserves" help and who doesn't, or we can decide to help anyone living a life that denies them of their dignity as human beings. We can reject the argument personal factors leading to their situation should determine whether or not they are helped.

AN INTRODUCTION TO POVERTY THEORY

Though a fundamental shift should be the long-term goal for how to address poverty, in the short-term, individuals and organizations have to learn and work within the current system. Given this context, let's explore how people have engaged with and described poverty and its alleviation in the past.

In 2000, the late Dr. Harrell Rodgers, Jr. published a book called *American Poverty in a New Era of Reform.* In the work, he described specific theories of the causes of poverty and divided them into two broad categories: cultural and behavioral theories and structural and economic theories. He describes structural and economic theories as "usually containing some behavioral component but argue that the main factor causing poverty is a lack of equal opportunities."[87] In contrast, cultural and behavioral theories, "argue that the only real cause of poverty is the behavior, values, and culture of people living in poverty."[88]

86 Harrell R. Rodgers, *American Poverty in a New Era of Reform,* (London; New York: Routledge, Taylor et Francis Group, 2015).

87 Ibid.

88 Ibid.

Some examples of these differences can be explained through books written by authors on both sides of the spectrum. Rodgers provided helpful summaries of the core arguments made by these authors, and I have done the same here to add context and clarity to prominent poverty theories.

CULTURAL AND BEHAVIORAL THEORIES

Let's start with major voices within the realm of cultural and behavioral theories. First, Myron Magnet, author of *The Dream and the Nightmare (1993)*, argued the basic cause of poverty is the culture and behavior of "the poor." He believed low-income people ended up in their situations because they lacked the initiative to take on the opportunities available to them. The major criticism of his argument was he focused on the highly visible underclass despite the fact most of "the poor" aren't as dysfunctional as he described.

The next important author was Charles Murray who wrote *Losing Ground* (1984). Murray argued welfare was the true enemy of "the poor" because it damaged incentives and motivations by making it more lucrative not to work. He argued the best way to reduce poverty is to abolish welfare.

On the same side of the spectrum, Lawrence Mead wrote two important books on poverty and welfare in the United States—*Beyond Entitlement: The Social Obligations of Citizenship* (1986) and *The New Politics of Poverty: The Nonworking Poor in America* (1993). He believed welfare systems didn't include enough requirements for its recipients, especially work requirements. He believed the welfare system did not place enough confidence in the abilities of "the poor" and long-term welfare dependence was the wrong solution for helping the able-bodied poor.

More recent works in this area include books like *The End of Poverty* published by Jeffrey Sachs in 2005. In his work, his core solutions for poverty alleviation center on factors like virtue ethics—such as compassion, discernment, and trustworthiness—to correct behaviors that perpetuate poverty. His work highlights the role of higher income countries funding and supporting lower income countries due to the harmful effects of life in poverty. To support his work and aid in his understanding of poverty, he lived in extreme poverty himself.

STRUCTURAL AND ECONOMIC THEORIES

On the other side of the poverty theory spectrum, there are structural and economic theories. One impactful author in this space is William J. Wilson, author of *The Truly Disadvantaged* (1987). He explored the relationship between civil rights laws and economic opportunity in the United States. He had four core hypotheses to describe his findings:

1. His first hypothesis was factors like slow economic growth and skills mismatch harm low-income, low-skilled workers—especially in the Black community—who lived in central cities.
2. His second hypothesis was increased unemployment led men to idleness and criminal activities.
3. His third hypothesis was civil rights and affirmative action laws made these issues worse because they led to selective out-migration.[89]

---

89 Selective out-migration is the trend of highly educated and highly skilled residents in impoverished areas moving into places like the suburbs.

4. His fourth hypothesis was due to selective out-migration, impoverished communities lost their best role models and leaders and were instead left with people who lacked human capital.

His critics argued he, as a Black scholar, did not focus enough on racial discrimination against the Black community as a contributing factor to poverty.

Micky Kaus with his work *The End of Equality* (1995) also made great contributions to structural and economic poverty theories. He argued welfare may not cause poverty, but it sustains it. He supported his point by noting before welfare, "the poor"—notably Blacks in the South—migrated to the North for work because they had no other choice. When welfare was introduced, they did have a choice. Either they could follow jobs or qualify for welfare and become idle. Many chose idleness.

In his work *Race Matters* (1993), Cornel West argued self-destructive behavior of "the poor" reflected not only economic but cultural failings in the United States at large. He argued increasing economic opportunities would not solve the fundamental problems facing low-income communities. Within low-income, Black communities in particular, he argued altering cultural values and de-emphasizing materialism, providing more government programs for struggling families, and encouraging Black leaders were all necessary.

James Tobin was a popular economist and Nobel laureate who had great influence on macroeconomic theories during the twentieth century. He is best known for his research on the relationships between financial markets and macroeconomics. He believed the impact of economic performance on poverty had decreased overtime for five core reasons:

1. First, he argued increasing amounts of the population were being excluded from economic opportunities because they lacked the necessary skills to obtain higher-paying jobs.
2. Second, better-paying jobs for low-skilled workers are moving outside of central cities.
3. Third, wage rates are decreasing because cheaper labor is available overseas.
4. Fourth, the welfare population increasingly includes female heads of households and poorly educated single males who Tobin argues are not pursing available opportunities.
5. Fifth, he argued the Federal Reserve Bank—as of 1994—was not allowing the economy to grow fast enough.

More recently, the book *Poor Economics* was published by Abhijit Banerjee and Esther Duflo in 2011. In the work, they lean on decades of research and hundreds of randomized control trials they conducted in their lab to learn more about the economics of poverty. They argue poverty alleviation work has failed in the past because we still don't thoroughly understand the nature of poverty. Their experimental approach to eradicating extreme poverty earned them the Nobel Prize in Economics in 2019.

In summary, the structural and economic theories argue poverty is caused by a lack of economic opportunities, inadequate government policies, and discrimination based on race and sex.

WHAT HAVE WE LEARNED SINCE?

In reviewing all of these theories, a few key themes stand out. Namely:

- Poverty is not one problem but rather a series of complex problems rooted in culture, behavior, societal structure, and economics.[90]
- A healthy economy is a crucial component of creating a healthy ecosystem for low-income individuals to pursue and take advantage of opportunities.[91]
- Individuals will not feel confident or prepared enough to pursue the opportunities available to them if they don't have the proper education, job training, or support like childcare.[92]

THE CURRENT POVERTY ALLEVIATION SYSTEM

So, how does all of this theory get applied today?

In the United States, the poverty alleviation sector can be thought of as a funnel system. Tax dollars are allocated and channeled down to donor governments and aid agencies. From there, the money is funneled to recipient governments who give the money to companies that work on aid projects to support struggling communities, build up infrastructure, and more.

The key players in this poverty space are the influential individuals at each node within the poverty alleviation system: government leaders, aid agency presidents and chairpersons, social entrepreneurs, celebrity philanthropists, nongovernmental organizations, and major corporations.

To make things a bit clearer, consider the following example: every year, the majority of law-abiding citizens in the United States give their money to the government in the form

---

90   Ibid.
91   Ibid.
92   Ibid.

of tax dollars. Let's assume, for the sake of this example, the US government collects US$1,000,000 in taxes. This number is nowhere near the real amount, but it keeps things simple.

This US$1,000,000 is then allocated across a variety of expenses. Most notable for this work, some of the money is allocated to aid agencies.

If you remember from the last section, about 1 percent of US tax dollars goes to foreign aid.[93] This means US$10,000 would go toward aid agencies.

The breakdown of this US$10,000 of foreign aid was also discussed: 20 percent to nonprofit organizations, 34 percent to multilateral organizations, 21 percent to governments, and 25 percent to an unspecified "elsewhere" category.[94]

How does this US$10,000 get spread out?

- US$2,000 to nonprofits
- US$3,400 to multilateral organization
- US$2,100 to governments
- US$2,500 to the "elsewhere" spending

Let's return again to our poverty alleviation funnel system example. The tax dollars—US$100,000—are allocated and funneled down to donor governments and aid agencies. From there, the money is funneled to recipient governments—US$2,100—who give the money to companies working on aid projects to support struggling communities, build up infrastructure, and more.

Assuming the nonprofits—US$2,000—and multilateral organizations—US$3,400—tax dollars support are being funded separately, that US$2,100 given to recipient governments has to stretch quite far to support the companies it

---

93 George Ingram, "What Every American Should Know about US Foreign Aid," Brookings, October 3, 2019.

94 Ibid.

helps (think costs like salaries, operating expenses, overhead, etc.) *and* their aid projects.

This small amount does not cover much in the grand scheme of things. Keep that in the mind the next time a nonprofit reaches out for a donation!

While it is great to have all of these people working on this critical issue, the results of their actions are not always aligned with the progress they are hoping to see.

DO THEY KNOW IT'S CHRISTMAS TIME? YES.

A helpful example of this misalignment was highlighted in the documentary *Poverty, Inc* which premiered in 2014. The filmmakers described the impact of the popular Christmas song, "Do They Know It's Christmas?" written by Bob Geldof and Midge Ure. While the song drew attention to some of the issues facing low-income countries and encouraged people to take action, it also perpetuated the stereotype of African countries being barren lands with no resources, no educated people, and no progress, which is not helpful for encouraging a new perspective of what the future of low-income countries could become.

Despite its controversy and heartfelt but misguided message, it had a major impact and encouraged many people to donate money to support relief efforts. Even my hometown priest shared that his mother donated her pension for a month to help support the famine relief efforts the song highlighted.

In the end, a lot of the relief money was used by Ethiopia's military dictatorship, which made the famine in the country worse by poisoning their enemies' farms. The famine was caused by the corrupt government at the time and its misuse of international aid. The popularity of the song and the entire movement led to millions of dollars in donations from people all over the world which is a positive effect from these kinds of campaigns. Despite this, it aided in spreading misinformation about the potential for Ethiopians to help themselves given the proper resources. Initiatives should not come at the cost of truth. With large, global campaigns, it is even more crucial to ensure funds are used correctly.

And lastly, Ethiopians did likely know it was Christmas time. Ethiopia is one of the oldest Christian nations in the world.[95]

THE PERILS OF PATERNALISM

Should large-scale, celebrity studded events raising large amounts of money for charities continue if they unintentional perpetuate harmful stereotypes?

At the moment, there is no right side of the debate.

Drawing attention to social problems is important for raising money, finding volunteers, and incorporating unique points of view into problem solving. However, if the attention is placed on negative factors—like "barren lands," a lack of education and progress, etc.—instead of on the potential for growth, it can promote harmful ideas.

The current system also enables paternalism, which is an important word to remember throughout this work. The Cambridge dictionary defines paternalism as "thinking or behavior by people in authority that results in them making decisions for other people that, although they may be to those people's advantage, prevent them from taking responsibility

---

95 Brian Stiller, Todd M. Johnson, Karen Stiller, and Mark Hutchinson, *Evangelicals around the World: A Global Handbook for the 21st Century,* (Nashville, TN: Thomas Nelson, 2015), 240.

for their own lives."[96] The word is helpful when describing the relationship between low-income and high-income individuals.

To take this idea out of the abstract, consider the tone of voice sometimes adopted by volunteers at soup kitchens, homeless shelters, or similar locales. Do you hear voices getting higher? Does it sound as if people are chatting with young children? That is one illustration of the impact paternalism can have on human interactions. In comparison to crippling debt, it sounds harmless; but the idea the rich need to take care of, shepherd, shelter, or guide the "helpless" poor allows for this current system to continue and creates larger divides between people from different income levels. Helplessness translates to childishness and high-income people treat low-income people as though they are not adults.

This example brings me to a point referenced within the documentary as well by Andreas Widmer, director of entrepreneurship programs at the Catholic University of America's Busch School of Business: "Within a harmful framework, successful innovation makes a harmful system more effectively harmful."[97] The eye-opening example shared in *Poverty, Inc.* to illustrate this point is the popular company Tom's Shoes. The enterprise has a business model many are familiar with: every time you buy a pair of shoes, a pair of shoes is given to a child in need.

---

96 Cambridge English Dictionary, Cambridge University Press, s.v. "Paternalism: Definition in the Cambridge English Dictionary."

97 Kris Mauren, James F. Fitzgerald, Michael Matheson Miller, Jonathan Witt, Simon Scionka, Tom Small, Magatte Wade, et al. 2015, 49:57—50:05, Poverty, Inc.

Again, a new layer of analysis is required. While on the surface, this sounds impactful and creates an easy way for people to engage with social issues, it is a short-term solution to a long-term problem. Think back to the fish proverb and the importance of teaching rather than giving, or the impact imported rice had on local food markets in Haiti.

In giving shoes, business is taken away from any local cobblers in the community who may have been supporting their families. Further, it begets the question: is the plan to continue giving shoes to this community in perpetuity? Would it not be better to provide tools for people to make their own shoes and eventually no longer need outside aid?

In this case, giving away shoes helps address the short-term need as many people in low-income communities do need shoes, but it does not address the underlying issues relating to *why* people in low-income communities can't afford to buy shoes.

Making changes within a broken system is not as effective as changing the system to address the needs of low-income populations.

CONCLUSION

This chapter outlined what poverty is, what some of its root causes are, and provided just a peek into the challenges facing low-income populations. From there, we looked at the major theories influencing poverty alleviation strategies, and we ended with an example of how poverty theory is applied to the current poverty alleviation system.

These concepts, ideas, terms, and frameworks are pivotal points referenced throughout the book. I have already mentioned why money is not enough to eradicate extreme poverty a few times now, but *just* education isn't enough either. Neither is *just* clean water. Or *just* nutritious foods. Those necessities are important for human survival, but we can do better.

This is not a book about helping *you* eradicate extreme poverty. Rather than seeking to "save the poor," we should seek out opportunities to help people living in extreme poverty save *themselves*.

As you continue through this book, you will gain more insights into what extreme poverty is and how it impacts people's lives. With this knowledge, my hope is you will be able to contribute to poverty eradication within your community *first* before looking beyond your backyard.

"Almost all electricity around the world, whether it's from coal or nuclear power, is just a steam engine. It's all still just water and heat. It speaks to how truly revolutionary the Industrial Revolution was that since then, it's really just been evolution."

—JOHN GREEN, AUTHOR AND CONTENT CREATOR[98]

98 CrashCourse, "Coal, Steam, and The Industrial Revolution: Crash Course World History #32," YouTube video, August 30, 2012.

THE PROMISE OF PRODUCTIVITY: INDUSTRIAL REVOLUTION

———

When I first started to gather information about the Industrial Revolution, I thought I was prepared. *I've taken US history classes.* I thought. *There's one anyway, and it was one hundred-ish years long.*

I was wrong.

According to experts like Klaus Schwab, it turns out there are four distinct industrial revolutions. Schwab is the founder and executive chairman of the World Economic Forum and author of the book *The Fourth Industrial Revolution*. He argues we are currently in the middle of the Fourth Industrial Revolution. Schwab describes these time periods as the appearance of "new technologies and novel ways of perceiving the world [that] trigger a profound change in economic and social structures."[99]

In this chapter, I will:

- dive into some of the details of these pivotal periods within history
- connect the Industrial Revolutions to how we view social classes today
- show why the Fourth Industrial Revolution is critical to helping improve the lives of today's Robins
- provide an example of how humans have managed to time travel in the 21st century

THE AGRARIAN REVOLUTION

The lives many of us live now are on par with the utopias envisioned by scholars of the Middle Ages. Around 270 years ago, the majority of the world's population lived at level one in dire, extreme poverty. Before the 1800s, most human power came from our own physical strength, followed by the use of animals, then elements like water and wind. Most humans at the time rarely owned or used objects outside of their communities—with the exception being the wealthiest of the population.

The period immediately before the Industrial Revolution was the result of the Agrarian Revolution. During this time period, around 80 percent of the world's population farmed.[100] As of 2018, approximately two billion people—

---

99 Klaus Schwab, *The Fourth Industrial Revolution*, (London: Portfolio Penguin, 2017.)

100 Simple History, "The Industrial Revolution (18–19th Century)," YouTube video, 2:37, October 1, 2017.

constituting roughly 26 percent of the world population—base their livelihoods primarily on agriculture.[101]

Between the eighteenth and nineteenth century, agricultural production increased, leading to larger population sizes and a boost in trade. As more machines were used in farming, less labor was needed, which freed up workers to enter industrial markets in urban areas.

Depending on who you ask, the Industrial Revolutions can be separated by what countries they impacted the most. For example, some argue the First Industrial Revolution predominantly impacted England while the Second Industrial Revolution predominantly impacted the United States. This understanding is a helpful way to divide the historical periods, so keep those countries in mind as we continue.

THE FIRST INDUSTRIAL REVOLUTION

The First Industrial Revolution lasted from around 1760 to 1840 and was primarily notable for the invention of the steam engine. I don't know much about science, but I do know when you heat up water, steam forms. This sounds basic, but this fact changed the course of history. Steam power helped largely agrarian societies industrialize and revolutionized human productivity.

Cotton mills, machines, ships, steamboats, trains, wagons, and more could all be made better, faster, and more efficient through steam power.[102] We have James Watt—in case you're wondering, yes, the unit of power is named after him—to thank for this. He improved the Newcomen steam

---

101 "Industrial Agriculture and Small-Scale Farming," Weltagrarbericht.
102 CrashCourse, "Coal, Steam, and The Industrial Revolution: Crash Course World History #32," YouTube video, 11:04, August 30, 2012.

engine that was popular at the time and ushered in these major changes.[103]

Before we continue, how does all of this historical context relate to extreme poverty?

A helpful way to conceptualize how income levels— remember the world's Robins, Drews, Taylors, and Camerons—influence life is to overlay that idea with developments during each industrial revolution.

Each income level can be roughly correlated to an industrial revolution to provide a clearer picture of what life is like.

Life during the First Industrial Revolution is the equivalent of life at level one today. Robins have access to basic technologies and rudimentary machines to make life easier and faster than doing everything by hand. This is life at less than US$2 a day.

Robins' homes are made from a natural material like mud and are very vulnerable to bad weather and theft because they have no locks. Robins' family members could die due to treatable illness and infections because of their lack of access to antibiotics or health clinics.

Robins are usually low-yield farmers or laborers with no savings. Given many people at level one also depend on farming for sustenance, life at level one can be paralleled with life during the Agrarian Revolution.

WHAT MADE GREAT BRITAIN SO... GREAT?

The Industrial Revolutions, especially the first one, are likely familiar topics for many, but my classes didn't cover the full scope. While the historical details of the Industrial Revolution made sense to me, I never stopped to consider why all

---

103 Ibid.

of these impactful changes happened in Britain instead of anywhere else in the world.

So, why England? If you are looking for a straightforward answer, you won't find one in this book. Unfortunately, I can't guarantee you'll find one in other books either.

What I will do instead is introduce a few popular answers.

Let's start with the Eurocentric reasons. Some historians argue Great Britain became the birthplace of the First Industrial Revolution because of its:[104]

- cultural superiority
- power accumulation
- supportive atmosphere for science and invention
- freer political institutions
- strong property rights
- smaller population size which supported the creation of labor-saving inventions

However, in the 1800s, Britain was *not* the most obvious choice for becoming a manufacturing dynamo. In fact, China, India, and a lot of Western Europe were in similar phases of development. Before the Industrial Revolution, the best indicator for whether or not a country would be successful was population size and growth rate. At the time, China had the largest population in the world, and it still does. With regards to growing market success, Indian cotton basically created the global cotton market. British manufacturers focused on machines as a means to increase their production and be more *competitive* against India.

If Eurocentrism doesn't quite explain it, what else could be responsible? Possibly geography. Some historians argue

---

104 This argument of cultural superiority is very outdated today—most modern arguments focus on power accumulation.

because Britain is an island, there was more peace and stability compared to the rest of Europe, freeing up more of the government's money for other things like supporting engineers and inventors.[105]

Natural resources played a role, too. The First Industrial Revolution was predominantly led by a push to discover and utilize different energy sources to make production faster. England's large, cheap coal supply near the surface made it easy to mine and easier to replace other forms of heat, like wood.

Lastly, some historians explain Britain's success through the high wages it paid workers. With higher wages, employees were able to buy more goods and further stimulate the economy. The reason why Britain paid high wages compared to other countries in Europe is unclear, but high wages and cheap coal also served as a reason for manufacturers to push for the development of machines to increase productivity while lowering the cost of production. Productivity growth during the Industrial Revolutions is part of what made them such pivotal moments in human history.

The opportunities within industrial labor drew large swaths of workers from rural areas. In 1750, only about 15 percent of Britain's population lived in towns. In 1850, over 50 percent of Britain's population lived in either a town or city.[106,107]

By 1900, a new world power was rising to the top: the United States. Other European countries like Germany,

---

105 Simple History, "The Industrial Revolution (18–19th Century)," YouTube video, 2:37, October 1, 2017.

106 CrashCourse, "Coal, Steam, and The Industrial Revolution: Crash Course World History #32," YouTube video, 11:04, August 30, 2012.

107 Ibid.

France, Switzerland, and Belgium had begun feeling the impact of industrial change as well.[108]

THE SECOND INDUSTRIAL REVOLUTION

The Second Industrial Revolution occurred from around 1870 to 1914 and was primarily defined by scientific innovations and mass production. During this time period, the United States went from having about one-third the per capita output of Britain to becoming the richest nation in the world.[109]

This transition occurred in the aftermath of the Civil War, which cost many lives but also left the United States with:[110]

- an improved financial system after introducing a national currency
- increased use of the telegraph
- led to the development of the transcontinental railway
- promoted industrialization by funding arms and clothing manufacturers

Level two correlates to the Second Industrial Revolution. With US$2 to US$8 of income per day, the world's Drews have access to electricity, though likely erratic, radios, chemical fertilizer for increased crop production, and telephones.[111] While Drews don't struggle with basic needs, there is still a lot of uncertainty in their lives. During the Second Industrial Revolution, life was uncertain for many individuals too. While the United States was thriving nationally, individuals

---

108 Simple History, "The Industrial Revolution (18–19th Century)," YouTube video, 2:37, October 1, 2017.

109 By GDP per capita, Qatar is the richest country in the world now. By nominal GDP, it's still the US—rampant wealth inequality places the US at number ten on the list by GDP per capita.

110 CrashCourse, "The Industrial Economy: Crash Course US History #23," YouTube video, 12:31, July 25, 2013.

111 "Income Level 2," Gapminder.

working in factories were struggling due to the pressure accompanying the industrial boom.

The United States had all of the necessary natural resources to thrive in an industrial boom as well—coal, iron, oil, and grain. Its increased population, growing from thirty-eight million in 1870 to seventy-six million in 1900, also provided more laborers and consumers.[112,113] The Supreme Court also interpreted laws in a business-friendly way that supported and encouraged innovation.[114]

As the nation became more industrialized and urban, key inventions like electric lighting, gasoline engines, radio, airplanes, chemical fertilizer, and telephones all transformed productivity, communication, and living standards in the United States. Even cars were improved during this period when Henry Ford introduced the idea of the assembly line to the United States' production to boost the creation of his Model T car. His idea revolutionized mass production.[115]

The Industrial Revolution also influenced where people lived. People moved to where the jobs were, specifically urban areas with factories. The year 1880 marked the first time when a majority of the United States' workforce worked non-farming jobs earning wages or owning businesses.[116]

At that time, only 6 percent of the US population lived in cities.[117] In the early 1900s, workers began to leave rural

112 CrashCourse, "The Industrial Economy: Crash Course US History #23," YouTube video, 12:31, July 25, 2013.
113 Ibid.
114 Ibid.
115 Jason Gauthier, "1870 Fast Facts—History—US Census Bureau."
116 Ibid.
117 CrashCourse, "The Industrial Economy: Crash Course US History #23," YouTube video, 12:31, July 25, 2013.

areas for urban ones with more factory jobs. By then, 40 percent of the US population lived in cities.[118] One-third of this population growth was due to immigration.[119]

THE THIRD INDUSTRIAL REVOLUTION

The Third Industrial Revolution began in the 1950s—or 1960s depending on who you ask—and was defined primarily by the advent of digital technology. It arguably ended at the beginning of the twenty-first century to make way for the start of the Fourth Industrial Revolution.

The Third Industrial Revolution can be overlaid with life for the world's Taylors. At level three, with US$8 to US$32 per day to work with, Taylors have running water, though it is likely cold, and their own transportation like a motorbike or a car.[120] People like Taylor have electricity, though still not necessarily consistent, and fridges to make things like studying and eating a balanced diet of diverse meals easier.

At the Taylors' level, people begin to save more time due to modern technologies like personal computers and the internet. Social mobility to level four looks like more of a reality for people at this level as well. This is similar to the impact of the Third Industrial Revolution.

The Third Industrial Revolution brought with it the introduction of technological advancements like semiconductors and the internet. The world transitioned from analog technologies to digital ones, such as antenna televisions to flat screens. This transition had far reaching effects on the world

---

118 "The Four Industrial Revolutions," Unit | Salesforce Trailhead.
119 CrashCourse, "The Industrial Economy: Crash Course US History #23," YouTube video, 12:31, July 25, 2013.
120 "Income Level 3," Gapminder.

of communication and energy as things became increasingly automated and globalized.[121]

THE FOURTH INDUSTRIAL REVOLUTION: THE FUTURE IS NOW

The Fourth Industrial Revolution is, well, now. Whether or not we have entered a Fourth Industrial Revolution is a new idea and up for debate. Regardless, the advent of cloud computing, social media, mobile devices, the Internet of Things, and data-driven everything are clear signs of the technologically advanced future.[122] Life during the Fourth Industrial Revolution is what life is like for the world's Camerons living at level four.

Camerons have plenty of diverse, nutritious foods to eat. They have finished twelve or more years of school (which their job requires). Most can travel abroad for vacation and eat out at restaurants. Camerons likely have several bank accounts, access to credit, and retirement accounts. Camerons enjoy access to the cutting-edge technology permeating life in high-income countries.

Schwab describes the Fourth Industrial Revolution as the beginning of "cyber-physical systems" that will transform the capacities of both people and machines.[123] The transformation will be rooted in the technology of the Third Industrial Revolution but will change the way technology interacts with society and our bodies.

---

121 "The Four Industrial Revolutions," Unit | Salesforce Trailhead.

122 The Internet of Things refers to physical devices like cellphones, computers, washing machines, and more that are connected to the Internet. This connection enables the devices to collect and share data.

123 Nicholas Davis, Thunderbird School of Global Management, and UCL Department of Science, "What Is the Fourth Industrial Revolution?" World Economic Forum, January 19, 2016.

This dramatic shift is contrasted by the fact that there are people in the world who have yet to see every aspect of the Second and Third Industrial Revolutions impact their lives. As the Fourth Industrial Revolution begins, the impacts of the Second and Third Industrial Revolution are still spreading.

Schwab identified the three core areas of concern for the Fourth Industrial Revolution:[124]

- inequality
- security
- identity

Inequality is a prevalent concern of the Fourth Industrial Revolution because the transition will mark an increased dependence on digital technology to drive innovation, change, and opportunity.[125] This is relevant for new industries that could create fewer jobs with more education and training requirements while increasing unemployment, particularly for low-skilled positions. In part three, details regarding the changes happening in work and career-planning in the twenty-first century will be discussed with more depth.

Shifts like these frequently impact the world's Robins and Drews more dramatically than the wealthy.[126] Though wealth

---

124 Ibid.

125 Ibid.

126 According to two articles from the World Economic Forum (WEF) discussing both the Fourth Industrial Revolution and the Reskilling Revolution, during the 1980s, 8.2 percent of new jobs were created in new industries and, during the 1990s, 4.4 percent of new jobs were created in new industries. This trend also disproportionately impacts lower income individuals who currently have the comparative advantage of providing a cheap labor source on their side As more jobs are created and destroyed as technology continues to advance, the WEF believes more than one billion people will need to learn new skills by as early as 2030. Without retraining opportunities, the divide between income levels will only

inequality has increased with each passing industrial revolution, it has hit new heights in the twenty-first century. For example, in January 2020 Oxfam released a report revealing the world's two-thousand plus billionaires have more wealth than over four billion people who make up 60 percent of the world's population.[127] To wrap your head around the depths of that level of inequality consider this: the richest twenty-two men in the world have more wealth than all women living in Africa.[128]

Schwab's next area of concern was *security*. In our increasingly digital world, conflicts can occur on more than just physical land, space, or air. Cybercrime is becoming an increased risk for governments who need to find new ways to regulate technologies and negotiate to maintain peace. Autonomous weapons, drones, biological and biochemical weapons, along with other advanced devices are all becoming options for current and future warfare.[129]

Schwab's last area of concern was *identity*. The Fourth Industrial Revolution includes technologies capable of changing us down to our DNA, which reshapes the depths to which technology and identity could interact.[130]

Today's technology and the technology of the future can either help or hurt humanity as we become closer and more connected than ever before.

---

continue to grow. These important changes and more will be discussed in part three.

127 Anna Ratcliff and Annie Thériault, "World's Billionaires Have More Wealth Than 4.6 Billion People," Oxfam International, January 20, 2020.

128 Ibid.

129 Nicholas Davis, Thunderbird School of Global Management, and UCL Department of Science, "What Is the Fourth Industrial Revolution?" World Economic Forum, January 19, 2016.

130 Ibid.

SOCIAL DARWINISM

Industrial changes were not all positive and certainly not all equal. New ideas were also introduced during the time period, notably social Darwinism, which helped explain away income inequality in industrialized economies.[131] Social Darwinism was a distortion of Darwin's theory. The idea argued the theory of "survival of the fittest" should apply to people and corporations because it considered corporations people.[132]

The concept was also used to support decreasing government regulations on business and to oppose creating laws to help low-income people. Social Darwinists blamed poverty on the inherent, evolutionary flaws of "the poor" and argued big companies were big because they were "fitter."[133]

CUTTING COSTS AND CHILD LABOR

During the First and Second Industrial Revolutions, the rate of business failure was quite high, leading manufacturers to focus on trying to reduce labor costs as much as possible to save money.[134]

Factory life was very difficult, and laborers often worked in very dangerous conditions for sixty hours a week or more with no pensions or injury compensation. An average of over thirty-five thousand people per year in the United States died on the job. Profit was always the top priority for factory owners.[135]

---

131 CrashCourse, "The Industrial Economy: Crash Course US History #23," YouTube video, 12:31, July 25, 2013.

132 Ibid.

133 Ibid.

134 CrashCourse, "The Industrial Revolution: Crash Course European History #24," YouTube video, 17:05, November 5, 2019.

135 Ibid.

In response to the poor conditions, adult workers formed unions at the local and occasionally national level, like the Industrial Workers of the World. Unions argued without equality in economic systems, the United States was becoming less free as it became more financially successful.[136]

To save money, major corporations used unpaid orphans as free child labor. Children often worked fourteen-hour shifts alongside adults, and deaths were common.[137] Industrial accidents happened frequently because many people did not fully understand steam powered machinery and all of the dangers that went along with it. In the minds of factory owners, child labor was beneficial because:[138]

- children were smaller and could perform tasks that were harder for adults
- it was more difficult for them to unionize
- they could pay children lower wages

If child labor sounds like a distant, historic social problem, it shouldn't.[139] As of 2018, over 218 million children between five and seventeen years old were employed and 152 million are victims of child labor.[140,141] Of those children, almost half work in hazardous conditions.[142] Unsurprisingly, many of these children live in low- and middle-income countries.

When a person is living in extreme poverty, anyone in the household who can work does work.

---

136 Ibid.

137 Ibid.

138 Yohuru Williams, "Sound Smart: Child Labor in the Industrial Revolution | History," YouTube Video, 2:12, November 27, 2016.

139 Ibid.

140 Reid Maki, Stop Child Labor, Child Labor Coalition, July 16, 2018.

141 Ibid.

142 Ibid.

Reformers arguing against child labor during the Second Industrial Revolution fought on the premise young children should be getting educated instead. This idea was based on the Factories Regulation Act of 1833 passed in England, and the goal was to improve working conditions for children in factories. It included regulations like:[143]

- changing the minimum working age to nine years old
- capping the workday for children between the ages of nine and thirteen at nine hours a day and children thirteen to eighteen at twelve hours a day
- not allowing children to work at night
- requiring two hours of schooling per day for children working

There were factory inspectors assigned to ensure the law was being followed, but the law passing did not guarantee children would stop being exploited. Many legal acts followed this one to deal with the harsh working conditions and terrible hours.[144]

It took the Great Depression to change factory attitudes in the United States. So many adults were out of work that labor unions and laborers advocated to take children out of factories so adults could take their jobs.[145] It was around this time legislators drafted laws to end child labor, starting with working hour restrictions and improved working conditions.

143 National Archives, "1833 Factory Act," The National Archives. The National Archives, May 23, 2019.

144 Ibid.

145 Yohuru Williams, "Sound Smart: Child Labor in the Industrial Revolution | History," YouTube Video, 2:12, November 27, 2016.

MODERNIZATION THROUGH EXPLOITATION

It's no coincidence around the same time slavery was abolished in major world powers like the United States (1866) and the United Kingdom (1833), the Industrial Revolution began on the backs of cheap labor in terrible working conditions where the quality of life between the haves and have-nots got more and more divided. Money had to be made somewhere and cutting labor costs by exploiting the powerless was one of the easiest ways to do it. The same practice of putting profits over workers can still be seen today.

As the 2008 documentary *The End of Poverty* highlights, "The European empires were built on riches stolen from the colonies and on cheap or free labor provided by the slaves. The gold mines of Brazil and the silver mines of Bolivia like Potosi provided the European empires with the initial capital needed to start and finance their industrial revolutions."[146]

During the early days of the First Industrial Revolution, industry booms increased demand for slaves. Slaves produced food for factory workers who could no longer depend on their farms for food and produced the tropic oils that kept machinery running along with the raw materials, like cotton, that were so crucial for advancement.[147]

Slavery was the backbone of modernization and industrial labor rose to take its place.

REDEFINING WOMANHOOD

The role of women in society also changed. Prior to the Industrial Revolutions, women predominantly worked on farms or in workshops; if not, they often worked as seamstresses

---

146 Beth Portello, Philippe Diaz, and Martin Sheen, 2010, The end of poverty?

147 CrashCourse, "The Industrial Revolution: Crash Course European History #24," YouTube video, 17:05, November 5, 2019.

or weavers. When industrialization first began, women who worked at home spinning or weaving started working in factories. Women could also be found in coal mines transporting coal.

Popular ideology at the time in countries like France and the United States emphasized motherhood and discouraged women from working by taking away their rights to own property. Many women at the time worked, though their wages belonged to their husbands.

Because of the horrific working conditions workers faced, women were encouraged to be "angels in the house" by raising children and maintaining their households.[148] This popular Victorian ideal was based on a poem written by Coventry Patmore entitled "Angel in the House," where he describes his angelic wife as a model for all women.[149] The "angel of the house" was expected to be passive, graceful, sympathetic, pious, and pure. The general idea was that submissive and sympathetic wives could be a source of comfort for their working husbands.[150]

The concept gained popularity in England and the United States throughout the nineteenth and twentieth century as a goal for middle-class women. It also aligned with the popular value system for women at the time referred to as the "cult of domesticity," which restricted women's influence to the home. The idea spread throughout the rest of society as well, especially after Queen Victoria followed its principles with her husband Prince Albert.[151]

---

148 Ibid.

149 *Angel in the House* was originally published in 1854 and revised through 1862.

150 *The Angel in the House*, March 2, 2011.

151 Ibid.

Now, women have transitioned away from the "angels in the house" ideal and are beginning to take on roles in the formal labor market. The impact of this new balance of responsibility between work and home life will be discussed with more detail in the third section of this book.

SOCIAL CLASS AND SOCIAL MOBILITY

While living standards among the middle income and wealthy improved, living standards for the industrial poor were low. Slums developed and diseases spread, fresh and safe supplies of water were few and far between in impoverished areas, and garbage, sewage, and animal waste could be found all over the street in most low-income enclaves.[152]

These conditions are far from gone. Many of the world's Robins and Drews live in the modern-day equivalent of these same slums, susceptible to disease, lacking access to safe drinking water, and struggling to find clean places to live and work.

Charles Dickens's novel *Hard Times* is a useful commentary on workers' struggles during the Industrial Revolution. It addresses the dehumanizing impact industrialization had on workers and reveals how in a world where profit is king and one's main concern is obtaining wealth, people can devolve into apathetic, selfish individuals with little regard for the greater good.

On that note, industrial capitalists of the Second Industrial Revolution—big names like Cornelius Vanderbilt, Andrew Carnegie, and Leland Stanford—are considered both "captains of industry" or "robber barons," depending

---

152 CrashCourse, "The Industrial Revolution: Crash Course European History #24," YouTube video, 17:05, November 5, 2019.

on who is telling the story. This contrast was primarily due to the fact their methods of building wealth were not entirely honorable. The industry leaders of the era often pushed their competitors out of business and treated their workers poorly with little regard for their health or safety.[153]

As I wrote at the beginning of the chapter, the Industrial Revolutions are responsible for how we view social classes today. All of the changes industrialization brought upon the labor force changed social classes entirely.

Before industrialization, social class was predominantly determined by status at birth.[154] After industrialization, social class began to be tied to wealth, such as the amount of land a person owned. This transition increased the possibility of social mobility in society.

The divide between the haves and have-nots became more noticeable during the First and Second Industrial Revolutions.

SOCIAL CLASS AND SOCIAL MOBILITY: A SHORT ILLUSTRATION

Pause for a moment and try to envision yourself as a rural farmer during the First Industrial Revolution. While the rest of your friends and family members are making the move to urban cities for lucrative jobs, you love your rural farm life— the peace, tranquility, and simplicity—too much to give it up. Despite the challenges you face making ends meet, nothing beats the pride you feel supporting yourself.

On the other hand, your close friend and neighbor Harold started working in the city as soon as he could. At first,

---

153 CrashCourse, "The Industrial Economy: Crash Course US History #23," YouTube video, 12:31, July 25, 2013.

154 According to the Encyclopedia Britannica, social classes are considered to be collections of individuals sharing similar economic circumstances.

your dynamic remained the same. Harold was working longer hours than usual, but the two of you could find time to chat throughout the month and catch up like old times.

As months went on and Harold began spending more time in the city than at home, things changed. He got a promotion to manager. He started making more comments about social class and etiquette, and his wife's behavior changed too.

His children started spending more time doing homework for school instead of playing with your children. You had a hard time explaining to your children why Harold's children had new toys like dolls, puzzles, rocking horses, wooden blocks, and marbles while they needed to miss school lessons to help you in the fields.

A year goes by and Harold moves into the city with his family.

After entertaining the idea of getting a factory job to manage your family's ever-increasing expenses, you head to the city on a whim. You are shocked to see Harold walking down the street. He is wearing clothes nicer than you have ever seen before with intricate buttons on his top and shiny buckles on his belt and shoes. You see him stop to say hello to someone who must be a friend or colleague and are surprised to discover he now speaks with a cultured accent.

When he begins walking your way, you stop him to say hello. He takes one look at you in your base attempt at looking dressed up, feigns confusion, and pretends not to recognize you at all.

This was an all too common occurrence in the nineteenth and twentieth centuries and has further influenced how social classes interact today.

BEAUTY IS PAIN: CREATIVE DESTRUCTION

The Industrial Revolutions changed the way we:[155]

- handle waste sanitation
- source water, food, and clothing
- value the education of young people
- understand the concept of childhood

They also exposed two important facets of market economics: productivity growth and creative destruction. Productivity growth is what has improved living standards and global income levels from the First Industrial Revolution until now.[156] Workers have been able to make more with less and in shorter periods of time. Creative destruction is what the author of *Naked Economics,* Charles Wheelan, describes as a necessary part of market economies. It "crushes losers" but is a "tremendous positive force in the long run."[157]

Creative destruction is the idea of destroying old methods of doing things to make room for new methods. It is most valuable for its benefits in the long term and is a useful concept in theory. In practice, most issues facing the world's Robins, such as the covering costs of rent, utilities, clothing, and school tuition, are all harder to cover in the short term due to creative destruction.

In this way, the beauty of progress in the long run is met with the pain of financial struggle for the "losers" in the great race toward higher productivity.

---

155 CrashCourse, "Coal, Steam, and The Industrial Revolution: Crash Course World History #32," YouTube video, 11:04, August 30, 2012.

156 Charles J. Wheelan, *Naked Economics: Undressing the Dismal Science: Fully Revised and Updated*, (New York: W.W. Norton & Company), 2019.

157 Ibid.

CONCLUSION: MODERN-DAY TIME TRAVEL

In the context of global history, 270 years is a tiny sliver of time, and yet with it came:

- new modes of transportation
- new methods of production
- a fundamental shift in social structure

Even our expectation of major advancements in technology and communication occurring in less than a century is rooted in our knowledge of the Industrial Revolutions. Understanding these major changes is what helps propel humanity forward, and being reminded of the bitter truths of the past is what can encourage positive changes today.

Every major revolution has winners and losers. How wide the gaps are between those who win and those who lose in this new era of technological development is up to humanity to decide.

Imagine someone from the 1800s traveling through time to today. Crazy, right? Not really. That's life at level one in 2020.

To help provide some additional clarity, consider the cost of recent iPhones in comparison to annual income at levels one and two. A 256 GB iPhone X costs US$1,149. That's about the equivalent of what someone like Drew at level two makes in a single year. For someone like Robin living on at or less than US$1.90 a day, their annual income is about the equivalent of a 64GB iPhone 8, or US$700.

These stark divisions in quality of life is why the concept of "leapfrogging," defined by the UN as the concept of "bypassing intermediate stages of technology through which countries have historically passed during the development process," is so critically important for people living at levels one, two, and three today.[158]

We have access to twenty-first century technology to fix nineteenth century problems. While individuals at level four race to develop ever more innovative solutions to their problems, people living at level one need access to essentials like:

- sanitation
- nutritious foods and clean drinking water
- education
- housing
- healthcare

Before we move forward, we need to pause and ask ourselves:

Is humanity really progressing if hundreds of millions of people are being left behind?

---

158 UNCTAD, Technology and Innovation Report 2018: Harnessing Frontier Technologies for Sustainable Development, United Nations publication, Sales No. E.18.II.D.3, New York and Geneva.

"In the twenty-first century, the real elite are those born, not in the right family or the right class but, in the right country."

—RUTGER BREGMAN, AUTHOR OF UTOPIA FOR REALISTS[159]

---

159 Rutger Bregman, Utopia for Realists, (London: Bloomsbury), 2018, 186

A TALE OF TWO NATIONS: RICHLAND VERSUS POORLAND

—

You can learn a lot about a person by taking a look at their passport.

In 2006, a global ranking of the world's passports called the Henley Passport Index began. [160,161]

The ranking is based on the amount of countries a passport holder can travel to without a prior visa. Between continuous research by the Henley & Partners Research Department and data from the International Air Transport Association, these rankings are updated annually. Japan, with visa-free access to 191 countries, and Singapore, with 190 countries, top the list. In contrast, Afghanistan and Iraq have visa-free access to twenty-six and twenty-eight countries, respectively.

---

160 "Henley Passport Index 2008 to 2020," Henley Passport Index, n.d.
161 Henley & Partners, 2020, Henley Passport Index, PDF.

In a world where your citizenship(s) or nationality can influence your opportunities, indices like these are a unique look at how the economic and political standing of a person's country of origin impact their life. As a 2016 article from the Dubai-based online business magazine, *Gulf Business*, described things, "Much like in business, in the world of passports, it's not what you know, but who you know."[162,163]

In this section, I will address questions such as:

- Why are some nations rich?
- Why are some nations poor?
- What does it take to make a country rich?
- Why is what country you live in so important for understanding extreme poverty?

BUILDING RICHLAND: THE EIGHT CORE FACTORS

To build wealth, individuals need the opportunity to create things with value. Though economics does not have a straightforward formula for making a country rich, traditional economics can provide a helpful framework. The School of Life, an education company made famous for its videos and blog posts answering life's big questions, outlined eight core factors to transform a country into a hypothetical place they described as "Richland."[164] Richland represents

---

162 Aarti Nagraj, "Why Certain Passports Have More Visa-Free Options," Gulf Business, November 12, 2016.

163 The world's wealthiest can pay for so-called "Golden Passport" investment programs that open them up to opportunities to travel, trade, and live all over the world. Countries offer citizenship in exchange for making a sizable investment into things like real estate or national development funds.

164 Jess Cotton, "How to Make a Country Rich," The Book of Life, February 27, 2019.

the height of material success for nations. The factors they discuss are:

- military security and law and order
- lack of corruption in institutions
- low amounts of red tape around employment legislation and taxation
- a well-educated, mobile, and flexible labor force
- high-grade infrastructure and good telecommunications
- fair, transparent, and competitive markets
- enforceable contracts
- low corporation tax

This seems simple enough, right?

Wars make it hard to feel safe and secure every day, start businesses, or make long-term plans, so nations should combat war with military security. Corruption in government leads to a lack of trust, so nations should establish structured governments. These government should create effective policies within sound political systems to decrease corruption and support the natural flow of economic cycles. Excessive regulation can lead to more corruption when people are tempted to pay bribes, so nations should reduce regulation.

If things can be laid out so easily, why are some nations still poor? Like many of the problems and solutions addressed so far, things are rarely as simple as they look on the surface.

BUILDING RICHLAND: WHAT IT TAKES—MENTALLY, EMOTIONALLY, AND CULTURALLY

In the context of wealth creation at a national scale, beyond the core factors for becoming Richland rooted in traditional economics, cultural factors also play a role. The School of

Life outlined these factors as well.[165] For example, what you do in a rich country often becomes a core part of your identity. Furthermore, the love people feel for themselves and for others is often linked to achievements. For residents of Richland, no matter how much wealth they obtain, there is always someone making more money to aspire to be and envy. This aspiration feeds into the anxiety people in this hypothetical Richland feel constantly and make it nearly impossible to be content.

In Richland, the consumer is at the heart of all commerce and can separate their experiences as a producer and consumer. This enables them to simultaneously oppose the challenges of work and maintain high expectations for their consumer experience. Maintaining an optimistic mindset in Richland is hard enough given the constant striving to earn more money and the anxiety faced daily. On top of those struggles is the news. In Richland, the news is always terrible and focused on all of the worst moments in life. Despite the stress inhabitants of Richland face primarily due to work, they rarely go on vacation. When they do, they prefer fun activities that cost a lot of money over the simple pleasures of life.

Purchasing habits in Richland are based on ever-changing trends followed by Richland's self-described individual thinkers. Rather than focusing on contemplation, wisdom, and philosophy, Richland praises glamour and wealth. Richland residents focus on the lives of the rich. They are constantly comparing the middle class and below to those at the very top of the wealth spectrum. Their obsession with the rich is rooted in the comforting notion Richland is a meritocracy. If you work hard, you can make it to the top.

---

165 Ibid.

There is no luck and little religion in Richland because everyone takes personal responsibility for their fate. The religious in Richland use it to differentiate themselves and maintain their individuality. Lastly, Richland's weather is rarely nice. It serves as a constant reminder that, in Richland, the only source of joy and goodness is work.

These cultural factors, more so than the eight core factors, are harder to implement because they call attention to the sacrifices of morals and mental health nations must make to build and grow wealth at a local and national level.

A SKETCH OF LIFE IN POORLAND

While Richland has all the trappings of a wealthy and advanced nation, Poorland is devoid of them all. Poorland is living at level one where needs go unmet and survival is a gift, not a guarantee. While Poorland was not detailed by the School of Life, I will attempt to extend their ideas to what a Poorland would look like through a short story about one of Robin's daughters, Gaia.

This "Poorland" is fictional and based on the factors highlighted for the similarly fictional Richland.

Gaia is the oldest child of eight in Robin's family. She was born in a small, tight-knit community where nearly everyone earns less than US$1.90 a day. Despite this, Gaia does not consider herself poor. Usually, Gaia can afford food, enough to feed her youngest siblings at least, and usually can spare a few moments a day to share what little she was able to learn at school. In Gaia's mind, things are fine. She has learned to appreciate the simple pleasures in her life like the crunch of a sweet apple after a hard day at work or the sound of innocent, hearty laughter from her younger siblings.

She stopped attending school at eight years old to help her parents at home. She occasionally takes on odd jobs to contribute to the family's income and also sells their crops at the local market. She does not have a formal, full-time job. She would never be able to jump through all of the hoops getting a job would require. However, she does not define herself through her work. She feels more closely tied to her relationships, not her job achievements. In Gaia's community, she is a sister, a role model, and a loyal friend.

Gaia can't afford to go on vacation, and she spends more time focused on earning money for food than on the lives of the rich, glamorous, and wealthy. Rather than following trends, her income is predominately spent on food and bills. Though she works hard daily, the thought of reaching the "top" is a faraway dream.

On an average day, Gaia starts her morning by reciting prayers with her family. Her religious beliefs make her feel closer to her community, where nearly everyone follows the same faith. She prays for everything—big and small:

- She prays people will choose to be honest and pay a fair price for her crops.
- She prays the police officers in her community will stop asking for bribes from her late at night when she returns home from the market.
- She prays her siblings will be able to stay in school longer than she ever could.
- She prays for a bike she can use to get to the market faster, though the poor roads—the few that have been built—make it hard to do anything other than walk.
- Most importantly, she prays she and her family will survive another day.

As the sun rises, Gaia is comforted by the promise of nice weather. It is her reminder joy and goodness come from more than her work.

THE SECRET TO SUCCESS: INSTITUTIONS

In his bestselling novel *Guns, Germs, and Steel*, Jared Diamond calls attention to the role geography and natural resources play in determining whether nations succeed or fail. While those factors do contribute to the success of nations, Daron Acemoglu and James Robinson, authors of *Why Nations Fail*, argue the organizational structure of societies, political institutions, and economics make the real difference between rich and poor lands. Instead, the real challenge lies in trying to understand why poor countries can't take advantage of solutions like investing in public goods, education, property rights, and innovation that have been laid out by scholars in the past.[166]

To further their point, they compare two towns: Nogales, Arizona and Nogales, Mexico. The Nogales towns are separated only by a fence. There is no difference in geography or climate between the two places and the cultures are quite similar as well. Yet, in Nogales, Arizona median income is higher, school enrollment levels are higher, crime rates are lower, and infant mortality is lower than in Nogales, Mexico. What is causing this disparity?

EXTRACTIVE INSTITUTIONS

Acemoglu and Robinson argue the different economic systems and political institutions in place in Mexico in contrast

---

166 Paul Rand, host. "Why Some Nations Prosper and Others Fail, with James Robinson (Ep. 37)," Big Brains, Podcast audio, December 2, 2019.

to the United States led to the creation of different incentives and opportunities for people in both countries. They argue there are two kinds of institutions: extractive and inclusive. What is an extractive institution? Extractive institutions, as defined by Acemoglu and Robinson, are institutions that "take away people's incentives and opportunities or they concentrate incentives and opportunities."[167] These are the corrupt systems making it harder for countries to operate equitably.

For example, an individual won't purchase a home or land because of fear of theft or weak property laws resulting from extractive institutions. In extractive institutions, wealth and opportunity is concentrated among the select few which increases the amount of inequality between the haves and have-nots.

INCLUSIVE INSTITUTIONS

In contrast, inclusive institutions "create broad based incentives and opportunities" for people by balancing private and social incentives.[168] A helpful example of this would be mechanisms like patent protection of ideas.

Putting inclusive institutions in place takes time. Each nation has a unique form of government resulting from decades, centuries, or millennia of effort and formation. Each nation has its own set of political, social, and economic problems it needs to find sustainable solutions for. The formation of an organized society is a diverse process.

---

167 Ibid.
168 Ibid.

PROPERTY RIGHTS: A SHORT ILLUSTRATION

As Gaia prays her prayers, big and small, Robin is praying too. Today, the family's land is threatened.

Robin's family has lived on the same land for generations. Robin's family has farmed the land, cared for the land, and shared memories on the land. The land is a part of the family's history.

Robin would like to use the land as collateral to buy more machinery and supplies to expand, but without formal ownership, the options for loans are limited despite the farm's bountiful harvests. One day, a developer knocks on Robin's door and says he would like to build the world's tallest skyscraper on Robin's land. The developer has dreams of turning the skyscraper into a popular tourist attraction and gaining global fame.

Robin protests because Robin doesn't want the land to be taken, but there are no contracts or paperwork to prove the family's generations of ownership of the land. Robin panics. The family's home, farm, and future are at risk.

Now, imagine the alternative: on Robin's eighteenth birthday, they receive a title deed for the family's land as proof of ownership. Decades later, when the ambitious developer knocks on Robin's door, Robin has a choice. Robin can decide to sell the land to the developer and move away or refuse the offer and stay on the land.

This is life with and without property rights.

THE POWER OF PROPERTY RIGHTS

Property rights are a critical component of a functional economy, effective government, and substantive development. They are some of the most basic rights in a free society. Security of ownership is essential to build wealth, establish order and boundaries, and have the confidence to make long-term investments that can be passed down for generations.

Without the security property rights provide, it is challenging to build up a successful economy. Despite the importance of property rights, as of 2017, only 30 percent of the world's population had a legally registered title to their land.[169]

So, what are property rights and why are they so important?

Property rights are the rights an individual has to a specific asset, whether tangible or intangible.[170] Within this, a person has the right to:

- use the asset
- restrict others from accessing the asset
- change or mortgage the asset
- transfer the asset to someone else
- earn income from the asset or license control of it
- protect their property rights

Property rights impact the asset value because when property rights are secure and protected, they have more value to people interested in buying or selling them. As of 2005, only one-third of all apartments in North Macedonia were registered.[171] In response, the Real Estate Cadastre and Registration Project, an initiative sponsored through the World Bank, helped to establish more strongly enforced property laws. Their primary focus was on supporting private surveyors.[172]

---

169 "Why Secure Land Rights Matter," World Bank, March 24, 2017.

170 Dr. Michael Albertus, "Class 8: Property Rights and Development," (lecture, University of Chicago, Chicago, IL, May 2, 2018).

171 "Why Secure Land Rights Matter," World Bank, March 24, 2017.

172 Surveyors update boundary lines and prepare sites for construction so that legal disputes are prevented. They make precise measurements to determine property boundaries. (Source: "Surveyors: Occupational

Between 2005 and 2015, the number of private surveyors in North Macedonia increased from fourteen to 249 along with the development of online services. With this increase, the amount of land surveying increased from 43 percent of the country to 99 percent of the country in the same time period.[173,174,175] Registering property sales or mortgages now takes days when before it would take months. As a result, the value of mortgages increased 450 million Euros to 3.4 billion Euros, which is attracting investors locally and internationally.[176]

This also helps to explain how property rights impact incentives as well. With more property rights, people have more of an incentive to purchase assets and make innovations that improve them to increase their value. The same can be applied to intellectual property rights. If property rights for intellectual assets are weak, people and companies will have less of an incentive to invest in innovation because it won't be worth it.[177]

Given this information, why don't all countries prioritize strong property rights?

Part of the risk is that governments strong enough to enforce property rights are also strong enough to violate them.[178]Among political elites, it is often more beneficial to concentrate power among a select few than to focus on

Outlook Handbook," US Bureau of Labor Statistics. US Bureau of Labor Statistics, April 10, 2020.)

173 "Why Secure Land Rights Matter," World Bank, March 24, 2017.

174 Ibid.

175 Ibid.

176 Ibid.

177 Dr. Michael Albertus, "Class 8: Property Rights and Development," (lecture, University of Chicago, Chicago, IL, May 2, 2018).

178 Ibid.

inclusivity. However, there are many benefits for governments instituting stronger property rights beyond the personal fulfillment of giving people more freedom:[179]

- Secure property rights often make it easier for governments to raise money because people trust the government to pay off their debts.
- People are more willing to borrow money and invest because there is greater predictability in the financial markets, and they can benefit from the gains.

When people can securely own their assets, they feel confident enough to make the type of long-term investments that can lift them out of poverty and improve their standards of living.[180]

Property rights are a fundamental component of empowering individuals in their pathway out of extreme poverty, but how does this relate to Richland and Poorland or the world's Robins?

CONCLUSION: LOCATION, LOCATION, LOCATION

The country you live in impacts nearly every aspect of your life. From the factors I have observed, this impact can be broadly categorized into opportunities and trust.

In Richland, individuals' lives are replete with opportunity and there is little reason not to trust the institutions in their lives, yet not everything is as perfect as it seems on a mental, emotional, and cultural level. In Poorland, the daily fight for survival takes precedence over most other elements of life and trust levels are low. Even the ground a person

---

179 Ibid.
180 Ibid.

lives on can be taken away at a moment's notice with little opportunity or basis for defense.

For the world's Robins, life in Poorland often means living with:

- poor quality of education and a narrow set of job options
- restricted ability to travel (for work, school, or leisure)
- reduced ability to learn employable language skills
- unstable housing and land circumstances
- decreased access to nutritious foods
- substandard infrastructure

For many of the world's Robins, the structural factors making their lives so challenging are beyond their control, and their government officials are not held accountable for their actions. This is frustrating and leads to resentment and distrust of the institutions that are supposed to improve their lives. A lack of trust in institutions influences a person's:

- perception of authority (e.g. government officials, police officers, etc.)
- bias toward nationalities perceived as foreign
- opinions of public marketplaces for goods and services
- views on the role and power of big corporations
- relationships with people in their community

You may be wondering: why not just move?

I will describe immigration with more depth in part two. For now, it is important to note while immigration is a possibility for some people, the costs of moving—financially, emotionally, and physically—are high.

In this chapter's earlier discussion of national institutions, the importance of inclusive institutions was raised. However, what works well in one nation to promote inclusive institutions will not necessarily work well in another.

As James Robinson shared in a podcast interview with the University of Chicago, "Whether or not a nation succeeds or fails depends on how the people in that society themselves organize that society, organize the institutions, [and organize] the rules that create different patterns of incentives and opportunities."[181]

These ideas are a helpful framework, but individuals with community-specific knowledge and expertise need to be involved in their successful implementation.

Effective institutions support building a trust-based relationship between the government and its citizens, provide access to the resources necessary for daily life, and ensure individuals have the opportunities and resources they need to succeed.

---

181 Paul Rand, host, "Why Some Nations Prosper and Others Fail, with James Robinson (Ep. 37)," Big Brains, Podcast audio, December 2, 2019.

"Poverty in the world cannot possibly be eliminated unless the poor themselves say: we insist on justice, not charity."

—CLIFFORD COBB, THE END OF POVERTY?
DOCUMENTARY PRODUCER[182]

---

182 Beth Portello, Philippe Diaz, and Martin Sheen, 2010, The end of poverty?

HOW YOU GIVE MATTERS

———

I'll never forget the Thanksgiving holiday I spent volunteering at my town's local soup kitchen, partially because the year prior my mother had somehow managed to convince me running a 5K on Thanksgiving Day was a good idea—anything sounded better than that—but primarily because of how fulfilled I felt having done a good deed.

I arrived in the morning excited to contribute. Having volunteered a few times in the past to fulfill school requirements, I was confident I knew the drill. I would be helping to prepare the food, clean up the serving hall, and serve the food as patrons arrived. Given my utter lack of cooking abilities, I didn't do much on the preparation end aside from moving ingredients between the storage room and the kitchen. Cleaning went by quickly with the help of some fellow volunteers, but it was during food service that I was able to shine.

I played an active role and served portions of both the main course and dessert items salvaged from a local restaurant. I made an effort to serve each person with a smile, and I convinced myself it made a difference. Little did I know my quick jaunt into the world of volunteering was exactly how *not* to help.

I was engaging in what I learned through my research is called "sympathetic giving," which has proven time and again to be an ineffective approach to helping low-income populations get back on their feet. Though the experience made *me* feel better and left a lasting impression on my well-intentioned heart, I can't recall the last time I went to volunteer at the soup kitchen today. It is, as I will now explain, for the best.

In this section, I will discuss:
- two distinct approaches to giving and how giving can sometimes cause more harm than good
- the importance of community-based work
- income redistribution
- how we can give more meaningfully

THE BEST APPROACH

Based on the theories introduced earlier—cultural and behavioral theories versus structural and economic theories—what is the best approach to addressing poverty?

There is no "best" approach.

Deciding how to address poverty in any area will require borrowing from both sides and trying to find compromises among methods. Only anti-poverty policies considering the diverse needs of its low-income populations can be successful. How nations, companies, and communities choose to tackle poverty all differ based on the kind of poverty being addressed as well as the personal capacities of the people who need to be helped.

Even how we give is important. There is another structural and economy poverty theorist relevant for this writing: James L. Payne. He wrote the book *Overcoming Welfare* (1998) and advocated for a concept he called "expectant giving."

His distinction between two types of giving, sympathetic giving and expectant giving, provide a helpful framework for understanding common approaches to poverty alleviation today.

Why is *how* we give so important? Because giving can be dangerous, like social media: a tool that can lead to good or evil. When used correctly, social media can be an incredible source for global connectivity, education, and communication, but when used incorrectly, a well-intentioned message, post, or photo can be warped and used to cause irreparable harm.

The same can be said of giving. When giving is done well, it provides resources and support people need to better themselves; but when given incorrectly, it leaves people worse off than they were when left to their own devices.

SYMPATHETIC GIVING

Sympathetic giving is a handout. The size of the gift is determined based on how much sympathy or pity we feel for the recipient.[183] An example of this would be giving money to a homeless person on the street. The more helpless they look (e.g. crippled, disheveled, etc.), the bigger the donation.

Until around two centuries ago, donors weren't wealthy enough to give this way often because many people were poor. As individual's wealth increased, the flow of handouts also increased.[184] These handouts led impoverished

---

183 James L. Payne, *Overcoming Welfare: Expecting More from the Poor—and from Ourselves,* (New York, NY: Basic Books), 1998.
184 Ibid.

people to live their lives under the assumption they would be helped by generous donors. This is what Payne described as the "aggravation principle" of sympathetic giving where "repeated giving prompted by the misfortune of recipients tends to increase the incidence of the misfortune."[185]

When I say things like "I volunteered at the soup kitchen over the holidays" or "I donated to a homeless person on the street today," it makes *me* feel good. This is a self-centered approach to giving that ignores the true needs of low-income populations and avoids looking deeper into whether or not my help is beneficial. Don't just ask yourself why you give, ask what the impact of your giving will be.

Are you giving to feel satisfied and fulfilled *within yourself*, because you want to be perceived as a good person, or because you want to improve the lives of *other people*?

If we say we care about helping the Robins of the world then we should help, but only when we are prepared to shift our attention away from ourselves and toward those we try to help.

It is cheaper to give money or material things away than it is to incorporate any sort of exchange or self-help programs. Though this type of giving is superficial and sometimes damaging, the consequences of arguing against sympathetic giving are large. For example, in the political world, voters and legislators want to see as many people being helped as possible, typically for the lowest price possible. If politicians started advocating for providing *less* help to people in need, they would lose votes.[186]

---

185 Ibid.
186 Ibid.

In general, attempting to share this view without context would lead to judgment. If you aren't willing to give, no one considers the idea that you are thinking about the downsides to constant giving over time. Instead, you are labeled as selfish, racist, sexist, or heartless. Yet, advocating against sympathetic giving is not advocating for *less* help. It's advocating for a *higher quality* of help.[187]

The differentiation between sympathetic and expectant giving is most important in cases of *repeated* giving, not one-off moments of hardship.[188] If a neighbor reaches out for help covering the cost of dinner for their family one night, the adequate reply is not to refuse all aid and force them to work. When people are in need, short-term solutions can be helpful. However, if a single night turns into every night for months on end, it is time to change the approach.

Before I continue, there is a notable exception to this discussion. For those who are incapable of helping themselves due to physical or mental restraints—the comatose, the elderly, babies, people diagnosed with debilitating psychiatric conditions—the effective way to help is through sympathetic giving.[189]

EXPECTANT GIVING

For those able to help themselves, an idea referred to as "expectant giving"—treating giving as a form of exchange—can fill the gap.[190]

---

187 Ibid.
188 Ibid.
189 Ibid.
190 Ibid.

Expectant giving involves "giving with a definitive expectation that the needy person will do something constructive in exchange for the help rendered."[191]

The idea of expectant giving was championed by a group of nineteenth century charity workers Payne referred to as "charity theorists," who were in between the religion-based approach to poverty alleviation dominating at the time and the social Darwinists of the era.[192] These theorists learned about the world's Robins and Drews by working with them and learning through observation. They found sympathetic giving was reinforcing the negative habits donators were hoping to alleviate.

Payne identified the charity theorists' four core conclusions shaping their interactions:[193]

1. Forming personal relationships between donors and recipients is necessary for effective charity.
2. Sympathetic giving is generally harmful.
3. Giving should focus on an optimistic future and address any correctable weaknesses.
4. Effective giving requires action from the recipient.

The most common exchange the charity theorists promoted was the idea of working in exchange for aid. This kind of aid is focused on the future and directed at helping the recipients thrive and achieve. It is a form of tough love and is considered a "hand up."[194]

The core of expectant giving is exchange between donors and recipients, which is why it is more complex and intellectually demanding than sympathetic giving. It requires its

---

191 Ibid.
192 Ibid.
193 Ibid.
194 Ibid.

recipients play an active role in helping themselves and in some cases involves hardships.[195] For example, a homeless shelter refusing recipients who won't shower is considered to follow a philosophy of expectant giving.

What sounds easier? Giving a person a dollar on your way to work or stopping to have a conversation to parse out what a person's deeper needs are first?

Giving money is not as valuable as giving a part of yourself—your love, your sympathy, your problem-solving ability, or your knowledge. As Payne said, "When charity reformers gather to discuss strategies and purposes, they should avoid focusing on the things needy people may lack. The plan they come up with may involve material assistance, but the focus should be on creating opportunities that let people fill their own needs."[196]

The charity theorists also advocated for a personalized approach to giving that focuses on creating genuine, voluntary relationships between donors and recipients. They called the idea "friendly visiting" and vestiges of it can still be seen in the work done through volunteer programs today. [197]

Expectant giving is challenging because it involves judgment on both sides. For the recipient, it requires self-judgement and a personal decision to work toward self-improvement. For the donor, it requires thoughtful and critical reflection on why people are poor, what people living in poverty need, what they should give in return for aid, and a clear assessment of whether or not the recipients have addressed their part of the exchange.[198]

---

195 Ibid.
196 Ibid.
197 Ibid.
198 Ibid.

This form of giving involves crafting requirements to fit the individual cases of each recipient. If this sounds like a lot to do at regional, national, and global level, that's because it is.

So, how can we make Robins wealthier *and* craft individualized poverty alleviation programs?

THE BEST PEOPLE TO HELP ROBINS ARE OTHER ROBINS

This is where a community-based development approach to poverty alleviation can shine; the people who know their communities well can make a difference without imposing the values of outsiders or trying to impose their beliefs and standards on other communities. Those foreign values may not align with the cultural norms of a particular city or neighborhood. Also, values change over time, so trying to impose one person's version of what is "right" at one point could, in a decade, be something different.

Rather than entering into discussion about people like Robin from a judgmental stance, take a moment to observe how they are living now, how they solve their problems, and how they engage with the world. Assume people are not stupid, they understand their problems better than you do, and are capable of solving their problems. Solutions from the world's Camerons can miss the mark in addressing problems faced by the world's Robins, Taylors, and Drews because assumptions cloud judgements and analysis.

More often than not, the solutions the world's Robins can find for their problems are just as innovative, if not more so, than the solutions of any outsider, and the solutions are based on the local resources available. From there, donors can see where their ideas could fit in. Not the other way around. All too often, Camerons have a tendency to impose their version of what is "insightful" or "imaginative" on Robins who are just as creative and capable when given the tools. Despite this oversight, Camerons are surprised when the outcome is not what they expect.

It is time for the world's Camerons to support and believe Robins are just as capable of living up to their potential as they are. Similar to what Payne wrote, rather than focusing on the material things Robins do not have, it would be more meaningful to create opportunities for Robins to fill their own needs.

Working closely with recipients and understanding the needs of others requires a level of trust, credibility, and closeness that community leaders are best positioned to develop. Community leaders can serve as mentors, communicators, and friends who represent the values and priorities most important to the populations they represent. At this level of giving, customizing aid to the specific needs of individuals becomes a natural byproduct of the types of relationships formed. This approach will be discussed with more depth in part three.

HOW CAN WE CHANGE?

It is okay to start small. For example, let's return to my soup kitchen experience. The volunteering effort, while well-intentioned, fed into a harmful system of giving. How could exchange be incorporated into that framework?

Soup kitchens could start implementing a small charge, and if recipients have no money at all to pay the small charge, they could instead work for food.[199] Payne described this difference in his work *Overcoming Welfare*: "Unrequited

---

199 Ibid.

giving does not represent the highest kindness; it is a truncated, defective charity. To give back, to give in return for gifts given, is how we express our gratitude, our pride, and our humanity."[200]

Expectant giving is not without its own set of challenges. While it sounds useful in theory, it is challenging to implement. Expectant giving is expensive and relies on high levels of enthusiasm and commitment not guaranteed to last throughout the entire duration of the programs or local efforts that focus on the philosophy.[201]

For example, consider welfare-for-education programs. In 1995, reformers in Ohio proposed welfare recipients in the United States should work toward a high school general equivalency diploma, which sounded empowering and beneficial in principle.[202] Rather than just giving welfare recipients money, why could they not add on a high school education requirement?

The costs of the program revealed how unrealistic it would be. Estimates indicated the cost of supplying necessary education and supervision would be US$8,892—in 1998, so US$140,312.49 in 2019—per recipient per year on top of all the welfare benefits they were already getting.[203]

Expectant giving brings with it another limitation as well. If it is not implemented on a broad scale, people can just go somewhere else where they can receive free things.[204]

Imagine if a person in need was searching for food available in their community when they'd hit a rough patch. One

---

200 Ibid.
201 Ibid.
202 Ibid.
203 Ibid.
204 Ibid.

soup kitchen charged every adult a quarter meal fee and every child five cents. The other was free.

Where would you go?

This influences the quality of donations as well. If people are paying for things, they expect a certain quality out of the goods that either matches or surpasses the price paid. This puts more pressure on donors than giving for giving's sake and thinking little of the implications.

WHY HAVE THINGS STAYED THE SAME?

Expectant giving isn't a new idea. Payne's book was published in the 1990s. So, why have things stayed the same?

While I can't unpack the complexities of the intersection between public policy and political games or understand the motivations behind social workers at the desks of welfare offices or nonprofits, I can call attention to a concept relating to this struggle: task commitment.

Task commitment, as defined by Payne, is "the general tendency individuals have to believe that what they are working on is worth doing regardless of the outcomes."[205] It is what leads employees to focus on expanding their programs to create larger impact and validate their importance, regardless of the results. This is the attitude sustaining failing programs.

With more time committed to a task, people stop thinking critically about their actions and the results of their work. Instead, employees focus on short-term repercussions—a consistent paycheck and a feeling of fulfillment for having contributed to helping the less fortunate.

---

205 Ibid.

In this mindset, some form of action is better than none at all—even at the expense of long-term, substantive change.

How do we avoid committing to the wrong task? If expectant giving is the next best step, how can we move forward? What should we be giving?

We can start by focusing on strategies that increase human capital.

Our best course of action is to determine how we can make the most positive change with the resources available to us. As more volunteers and community leaders take the time to develop personal relationships with the people who they help, they will be able to identify and address root causes of their problems.

Beyond material items, Robins need opportunity. Beyond money, Robins need to build wealth.

INCOME REDISTRIBUTION

At this point, you may be thinking, *I know the answer now. Just take all of the excess money from the Camerons of the world and give it to the Robins of the world. Problem solved. Easy-peasy. One person can't spend all of those billions anyway, and besides, the rich should be donating more money more often.* Or maybe you're noticing the growing trend that just money won't cut it. Either way, this is a helpful time to address why pure income redistribution as a policy reform strategy won't be as straightforward as it may seem.

The general assumption behind the debate of income redistribution is that someone like Robin will always benefit from a system of redistribution and the real argument lies in whether or not it is ethical to take from Taylor and Cameron and give the money to Robin and Drew.[206]

Those who support income redistribution argue Taylor and Cameron are wealthy because of inheritance, luck, or the few cases of hard-work within rags-to-riches stories all rooted in expansive social networks and high-powered connections. Those who oppose income redistribution argue forcing Taylor and Cameron to give their money to Robin and Drew is wrong because it punishes the wealthy for their hard work and sacrifices to earn their money.[207]

Regardless of whether the money is deserved or not, forcing Taylor and Cameron to give money to Robin and Drew ends up hurting Robin and Drew more than helping them. Furthermore, because the giving is forced, Camerons won't feel good about helping Robins. Instead, they will feel resentment.

But, let's break down this idea even further by taking a look at some numbers.

The combined net worth of *Forbes'* list of the world's four hundred richest people is about US$2.4 trillion.[208]

Yep: $2,400,000,000,000

However, that number is not stored away in rooms filled with paper money. Rather, it is what the Foundation for Economic Education described in a 2017 article about intergenerational poverty as "the estimated monetary value of all the assets they own."[209] It basically means things like office

206 Ibid.

207 Ibid.

208 Sean W Malone, "10 Solutions to Intergenerational Poverty: Sean W. Malone," FEE Freeman Article, Foundation for Economic Education, August 29, 2017.

209 Ibid.

buildings, computers, employee salaries, pensions, and any other components of the businesses and assets those individuals own are all included in that value.

So when you see headlines about businessmen like Jeff Bezos being worth billions—and within the decade, possibly trillions—of dollars, remember those big numbers are because Amazon has billions of dollars in assets, including the value of "their warehouses, trucks, servers, and the actual stuff they keep in stock for people to purchase."[210] To quickly access that money, Bezos would need to sell Amazon's buildings, liquidate all of Amazon's inventory, and more—assuming there are people willing to buy all of those assets too.

Why is this important in the context of extreme poverty? Because those assets can't easily be transferred as income to the world's Robins.

But wait, the Foundation for Economic Education article I referenced earlier tried to do this anyway.

Let's say the US$2.4 trillion spread out among the world's richest could be quickly converted to cash. And, let's say the money was divided across the entire US population evenly. There are approximately 329 million people in the United States.[211]

Every single person in the United States, regardless of income, would get about US$7,300. Once.

Even if only the bottom 20 percent of the US population—assuming the 20 percent only consists of the poorest approximately sixty-five million people in the United States—were given the money, the payments would be about US$36,500. Once.

---

210 Ibid.
211 "US and World Population Clock," Population Clock, US Census Bureau, n.d.

Spread out across the approximately six hundred million people living in extreme poverty globally, each Robin would receive US$4,000. Once.

The additional one-time income would be great, but after the money runs out and debts are paid off, where would that leave us?

Beyond that, every rich person who owned a large, successful company would suddenly have nothing to show for it and the "reward" for building up a large company would essentially be a punishment.

Depending on income, redistribution is just another form of sympathetic giving.

Sympathetic giving is a harmful system of disempowering low-income individuals and assuming these populations are incapable of helping themselves when given the proper education and training.

Outside of the hypothetical scenarios, the method has also been tried before. In fact, Payne shared a helpful example in *Overcoming Welfare*—the US tax on powerboats initiated in 1990. The government assumed it would be a luxury tax, but the true repercussions hurt the Robins more than the Camerons. The tax led to boat sales declining, which pushed the suffering businesses to lay off workers and led those workers into poverty. The result was so harmful Congress repealed the decision.[212]

But that was then, and this is now. If redistribution isn't the band-aid solution, then what can be done? How can we uplift the world's Robins? Or rather, how can we support the Robins of the world in uplifting themselves?

---

212 James L. Payne, *Overcoming Welfare: Expecting More from the Poor—and from Ourselves,* (New York, NY: Basic Books), 1998.

Rather than giving thoughtlessly, we can focus on methods of assisting that work toward helping people get back on their feet. Mentorship costs nothing but time, yet it can be valuable for an ambitious individual who needs to learn the skills or gain the self-confidence necessary to succeed. As with many expectant giving solutions, it requires more effort and more investments into personal relationships. Beyond that, it is harder to quantify the results of the relationships which leads to the solution often being overlooked.

CONCLUSION: THE FOUR HOWS

The Robins of the world need your time, your knowledge, and your connections more than your handouts.

Actions rooted in the expectant giving framework require being more thoughtful about aid programs and what their effects are or will be. This is a challenge.

"We don't have the time," many people argue.

Yet, the issue right now is not enough time is being invested into solving these problems in an effective and sustainable way. Instead, there is more of a focus on the quantity of the people being served and less effort spent on whether or not the programs are helping people in the long run. And, of course, the staff members hired to work on these issues will continue to convince themselves their work matters to feel important and impactful, though the appropriate response would be a mindful critique.

In working toward more meaningful solutions, consider the four hows:[213]

---

213 Payne's original questions were as follows: Who are our recipients and how should our program help them? How do we know we are helping them? In what way might our program be harming recipients (or others)?

1. How are your actions helping those in need?
2. How do you know you are helping?
3. How could your actions be harmful?
4. How can you learn more about the needs of those you are helping?

On a small scale, focusing on individuals and how their actions impact these issues, consider this simple solution: if you don't have the time to consider the long-term effects or repercussions of what you give, then stop giving material things. Choose to be more thoughtful and intentional with your actions. In part three, I will expand on this idea in more depth with a particular focus on helping all of us to determine how we can help.

However, we should be wary of avoiding all action in the hopes of finding the perfect solution. As Voltaire once said, "The perfect is the enemy of the good."

I have been drawing attention to past efforts in part one, not to attack or to critique them, but to call attention to moments where people, organizations, and government programs have tried. Each attempt at addressing poverty, whether successful or unsuccessful, draws us closer to effective solutions.

How can we bring about more direct personal contact between helpers and helped?

PART 2

UNPACKING THE PROBLEM

POVERTY MINDSET

"If English is your first language, take one step forward!" my program coordinator yelled in the courtyard of our largest local museum.

I confidently stepped forward, along with the majority of the group. Solid start. Nothing to be nervous about...yet.

In my junior year of high school, I was a member of a city-wide leadership development program. As part of the program, we participated in a "privilege walk," which is an exercise designed to help people understand how levels of privilege vary from person to person.

"If you were raised in a single parent household, take one step back."

I gulped nervously and stepped back. It was the first of many to come. By the end of the exercise, I found myself somewhere in the middle of the pack. I was behind the students with housemaids and high-powered social connections, but ahead of others who had faced hardships like being raised in rough neighborhoods or going without meals when money was tight at home. At the time, I was just relieved to have not been too far in the back.

As one of the few Black students in the program, I didn't need any more reasons to stand out. To this day, I remember making nervous eye contact with my Black friend. We glanced at our friends near the front, but our moment of silent solidarity was more valuable than the things we already knew about some of the more privileged students in our group.

My personal experience with this exercise was memorable because of the sentiments shared by the girl who ended up finding herself furthest from the front. She was white, surprisingly, but what shocked me most wasn't the color of her skin but the happiness she exuded.

She shared that even though she didn't have as much as the rest of us, she was content with her life. She felt loved and sustained by the support of her family, and she didn't realize how much she didn't have until the exercise. I share this to say we are all born into situations we have no control over, and those situations shape everything from the clothes we wear to the mindsets guiding our interactions with others and within ourselves.

The long-term value of exercises like the "privilege walk" has been called into question in recent years by some who argue it exploits the stories and hardships faced by the less privileged and centers its focus on the most privileged in the group. The most privileged receive an eye-opening lesson while those with the least privilege are forced to face facts they already know—they are marginalized and oppressed.

Poverty can have deeply damaging effects on our psyches. Our economic and financial security influence how we make decisions, how we plan for the future or if we consider the future, and how we identify ourselves.

In this chapter, I am going to draw closer attention to the relationship between poverty and psychology. Why is this relationship so critical to our understanding of extreme poverty? Because unlike other impediments on our health, no amount of medicine, therapy, or treatment can directly make a person less poor. We know life in poverty is hard, but with more detail about the psychological effects, we can gain a better understanding of *why* it is so hard. Essentially, rather than treating the symptoms of poverty, we can begin to understand and eliminate its causes.

Let's begin.

FAST VERSUS SLOW LIFE HISTORIES

Life history theory is a helpful starting point because it relates to how organisms allocate resources for survival and reproduction.[214] Within this theory, there are two primary strategies to help explain the trade-off in resource allocation: the fast path and the slow path. For humans, these paths are rooted in the experiences and environments faced during childhood.[215]

On the fast path, people grow, well, faster. They start puberty earlier, have more children, and age faster.[216] Fast path people focus on short-term, immediate benefits rather than the long-term repercussions. On the slower path, the opposite occurs. The slow path leads people to focus on the long-term and forego instant gratification in favor of greater gains in the future.[217]

---

214 Dr. Jean Decety, "Social influence and decision-making," (lecture, University of Chicago, Chicago, IL, November 5, 2019).

215 Ibid.

216 Ibid.

217 Ibid.

Is there a *better* option between the two paths? Not exactly. Determining which path is better depends on context and who is making the decisions. Both paths have benefits and costs. On the fast path, people are more adaptive in uncertain situations.[218] On the slow path, people are more adaptive in safer situations.[219]

Where do Robins fit into all of this? Being poor does not automatically place Robins in the fast path. In fact, for the Robins of the world, the importance is on the predictability of any given environment.[220] What makes life feel "unpredictable"? Aside from the uncertainties of living in poverty, anything from frequent moves to an absent parental figure can all impact whether or not a person feels secure. The more predictable an environment is, the more likely a person is to develop a slow life strategy and vice versa for fast strategies.[221]

GROWING UP POOR

Growing up in poverty can influence a person's development trajectory cognitively, emotionally, and even physically. Low-income children are more likely to face physical stress and psychological stress. Constant exposure to taxing events wears on a person's natural capacity to handle stress and respond to external pressure.[222,223]

Researchers are working toward gathering more data about the relationship between development trajectories

218 Ibid.

219 Ibid.

220 Ibid.

221 Ibid.

222 Gary Evans et al., "Childhood Poverty, Chronic Stress, Self-Regulation, and Coping," Child Development Perspectives, Volume 7, No. 1 (2013): 43–48; DOI: 10.1111/cdep.12013

223 Ibid.

and early childhood poverty, as well as the specific factors of what make up poverty, stress, and coping processes. A core question to be answered is how the duration of exposure to poverty influences development and whether there is a significant difference between short-term, early deprivation and "repeated experiences of poverty over life."[224]

What contributes to low-income children lagging behind their more affluent peers? Studies call attention to a few factors:

1. The difference in parental investment.
   a. For low-income children, there are typically fewer books and learning materials at home for intellectual stimulation and language learning. There are also fewer toys around and more exposure to television.[225,226,227]
   b. Parents in low-income households don't read to their children as much as their higher-income peers, and fewer words are spoken at home which also makes intellectual development a challenge.[228]
   c. Beyond this worry about making ends meet, poor sleep quality and fatigue, balancing several jobs to pay bills, and more result in having less energy to pay attention to and care for their children.

---

224 Ibid.

225 R.H. Bradley et al., "Socioeconomic status and child development," Annual Review of Psychology (2002): 53, 371–399

226 G.J. Duncan, J. Brooks-Gunn, "Consequences of growing up poor," New York, New York, 1997.

227 Russell Sage Foundation, G.W. Evans, "The environment of childhood poverty," American Psychologist (2004): 59, 77–92.

228 E Hoff et al., "Socioeconomic status and parenting," In M.H. Bornstein (Ed.), Handbook of parenting, 2nd ed., 2002, 231–252.

2. The higher likelihood for low-income parents to be harsher to their children and have less time to be attentive to their children.[229,230,231]

   a. Corporal punishment is more common in low-income households than high-income ones, and there is a higher likelihood of parental conflict. Less attention is referring to the lower amount of attention and support provided in the household like helping with homework or job applications.[232]

3. The elevated level of chronic stress low-income students experience.[233]

   a. Constant exposure to stress damages children biologically and psychologically.[234]

The financial strain low-income parents experience inhibits their parenting abilities. However, this does not happen in every low-income family. Take, for example, the girl in my leadership development cohort. Despite her circumstances, she felt content and happy with her life. Not every low-income family's experience leaves a negative mark on their children's lives, but the impact still needs to be studied.

---

229 R.H. Bradley et al., "Socioeconomic status and child development," Annual Review of Psychology (2002): 53, 371–399

230 R.D. Conger et al., "An interactionist perspective on the socioeconomic context of human development," Annual Review of Psychology (2007): 58, 175–199.

231 K.E. Grant et al., "Stressors and child and adolescent psychopathology: Moving from markers to mechanisms of risk," Psychological Bulletin (2003): 129, 447–466.

232 Ibid.

233 Gary Evans et al., "Childhood Poverty, Chronic Stress, Self-Regulation, and Coping" Child Development Perspectives, Volume 7, No. 1 (2013): 43–48; DOI: 10.1111/cdep.12013.

234 Ibid.

SCARCITY MINDSET

Growing up in poverty impacts a person's ability to make decisions, and this influence is not restricted to childhood. Across all age groups, people living in poverty make decisions that tend to focus on coping with current, stressful situations rather than on future goals.[235] Poverty can be considered as living in a state of "scarcity," which can be defined as a lack of any good or service.

Scarcity can also shift a person's focus. For example, scarcity shifts low-income individuals' attention away from the future and toward the present, leading to overvaluing the importance of the present. Being poor and worried about fulfilling basic needs uses up mental energy and capacity that could be dedicated to other tasks.[236] A psychology experiment can show what this shift in mindset looks like in practice.[237]

Researchers Anuj K. Shah, Sendhil Mullainathan, and Eldar Shafir conducted an experiment with 137 participants playing *Family Feud*—a television game show where two families guess the most popular answers to survey questions to win cash and prizes. Some participants could see previews of the next round's question and others couldn't. All participants could borrow more time at a predetermined cost.

The results revealed low-income participants performed the same with and without previews of the next question. Meanwhile, high-income participants performed better with

---

235 Anuj K. Shah et al., "Some Consequences of Having Too Little," *Science Magazine*, Volume 338 (2012).

236 Anandi Mani et al., "Poverty Impedes Cognitive Function," *Science Magazine*, Volume 341 (2013).

237 Anuj K Shah et al., "Some Consequences of Having Too Little," *Science Magazine*, Volume 338 (2012).

previews. This is not for lack of time, either. The low-income participants over-borrowed additional time. Even if they had used some of the borrowed time to look at the previews of the next questions, they could have done better.[238]

This experiment revealed that while the high-income participants used the preview of the next questions to save more time, the low-income participants were too focused on their current rounds to benefit despite the advantage of borrowed time.[239]

They highlighted a few potential explanations:[240]

1. While low-income individuals are great at making quick, short-term decisions, it is harder for them to make long-term ones.

2. Scarcity creates a "cognitive load" that diminishes general performance.

Cognitive load "relates to the amount of information that working memory can hold at one time."[241] The core of the second argument is that cognitive load is the result of a more focused engagement with specific problems and this attention leaves less mental resources available for other problems.[242]

This doesn't mean people living on low incomes are not future-oriented. Many are. Rather than doing things considered to be future-oriented like saving money, their savings are focused on **specific** future expenses—again focusing on

---

238 Ibid.

239 Ibid.

240 Ibid.

241 The Mind Tools Content Team, "Cognitive Load Theory," MindTools, 2019.

242 Ibid.

particular problems rather than giving other problems their full attention.

As the researchers observed, "a scarcity mindset leads people to choose the most convenient response to pressing demands, leading to constant financial juggling."[243] Understanding a scarcity mindset is important because scarcity can be applied to other material and physical resources aside from money, including issues like allocating your limited amounts of time.

For Drews, Taylors, and Camerons, something like being busy is more often than not a short-term inconvenience remedied with a vacation or an assistant. For Robins, poverty is a long-term disadvantage with no quick fix.

If you were standing at the edge of a cliff with nothing preventing you from falling but a thin rope, would you be able to confidently make a decision about whether or not you should change your major or your career or where you live?

When you feel afraid, stressed, or under pressure, it is harder to make serious decisions, especially long-term plans about the future. Poverty brings immense amounts of continuous stress for those who suffer under its weight. Poverty reduces cognitive function because concerns related to poverty take up a lot of mental energy. Reminding someone of their financial concerns has the same cognitive consequence as losing a full night of sleep.[244] Living in poverty makes it harder to make decisions.

Further, living in poverty makes bad decisions more impactful. The mistakes that the world's Robins make can

---

243 D. Collins et al., "Insufficient Funds," R.M. Blank, M.S. Barr, Eds. (Russell Sage Foundation, New York, 2009), chap. 4.

244 Anandi Mani et al., "Poverty Impedes Cognitive Function," *Science Magazine*, Volume 341 (2013).

lead to worse outcomes than the mistakes of those with higher incomes, and the mistakes carry on with future generations as well.[245,246]

The relationship between poverty and decision-making is circular. As the behavioral insights team at Joseph Rowntree Foundation described it, "Decisions made by individuals can make a difference to their poverty status but these decisions are significantly influenced by how choices are presented and the context in which they are made, including in the context of poverty itself."[247]

Why do low- and high-income people act differently? There are two dominant responses to this question within psychology research:

One explanation is "the poor" make decisions best for them given their economic contexts. Often, their decisions are based on their low incomes. The other dominant explanation is poverty shapes their preferences and increases their likelihood of making mistakes in decision-making.[248]

Researchers Leandro Carvalho, Stephan Meler, and Stephanie Wang advocate for a third view in their research paper entitled "Poverty and Economic Decision-Making: Evidence from Changes in Financial Resources at Payday" that conflicts with both sides of the debate. Their hypothesis states scarcity negatively impacts cognitive function, which leads to errors in decision-making and a focus on short-term

245 M. Bertrand et al., *The American Economic Review* (2004): 94, 419–423.
246 M. Bertrand et al., *Journal of Public Policy & Marketing* (2006): 25, 8–23.
247 Kizzy Gandy et al., "Poverty and decision-making: How behavioral science can improve opportunity in the UK," Joseph Rowntree Foundation Behavioral Insights Team, 2016.
248 Leandro Carvalho et al., "Poverty and Economic Decision-Making: Evidence from Changes in Financial Resources at Payday," *The American Economic Review* (2016): 106(2): 260–284. doi:10.1257/aer.20140481

problems highlighted earlier in the section. This is in line with the second dominant explanation, but their research did not support their hypothesis.[249]

They conducted a study observing how changes in finances around payday influence economic decision-making. Short-term variations in income were treated as a proxy for general changes in financial status. The results of their study showed before and after payday, participants took similar amounts of risks and performed similarly on a number of cognitive tasks meant to test the relationship between financial security and ability.[250]

They found liquidity constraints, not scarcity, were the reason participants were focused more on the present before payday and had less self-control.[251] The paper indicates short-term variations in income don't create cognitive deficits. However, more work needs to be done to understand the impact of long-term, more permanent income scarcity.[252]

SOCIAL CONSEQUENCES

In 2016, researchers Carina Mood and Jan Jonsson set out to determine the effects of poverty on social relationships, political participation, and activity in organizations. After studying the results of over three thousand participants, they concluded that poverty does have negative consequences on social life. The consequences are greater for relationships with friends, relatives, and political participation than social support or organized activities.

---

249 Ibid.

250 Ibid.

251 According to Businessdictionary.com, a liquidity constraint is an inability to make a purchase due to a lack of cash.

252 Ibid.

The results of their study indicated a lack of cash leads to a "deterioration of social relations and participation."[253] Being poor makes it harder to participate in society "on equal terms with others."[254] In the long run, this leads to poorer individuals being excluded or choosing to withdraw from social and civic life out of shame.[255]

People who fall into poverty face weakened social relations and decreased social participation. People who escape from poverty have stronger social relationships and are more active social participants.

There was a notable exception to this general rule: when someone is in need due to something like a sickness or a personal problem, there are fewer negative consequences for closer social relations. Why is this the case?

Mood and Johnson argue it is because these types of relationships are often "unconditional."[256] They determined the social response to economic deprivation is the "strongest predictor of social outcomes," not income poverty.[257]

POVERTY IDENTITY

A person's financial status can influence their social identity and behavior. This concept is relevant for low-income

253 Carina Mood et al., "The Social Consequences of Poverty: An Empirical Test on Longitudinal Data," *Social Indicators Research* (2016): DOI: 10.1007/s11205-015-0983-9

254 Ibid.

255 A. Poor Sen, relatively speaking, Oxford Economic Papers (1983): 35, 153–169.

256 Carina Mood et al., "The Social Consequences of Poverty: An Empirical Test on Longitudinal Data," *Social Indicators Research* 2016: DOI: 10.1007/s11205-015-0983-9

257 Ibid.

populations and relates to the idea of a "poverty identity"[258] discussed at length in a research paper written by Sachin Banker, Syon Bhanot, and Aishwarya Deshpande titled "Poverty Identity and Competitiveness."

Have you ever considered what social groups influence your identity? Are you affiliated with a social group that has particular behaviors or beliefs associated with it? Do you act differently in those various groups?

In the same way your behavior may change depending on what social context you find yourself in, a person living on a low income may change their behavior as they adapt to life in poverty. Their behavior begins to change based on the actions and the decisions associated with their social group. Research has shown our preferences are shaped by social groups—affiliations as diverse as race, religion, history of charitable giving, or a criminal past all tie into the behaviors shaping who we are and how we present ourselves to the world. [259,260,261,262,263,264,265]

258 Sachin Banker et al., "Poverty Identity and Competitiveness," *Journal of Economic Psychology*, Volume 76, issue C, (2020); DOI: 10.1016/j. joep.2019.102214

259 G.A. Akerlof et al., "Economics and identity," *The Quarterly Journal of Economics* (2000): 115(3):715–753.

260 D.J. Benjamin et al., "Social identity and preferences," *American Economic Review* (2010): 100(4):1913–1928.

261 Y Chen et al., "Group identity and social preferences," *American Economic Review* (2009): 99(1):431–457.

262 D.J. Benjamin et al., "Social identity and preferences," *American Economic Review* (2010): 100(4):1913–1928.

263 D.J. Benjamin et al., "Religious identity and economic behavior," *Review of Economics and Statistics* (2016): 98(4):617-637.

264 J.B. Kessler et al., Identity in charitable giving, Management Science (2016).

265 A Cohn et al., "Bad boys: How criminal identity salience affects rule violation," *The Review of Economic Studies* (2015): 82(4):1289-1308.

Furthermore, the public stigma associated with poverty also has a negative impact on social interactions. As the recent paper from Banker et al. described, "Those who experience financial difficulties even fail to take advantage of benefits offered at no cost to the recipient because they wish to avoid the associated stigma."[266]

Poverty identity also influences the likelihood a person will compete. Banker et al. found impoverished individuals "may select away from competitive environments" and "perpetuate their impoverished status."[267]

As a person begins to understand themselves to be poor, this self-understanding harms their perceptions of their abilities.[268] They begin to associate themselves with the harmful stereotypes surrounding "the poor," like laziness.[269,270,271,272]

A person living in poverty develops a feeling of "learned helplessness" that makes it harder to feel in control of their lives and begin to assume competitive opportunities are not

---

266 R.J. Kissane, "What's need got to do with it? Barriers to use of non-profit social services," *Journal of Sociology & Social Welfare* (2003): 30:127.

267 Sachin Banker et al., "Poverty Identity and Competitiveness," *Journal of Economic Psychology*, Volume 76, issue C (2020): DOI: 10.1016/j.joep.2019.102214

268 Ibid.

269 HR Kerbo, "The stigma of welfare and a passive poor," *Sociology & Social Research.* (1976).

270 C.C. Hall et al., "Self-affirmation among the poor: Cognitive and behavioral implications," *Psychological Science* (2014): 25(2):619-625;

271 P.M. Horan et al., "The social bases of welfare stigma," *Social Problems* (1974): 21(5):648-657.

272 R Rogers-Dillon, "The dynamics of welfare stigma," *Qualitative Sociology* (1995): 18(4):439-456.

for "people like them."[273,274] To combat this mentality, the researchers introduced verbal self-affirmations, in the form of personal conversations highlighting positive traits, to some of their subjects in an attempt to increase their competitive spirit.

After trying the verbal self-affirmations, they found that living on a low income does lead a person to use their financial status as a defining element of their identity. This confirms prior research that individuals "frequently self-identify" with their disadvantaged status.[275] The affirmations exercise also revealed building up confidence prior to competitive opportunities encourages and increases a person's levels of competitiveness in those environments.

Lacking the self-confidence required to compete influences whether or not a person takes risks like applying for selective opportunities such as higher education or jobs. Deciding *not* to compete further reinforces the negative self-image taken on by someone living in poverty.

Think about it this way: the guaranteed way to lose a competition and maintain your belief you would have lost is to never enter it.

ASPIRATIONS FAILURE

A lack of self-confidence and hope can lead to "aspirations failure," defined as a "failure to aspire to one's own

---

273 Sachin Banker et al., "Poverty Identity and Competitiveness," *Journal of Economic Psychology*, Volume 76, issue C, (2020): DOI: 10.1016/j.joep.2019.102214.

274 Ibid.

275 K Hoff et al., The whys of social exclusion: Insights from behavioral economics (English). Policy Research working paper: no. WPS 8267 (2017).

potential."[276] Aspirations failure is a "consequence of poverty, rather than a cause."[277] If high- and low-income individuals have similar aspirations, a low-income person's circumstances lead to their efforts not creating as many benefits as would be created for a high-income person.[278]

All things equal, a low-income individual has to make a greater effort than a high-income person to achieve the same level of wealth.[279] With this reality in mind, someone living in poverty is more likely to have their aspirations negatively impacted, which reduces their effort and continues a negative trend away from developing long-term, lofty goals. The low-income individual therefore has two reasons to put in less effort:

1. Their benefits are lower for the same amount of effort.
2. Their aspiration levels (which relates to benefits) are lower as well.

Poverty makes it harder to aspire to higher goals which contributes to its persistence over time.

HOPE: A SHORT ILLUSTRATION

Consider the following example: you enter school as a five-year-old in pre-school with little knowledge of the world around you. Before you start kindergarten, you and your friend Sophie are divided into the "gifted track" and the "traditional track."

Sophie loves math, has parents who have been reading to her since she was in the womb, and speaks three languages

---

276 Patricio S Dalton et al., "Poverty and Aspirations Failure," *The Economic Journal*, 126 (2016): 165–188. Doi: 10.1111/ecoj.12210.

277 Ibid.

278 Ibid.

279 Ibid.

fluently. She tests into the gifted track. Your parents are too busy working to pay bills to read to you, which leaves you to spend your time watching TV or playing in the park. Though your parents would like to spend more time with you, they are prioritizing being able to provide food, shelter, and clothing for you and your siblings. Before you have gotten a handle on your multiplication tables, your future as been laid out in front of you.

By the third grade, you noticed the smarter students in class got more attention from teachers and received all of the awards. You started to resent your remedial classes for reading and math, and you rebelled by messing around in class and distracting your middle-of-the-pack peers. You are already starting to lose hope for your future and set your expectations lower.

Flash forward to middle school and Sophie has already surpassed you. She competes in national spelling bees and has been targeted by some of the best high schools in the nation to join their Advanced Placement or International Baccalaureate programs. She recently started participating in both violin and piano competitions, too. You, on the other hand, are far behind and losing even more hope for your future. Sophie has received all of the benefits from being labeled early on as "smart" and being identified as a student with vast potential.

You and Sophie used to be close friends. Now, you make fun of her for spending all of her time studying, and she looks down on you for not trying hard enough in school. Her label has boosted her self-confidence to the point where there is a social divide between the "gifted" students like her and the "traditional" students like you who didn't make the cut.

You are now in different worlds, and this divide is reaffirmed by teachers, parents, and school administrators constantly. If Sophie gets in trouble, she gets a warning and a reminder she shouldn't risk her bright future. If you get in trouble, you get detention, suspension, or even expelled. Your hope continues to dwindle.

In high school, the divide gets worse. While Sophie is always presented with opportunities to develop, improve, and shine both in and outside of the classroom, your lack of the "gifted" label leaves you exiled to the back of the classroom. By now, your hope is nearly gone, and you rarely think about or plan for your future. You were never labeled "smart" like Sophie. You were never even given a chance.

One day in your junior year of high school things change. You are assigned a guidance counselor who believes in your success and pairs you with a private tutor determined to help you get into a good university. If you improve your grades and score well on your standardized exams before the end of the academic year, you could get into a state university! Excited by your first glimmer of educational hope and encouraged by the fact someone believes in you and your success, you study hard and get the grades you need to be a competitive applicant.

Before that year and the support, higher education had been nothing but a distant dream. After all, you were left behind and considered to lack the potential your "gifted" peers had from the beginning. Without hope, you spent your time outside of class doing anything but studying to distract yourself from your harsh reality. You were deemed "not good enough" by the education system before realizing you had any sort of chance.

This is life with and without hope.

HOPE WITHIN THE POVERTY TRAP

The poverty trap is the self-reinforcing cycle continuing to perpetuate poverty. Imagine the same education example but with no hope of a private tutor or a guidance counselor to increase your chances of getting into a university. Your grades would never improve because you would have no incentive to improve them, and your teachers would continue to focus on other more talented students in your classes instead of you—you with no future, no hope, no ambition, and no role models.

This same logic can be generalized to any situation where there is a certain threshold requirement to be met before a situation becomes desirable. If you know you will never make it to college or a high-paying job, why keep studying? If you think you will always be poor, why cut your spending in favor of investing in a seemingly hopeless future?

Hope is a building block for our future capacities. Just a small amount of hope is enough to help a person develop their potential. In contrast, hopelessness destroys a person's will and ability to invest in their futures. Nobel prize-winning economist Esther Duflo called attention to an unsettling truth: "low-income populations might be so convinced that they will always be poor that it creates a self-fulfilling prophecy."[280] Basically, expecting negative outcomes, like reduced cognitive performance and antisocial behavior, leads to negative outcomes.

Given this context, it is important to consider solutions to extreme poverty that increase hope by drawing attention to opportunities and the potential to meet future goals.

---

280 Esther Duflo, "Lack of Hope and the Persistence of Poverty," (lecture, University of Cambridge, Cambridge, England, 2012).

On the other hand, the researchers who created the 2015 World Development Report, "Mind, Society, and Behavior," determined that "development professionals are not always good at predicting how poverty shapes mindsets."[281] In particular, the report consolidated survey data from a variety of development professionals and determined many of them perceive "the poor" to be "less autonomous, less responsible, less hopeful, and less knowledgeable than they in fact are."[282]

With more research and data, a more complete picture of life in extreme poverty is forming. Misconceptions that understate meaning, purpose, and hope are being brought to the forefront of development work. More research into the role hope plays in shaping and influencing mindsets will be helpful when trying to understand the realities of life in extreme poverty in the future.

COMMUNITY TRUST

One way to uplift and empower low-income populations is through building up community trust. Why is community trust so important within the context of individuals living in extreme poverty? When low-income individuals trust more, they make fewer present-biased decisions and discount the future less.[283]

How is this possible?

---

281 World Bank. 2015. World Development Report 2015: Mind, Society, and Behavior. Washington, DC: World Bank. DOI: 10.1596/978-1-4648-0342-0. License: Creative Commons Attribution CC BY 3.0 IGO

282 Travis J Lybbert et al., "Poverty, Aspirations, and the Economics of Hope," University of Chicago Press (2018).

283 Martha J. Farah et al., "Trust and the poverty trap," Proceedings of the National Academy of Sciences of the United States of America, Volume 114, No. 21 (2017): 5327-5329.

When an individual has trust in a community, it reduces how severe financial need feels and how helpless they may perceive their situation to be. This makes it easier to prioritize long-term planning over immediate gratification. Low-income populations are more pessimistic about future benefits and their ability to miss out on present payoffs in favor of future gains. Their perspective on situations influences their behavior.

Because putting less focus on the future can be considered both a cause and effect of poverty, Martha J. Faraha and Cayce J. Hook refer to it as the "poverty trap" in their 2017 research paper entitled "Trust and the Poverty Trap."

Essentially, being poor leads to decisions that deepen poverty and keep people "trapped" in a negative cycle. Faraha and Hook describe "the poor" as having adapted to their economic status by developing a culture that "prioritizes immediate gratification over future benefits."[284] They also referred to the scarcity mindset that influences cognitive and decision-making abilities.

Trust in others is a necessary component for believing future, or delayed, rewards will come. This trust is easier to develop with a high income. Community trust is a "buffer from crises" such as urgent financial need. The trust makes it easier to decrease need-based discounting.[285]

In addition to a lack of trust, a lack of hope could also contribute to the negative relationship between low-income populations and decision-making.[286,287]

284 Ibid.

285 Esther Duflo, "Lack of Hope and the Persistence of Poverty," (lecture, University of Cambridge, Cambridge, England, 2012).

286 Travis J Lybbert et al., "Poverty, Aspirations, and the Economics of Hope," University of Chicago Press (2018).

287 Esther Duflo, "Lack of Hope and the Persistence of Poverty," (lecture, University of Cambridge, Cambridge, England, 2012).

These results are not meant to simplify the relationship between the scarcity mindset and poverty to a lack of trust. The multidimensional nature of poverty and its many causes were discussed in the first part of this book and reflect both how and why the relationship between decision-making and trust is as complex as poverty itself.

However, the impact of factors like hope and trust show how people view themselves, their strengths and weaknesses, and their possibilities for the future.

Hope and trust can either continue to perpetuate poverty or relieve it.

GROWTH VERSUS FIXED

In 2006, Carol Dweck published a book called *Mindset: The New Psychology of Success* that popularized two terms her research introduced in the late nineties:

1. fixed mindset—the idea that qualities such as intelligence, basic abilities, and talent are static and can't be changed
2. growth mindset—the idea that qualities such as intelligence, basic abilities, and talent can be developed with time, experience, and effort

In 2016, Susana Claro, David Paunesku, and Carol Dweck conducted further research to explore the relationship between having a growth mindset and academic achievement. In their research, they confirmed a commonly held belief about academic success and achievement: it is strongly influenced by socioeconomic background and an individual's beliefs about their abilities.[288] However, they found a growth mindset is comparably strong.

---

288 Susana Claro et al., "Growth mindset tempers the effects of poverty on academic achievement," Proceedings of the National Academy of

While low-income students were less likely to have a growth mindset, those that did were somewhat protected from the influence poverty has on achievement. Their results showed the "lowest 10th percentile of family income who exhibited a growth mindset showed academic performance as high as that of fixed mindset students from the 80th income percentile."[289]At every socioeconomic level, students with growth mindsets outperformed students with fixed mindsets.

Students with fixed mindsets avoid situations they may fail in because the experiences undermine their self-confidence and sense of intelligence. Students with a growth mindset seek out difficult tasks and challenges to increase their abilities. For students from low-income households, the realities of their economic situation can lead them to develop a fixed mindset that inhibits their intellectual capacity.

The results of this study highlight how structural, economic, and psychological inequalities intersect. It also provides a source of hope. Knowledge is power. If we know having a growth mindset can improve a students' life academically, then having a growth mindset can impact other areas of their lives as well. While in recent years debates surround the ability to teach someone how to have a growth mindset have raged on, the fundamental finding remains: a growth mindset can overcome the damaging impact of a low socioeconomic level.

Sciences of the United States of America, Volume 113, No. 31 (2016): 8664-8668.

289 Ibid.

CONCLUSION

Having a growth mindset can't magically lift people out of extreme poverty and "encouraging self-talk" doesn't pay bills. However, being aware of poverty's psychological impact can provide helpful context for how to address and discuss the impact of poverty on both life and survival for the world's Robins.

In this chapter, we covered a lot of information about why life in poverty quite literally changes the way you think. Before getting discouraged about the statistics and figures proving poverty's negative impacts, consider this: identifying a problem is first step toward solving it. There is still work to be done, but there are some glimmers of hope within the developing knowledge we have about things like scarcity mindset and poverty identity.

Building up community trust is a helpful starting point. While we learn more through research in years to come, we can take action daily by choosing to be good neighbors and reaching out to others. Remember poverty is relative, and hardship is perceived based on your context. While you may not engage with Robins daily, your neighbor who lost their job and is now waiting for unemployment benefits or the homeless person you pass by on the street during your daily run are both in need, too. As I wrote earlier, simply knowing someone else cares and could help in times of hardship reduces how severe and helpless financial need feels.

Start from where you are. Your community needs your active engagement and investment in improving life for everyone in it. Increasing hope can start with encouraging determination and ambition among Robins and improving education. I don't mean education in subjects like science or math or the humanities, though those are important.

Rather, I'm referring to education in confidence building and self-worth.

There is no question life in poverty is challenging and has impacts beyond mere financial need. Understanding this is a step in the right direction, but we can't stop there. Everyone is capable of succeeding when given the opportunities and resources, but individuals living in extreme poverty face mental barriers that make it even harder for them to realize their potential and believe in their capacity to succeed.

Within a system of paternalism, this would be a barrier that would be quickly dismissed. When children don't believe in themselves, what do parents typically do? Maybe give a pat on the back, share an encouraging word, or simply aid in completing the task. In a system of paternalism, everything centers on the person who is helping, and their skills, solutions, and values. The person being helped is a mere afterthought. Everything is organized around and without those who are in need. Paternalism manifests itself in individuals in ways that seem benign at first glance. It can take the form of the voice in your head wondering, "where do *I* fit into solving this problem?" Instead, ask yourself the four hows introduced in part one:

1. How are your actions helping those in need?
2. How do you know you are helping?
3. How could your actions be harmful?
4. How can you learn more about the needs of those you are helping?

Within a system of partnership, potential is unleashed. In a partnership model, when people don't believe in themselves, they can build self-confidence through education and opportunity. They are taught how to do necessary tasks for themselves to gain success, they can teach others in their community, and they build on that knowledge in the future. The knowledge they gain can turn into opportunity and connection, and the positive cycle continues. This counters the harmful mental effects of poverty because Robins begin to see how capable they truly are. These internal lessons are crucial for building self-worth. Partnerships *uplift and empower* Robins.

In a world where profit is king, choosing to believe in your value beyond your financial assets is radical. We know the poverty mindset exists, but so does the growth mindset. Breaking down the harmful impact of the poverty mindset starts with building up the self-worth of the world's Robins.

"Gender inequality cuts across every single country on Earth. No matter where in the world you are born, your life will be harder if you are born a girl."

—MELINDA GATES, CO-CHAIR, TRUSTEE, AND FOUNDER OF THE BILL & MELINDA GATES FOUNDATION[290]

---

290 Bill and Melinda Gates, 2019. "Examining Inequality," Gates Foundation. 2019

WHO RUNS THE WORLD?

———

When I first started my research for this book, I was determined not to incorporate gender. I tried to convince myself poverty is a genderless social constant.

It's not. Poverty doesn't have to be a social constant, and it is certainly not genderless.

Gender roles are a core part of:
- how capital is accumulated and distributed
- how job tasks, titles, and pay are determined
- how children are raised
- how daily life in the home is experienced

In this chapter, I will explore why women's empowerment must be a priority if humanity is serious about eradicating extreme poverty. Uplifting over 600 million people out of *extreme* poverty will require *extreme* measures, like a paradigm shift ensuring half of the global population has fundamental rights, privileges, and respect.

THE BIG PICTURE

More often than not, negativity surrounds the narratives of the treatment of women around the world. However, things are not all bad. There are pieces of hope to hold onto. Women's rights have advanced substantially in the past twenty years alone. For example, Iceland became the first country in the world to legally enforce equal pay in 2018.[291]

Further, in contrast to stories about sexual discrimination at birth, the Indian village Piplantri plants 111 trees every time a girl is born to ensure the trees survive and grow as the young girls do in the community.[292] The tree-planting program is a way to encourage families to celebrate girls and combat female feticide.[293] Village residents also collect money and create a deposit account for the girl to support her through adulthood. As part of the program, the parents sign contracts stating their daughters will receive a full education and not be married before eighteen years old.[294]

Beyond this, the United Nations Entity for Gender Equality and Empowerment of Women revealed income trends for households headed by women is positively rising due to their own increased earnings or cash transfers, and these changes tend to benefit children.

The trends are not all positive, though. For example, the average girl in sub-Saharan Africa ends school two years earlier than the average boy, and one-fifth of girls globally

---

291 Sif Sigmarsdóttir, "Once More, Iceland Has Shown It Is the Best Place in the World to Be Female | Sif Sigmarsdóttir," *The Guardian*. Guardian News and Media. January 5, 2018.

292 "This Indian Village Plants 111 Trees When a Girl Is Born," 2019, Earth Day, November 18, 2019.

293 Urvija Banerji, 2017. "An Indian Village Plants 111 Trees Every Time a Girl Is Born," Atlas Obscura. Atlas Obscura. March 22, 2017.

294 Ibid.

are married before they turn eighteen, which reduces options and personal freedoms for young girls to pursue further education or job opportunities.[295,296] In addition, one-third of women globally are victims of gender-based violence.[297]

Why are women's rights so critical to discussions about extreme poverty? To start, uplifting and empowering women is a core facet of uplifting and empowering entire communities. Studies have shown higher female incomes in households lead to higher expenditures invested into the human capital of children, which relates to income spent on essentials like education, health, and nutrition.[298,299]

UNPAID CARE WORK

As Elaine Welteroth once said, "Women are taught to work hard and to play by the rules. We are taught to never overstep, to stay in our lane, to keep our head down, to go with the flow, to never be too loud or disagreeable. Not to be bossy. Not to be pushy. We are not encouraged to know our worth, let alone demand it...Women aren't taught to get comfortable with making people uncomfortable."[300]

---

295 Bill and Melinda Gates, "Why We Swing for the Fences," Gatesnotes.com. February 10, 2020.

296 Ibid.

297 Ibid.

298 M. Bussolo, R.E. De Hoyos, and Q. Wodon, "Could Higher Prices for Export Crops Reduce Women's Bargaining Power and Household Spending on Human Capital in Senegal?" in Bussolo and De Hoyos (eds.), 2009. Gender Aspects of the Trade and Poverty Nexus—A Macro⊠Micro Approach, World Bank, Washington DC;

299 Backiny⊠Yetna, Q. Wodon, M. Bussolo and R.E. de Hoyos, "Gender Labor Income Shares and Human Capital Investment in the Republic of Congo. mimeo," World Bank, Washington, DC, 2009.

300 Elaine Welteroth, *More Than Enough: Claiming Space for Who You Are (No Matter What They Say).* Random House (2019), 221

It is this submissive mindset and treatment that provides a backdrop to the silent, essential force of our global economy: unpaid care work. The International Labor Organization (ILO) defines unpaid care work as relating to three categories of activities:[301]

- domestic work within the household
- caregiving work for household members
- community services and help to other households

The ILO argues the gender gap within the realm of unpaid care work can be paralleled with gender inequality more broadly because women represent a larger portion of the informal employment sector at 4.6 percent more representation than men.[302] This difference has negative repercussions for women. They spend more time on unpaid care work and have less time to dedicate to the labor force.

According the Organization for Economic Co-operation and Development (OECD), women do most of the unpaid work around the world.[303]

What do the numbers look like for these inequalities?

- In Mexico, women spend approximately forty-five hours a week on unpaid work in contrast to men's sixteen hours a week. [304,305]

---

301 King's College, "Women's Unpaid Care Work Has Been Unmeasured and Undervalued for Too Long," King's College London. King's College London. January 14, 2020.

302 "Facts and Figures: Economic Empowerment," n.d. UN Women.

303 The OECD defines unpaid work as routine housework, shopping, care for household members, volunteering and travel related to household activities.

304 Payman Taei, "Visualizing Women's Unpaid Work Across the Globe (A Special Chart)," Medium, Towards Data Science, March 8, 2019.

305 Ibid.

- In India the inequality is even worse, at approximately forty-two hours a week for women compared to men's seven hours a week. [306,307]

What about for more equal countries?

- In Sweden, women spend approximately twenty-five hours a week in contrast to men's nineteen hours.[308,309]
- In Norway, women spend approximately twenty-seven hours in contrast to men's twenty hours.[310,311]

This divide starts early in women's lives as well. Among girls between the ages of five and fourteen globally compared to young boys of the same age, 160 million more hours *per day* are spent on unpaid household chores, fetching water, and collecting firewood.[312] This gap increases with age and peaks between the ages of twenty-five and forty-four, which is the prime time for traditional career-building.

Beyond the work implications, this also influences how often both men and women enjoy their leisure time.

In most countries women "work more and play less" than men, with gaps for hours spent on leisure time like twenty-three hours (women) versus thirty-four hours (men) in

---

306 Ibid.

307 Ibid.

308 Ibid.

309 Ibid.

310 Ibid.

311 Ibid.

312 King's College, 2020, "Women's Unpaid Care Work Has Been Unmeasured and Undervalued for Too Long" King's College London, King's College London, January 14, 2020.

Portugal and thirty-eight hours (women) versus forty-six hours (men) in Greece. [313,314,315,316,317]

The gaps are not large everywhere. In Denmark, women and men spend around thirty-eight hours and forty hours respectively on leisure time; in Norway, women and men both spend around forty-three hours on leisure time. [318,319,320]

During the 19th International Conference of Labor Statisticians in 2013, unpaid care work was formally recognized as a form of work. This transition of status shed light on the economic contribution of unpaid care work, which is estimated to be roughly US$10 trillion per year, but more work needs to be done to formally validate women's contributions in this area.[321]

What about women involved in the more formalized job market?

Globally, women are less likely to participate in the labor force than men. Their participation rate is 63 percent compared to 94 percent for men among individuals between

313 Taei, Payman, 2019, "Visualizing Women's Unpaid Work Across the Globe (A Special Chart)," Medium, Towards Data Science, March 8, 2019.

314 Ibid.

315 Ibid.

316 Ibid.

317 Ibid.

318 Ibid.

319 Ibid.

320 Ibid.

321 King's College, 2020, "Women's Unpaid Care Work Has Been Unmeasured and Undervalued for Too Long," King's College London, King's College London, January 14, 2020.

the ages of twenty-five and fifty-four.[322,323,324] Of women who do actively participate, women are more likely to be unemployed.

As of 2017, the global unemployment rate for men was 5.5 percent compared to a rate of 6.2 percent for women.[325,326] For women who do work, they are paid less than men. According to the UN, women earn 77 percent of what men earn on average.[327] The difference is even more stark in low- and middle-income countries where self-employment is more dominant.

With the money women earn, they have less access to financial institutions or even bank accounts. Only 58 percent of women worldwide have accounts at formal financial institutions, compared to 68 percent of men.[328,329]

THE TRUE HEAD OF THE HOUSEHOLD

Among these unpaid care working heroes are also women who are the formal heads of their households.

---

322 UN Women defines participation rate as the rate of individuals who work or are actively searching for work.
323 "Facts and Figures: Economic Empowerment," 2018, UN Women, July 2018.
324 Ibid.
325 Ibid.
326 Ibid.
327 Ibid.
328 Ibid.
329 Ibid.

Female headed households are becoming increasingly common globally, and these households tend to be especially vulnerable to poverty.[330,331,332]

But what makes life so challenging for women who head households? Researchers Stephan Klasen, Tobias Lechtenfeld, and Felix Povel call attention to four core reasons in their piece "What about the Women? Female Headship, Poverty, and Vulnerability in Thailand and Vietnam" published in 2011.[333]

1. *Women in low- and middle-income countries don't have access to land.*[334]

In part one's section on rich versus poor nations, I explained why property rights are a basic right within a functional economy. Those points are important for women living in rural households with a heavy dependence on land access.

Land is unequally distributed between men and women. As a 2017 report from the World Economic Forum noted:

"Women own less than 20 percent of the world's land. A survey of 34 developing nations by the United Nations Food and Agriculture Organization puts that percentage as low as

---

330 M. Budowski, R. Tillman and M.M. Bergman, "Poverty, Stratification, and Gender in Switzerland," *Swiss Journal of Sociology* (2002): 28, 2, 297-317;

331 M. Buvinic and G.R. Gupta (1997), Female-Headed Households and Female-Maintained Families: Are They Worth Targeting to Reduce Poverty in Developing Countries? Economic Development and Cultural Change, 45, 2, 259-280.

332 V.M. Moghadam, "The feminization of poverty: notes on a concept and trend," Women's Studies Occasional Paper 2, Illinois State University, 1997.

333 Stephan Klasen, Tobias Lechtenfeld, and Felix Povel, "What about the Women? Female Headship, Poverty and Vulnerability in Thailand and Vietnam," Georg-August-Universität Göttingen, Courant Research Centre, March 2011.

334 Ibid.

10. This is staggering if you consider that half of the world's population is women. More than 400 million of them farm and produce the majority of the world's food supply. Yet female farmers lack equal rights to own land in more than 90 countries."[335]

This inequality is driven not only by gender discrimination through culture, but gender discrimination through law as well. In particular, inheritance and title laws are more favorable toward men.[336]

  2. *Women lack access to formal credit markets.*[337]

This is primarily because women do not own the collateral, like land or property, to back their loans.[338,339,340] Without collateral, women can sometimes get male figures like their husbands or male relatives to co-sign for them, but it is not guaranteed the males in a woman's household will be willing to co-sign.[341]

---

335 Monique Villa, "Women Own Less than 20% of the World's Land. It's Time to Give Them Equal Property Rights," World Economic Forum. January 11, 2017.

336 E. King, S. Klasen, and S. Porter, "Women and Development," Copenhagen Consensus 2008 Challenge Paper, Copenhagen, Denmark, 2007.

337 Ibid.

338 D.J. Storey, "Racial and Gender Discrimination in the Micro Firms Credit Market? Evidence from Trinidad and Tobago." *Small Business Economics* (2004): 23(5), 401–22.

339 A. Diagne, M. Zeller, and M. Sharma, "Empirical Measurements of Households' Access to Credit and Credit Constraints in Developing Countries: Methodological Issues and Evidence." IFPRI FCND Discussion Paper No. 90, International Food Policy Research Institute, Washington DC., 2000.

340 M. Ratusi and A.V. Swamy, "Explaining Ethnic Differentials in Credit Market Outcomes in Zimbabwe. Economic Development and Cultural Change (1999): 47, 585–604.

341 M. Fafchamps, "Ethnicity and Credit in African Manufacturing. Journal of Development Economics," (2000): 61(1), 205-35.

3. *Insurance markets in low- and middle-income countries do not provide adequate protections of assets.*[342]

This is particularly harmful for women in places where they do not have pension systems or property rights in place. Even health insurance for women is hard, if not impossible, to obtain without access to a spouse working in the formal sector.[343]

4. *Women lack access to the labor market.*[344]

While this divide is made most prominent through the wage gaps between women and men, the lack of access is also rooted in other factors. For example, women are often indirectly discouraged from pursuing formal work due to the time they spend at home completing domestic work during the normal workday. It is both hard and competitive to find employers willing to create a more flexible schedule.

As more women have taken on jobs in the formal working world, this shift has begun to impact household structures as well. Women are more likely to work a double day. A double day is when a woman handles both domestic work and formal work, typically as the primary breadwinner of a household.[345]

---

342 Stephan Klasen, Tobias Lechtenfeld, and Felix Povel, "What about the Women? Female Headship, Poverty and Vulnerability in Thailand and Vietnam," Georg-August-Universität Göttingen, Courant Research Centre, March 2011.

343 World Bank, "World Bank Policy Research Report 2001: Engendering Development: Through Gender Equality in Rights, Resources, and Voice." Oxford University Press, New York, 2001.

344 Stephan Klasen, Tobias Lechtenfeld, and Felix Povel, "What about the Women? Female Headship, Poverty and Vulnerability in Thailand and Vietnam," Georg-August-Universität Göttingen, Courant Research Centre, March 2011.

345 V.M. Moghadam, "The feminization of poverty: notes on a concept and trend." Women's Studies Occasional Paper 2, Illinois State University, 1997.

These double day shifts are thought to be part of the reason why women, especially women who are heads of household or the primary breadwinner, can "transmit poverty to the next generation" because their double day keeps them from fully providing for their families.[346]

Beyond this, the lack of opportunity to pursue formal education compared to their male peers of the same age keeps women from pursuing jobs, especially high paying jobs, in the future. This is worsened when households invest less in girls' education, which directly links to girls' inability to pursue the same labor opportunities as men.[347]

EDUCATION

As of 2018, fifteen million girls will never learn to read or write in primary school compared to ten million boys.[348] When income is taken into consideration, the implication for the world's Robins are even more stark. In India in particular, girls from low-income families are twenty-two times less likely than girls from high-income families to attend school and five times more likely to be married off before turning eighteen.[349,350]

Women with less education end up having more children, too. In sub-Saharan Africa in particular, women with

---

346 R. Mehra, S. Esim, and M. Simms, "Fulfilling the Beijing Commitment: Reducing Poverty, Enhancing Women's economic options," International Center for Research on Women, Washington DC, 2000.

347 World Bank, "World Bank Policy Research Report 2001: Engendering Development through Gender Equality in Rights, Resources, and Voice," Oxford University Press, New York, 2001.

348 Joe McCarthy, "Women Are More Likely Than Men to Live in Extreme Poverty: Report," Global Citizen, February 16, 2018.

349 Ibid.

350 Ibid.

no education give birth approximately seven times, with primary school education women give birth approximately six times, and with secondary education women give birth approximately four times.[351,352,353]

While the implications this has for women in the job market has already been explored, a lack of focus on women's education has further repercussions, particularly for child survival. In Hans Rosling's book *Factfulness*, he argues "half the increase in child survival in the world happens because the mothers can read and write"[354]

In fact, a 2013 UNESCO report titled "Education Transforms Lives" found "if all women had a primary education, there would be 15 percent fewer child deaths, saving 900,000 lives" and that "if all women had a secondary education, child deaths would be cut in half, saving 3 million lives."[355,356] With better educated parents, there is a higher chance future generations will survive.

Young girls in low- and middle-income countries also face gender-specific obstacles to accessing their education. For example, monthly menstruation cycles keep young women out of classrooms around the world. Missing days at school can lead girls to drop out altogether and puts women at risk of ending up as child brides or young mothers.

---

351 UNESCO, "Global Education Monitoring Report 2019: Migration, Displacement and Education—Building Bridges, not Walls," Paris, 2018.

352 Ibid.

353 Ibid.

354 Hans Rosling, Ola Rosling, and Rönnlund Anna Rosling, *Factfulness: Ten Reasons Were Wrong about the World—and Why Things Are Better than You Think*. London, Sceptre (2019), 139.

355 UNESCO, 2013, Education Transforms Lives, Paris.

356 Ibid.

For young women and girls on their periods, access to sanitary products and clean, safe bathrooms are both critical. Unfortunately, this is not the reality for all women. Period poverty, defined by Bodyform as a lack of or limited "access [to] sanitary products and having a poor knowledge of menstruation often due to financial constraints," is a global issue not restricted to low- and middle-income countries.[357]

According to a representative survey of one thousand girls and young women ages fourteen to twenty-one conducted by Plan International UK, 1 in 10 girls can't afford to buy menstrual products.[358] Their research also revealed 49 percent of girls in the United Kingdom have missed at least one day of school due to their periods.[359] In a single academic year, over 137 thousand students miss school because of period poverty.[360]

These findings led Monica Lennon, a member of Scottish Parliament, to call for free sanitary products to be used in school and an increased focus to be placed on providing sanitary products in homeless shelters, local charities, and food banks. In March 2019, the government announced a program to provide free sanitary products across secondary schools and colleges.[361]

EDUCATION: EMBRACING COMPLEXITY

While the statistics surrounding women and education have received more attention in recent years, there has been

357 "What Is Period Poverty?" Bodyform, September 20, 2018.
358 "Plan International UK's Research on Period Poverty and Stigma," Plan International UK, December 20, 2017.
359 Ibid.
360 "What Is Period Poverty?" 2018, Bodyform, September 20, 2018.
361 Ibid.

push back from researchers who have observed attendance records don't reflect the drastic impact often cited. In 2006, researchers Emily Oster and J-PAL affiliate Rebecca Thornton conducted a randomized trial involving reusable menstrual cups with 198 Nepalese girls living in Chitwan, Nepal, in seventh and eighth grade. Nepal is a particularly important area to study with regards to period poverty because the harmful, sexist practice of having girls stay in period huts called "Chhaupadi" still occurs, despite being made illegal in 2017.[362]

Half of the group received training on the proper use of menstrual cups and were given a menstrual cup. Only 2 percent of the girls in the study reported using pads, which the researchers argued indicates the price of sanitary products, especially more expensive options like menstrual cups, keeps them from purchasing those products.[363]

The results of the study indicated the introduction of menstrual cups did not reduce the already small number of schoolgirls missed due to menstruation—about half of a school day per year. In directly comparing girls who used the cups with girls who didn't, girls who didn't use the cup only had slightly lower attendance.

The study found that "On days when they were not menstruating, girls attended school 85.7 percent of the time, compared to 83 percent of the time during their periods."[364] This is the equivalent of about 0.35 school days per year.[365]

---

362 Danielle Preiss, 2017, "Law in Nepal Sets Penalties for Forcing a Woman into a Menstrual Shed," NPR, August 10, 2017.

363 Abdul Latif Jameel Poverty Action Lab (J-PAL), "Menstruation as a barrier to education?" June 2011.

364 Ibid.

365 Ibid.

The results of this study are an important reflection of why "rigorously testing programs" is so critical.[366] The almost half of the Nepalese girls in the study highlighted they missed school due to the periods, which made providing sanitary products seem like a simple and obvious solution.[367]

The root causes of girls' low school attendance are more complex than one problem.

Other randomized studies referenced in the paper highlighted solutions like:

- telling parents their children can earn more with each additional year of schooling they complete[368]
- improving student health through treatment of intestinal worms[369]
- reducing the cost of schooling with free uniforms[370]

All of these remedies had a larger impact on female school attendance.

Another deterrent for women's education is the higher likelihood of young pregnancy leading girls to leave school early. Beyond young girls in particular, there are over 200 million women in low- and middle-income countries who

---

366 Ibid.

367 Ibid.

368 Trang Nguyen, "Education and Health Care in Developing Countries," Education and Health Care in Developing Countries, Dissertation, Massachusetts Institute of Technology, Department of Economics, Massachusetts Institute of Technology.

369 Edward Miguel and Michael Kremer, "Primary School Deworming in Kenya: The Abdul Latif Jameel Poverty Action Lab," The Abdul Latif Jameel Poverty Action Lab (J-PAL), n.d.

370 David Evans, Michael Kremer, Mūthoni Ngatia, "The Impact of Distributing School Uniforms on Children's Education in Kenya," November 2009.

do not want to get pregnant but are not using modern contraceptives.[371]

Without the ability to plan when they get pregnant, it is harder for women to stay in school, apply for and obtain more lucrative jobs, or develop the skills to care for their children. If women are given more control over this life-altering portion of their lives, then that impact can be passed along to their families, their communities, and beyond.

Women with better educations can pursue better opportunities, make more money, and support their families. However, these changes will take time. Centuries of negative treatment toward women will need to be challenged and corrected to see substantive progress. Even a few days improvement in school attendance for women can lead to positive results. These small improvements are just as important as larger strides because they indicate change is happening.

ECONOMIC MOBILITY THROUGH WORK

Women can support their families through work, but how do women living in extreme poverty do this?

As an example, let's consider the work women living in extreme poverty do in clothing factories.

Working conditions in these factories are not satisfactory. Women often find themselves in unsafe environments with many accidents, occupational diseases, and even death.

One of the worst factory incidents in the twenty-first century and a helpful example of how terrible conditions can be is the Rana Plaza factory collapse in Dhaka, Bangladesh. Rana Plaza was a building that contained multiple clothing

---

371 Bill and Melinda Gates, 2020, "Why We Swing for the Fences," Gatesnotes. com, February 10, 2020.

factories. The garment workers made items for major fashion brands. The collapse killed at least 1,132 people and injured more than 2,500.[372,373] The issue was not a lack of awareness, either. A mere five months earlier, over one hundred workers died in a tragic accident involving a burning Tazreen Fashions factory outside of Dhaka.[374]

Why do women take on these jobs in such terrible conditions? Is it worth the risk?

For many women and families, it is. The work is a matter of short-term sacrifice in favor of long-term opportunity and the ability to provide for both children and family members.

Women often keep their jobs in poor conditions because the pay is better compared to alternatives. If you recall from the chapter on the Industrial Revolution, similar decisions were made by workers forced to work in the harsh factory conditions because those jobs provided the best wages at the time. This is yet another example of how the world's Robins are stuck in the nineteenth century when it comes to working conditions and the types of jobs pursued.

By the standards of high-income countries, workers, especially women, are paid very little. As Charles Wheelan highlights in his book *Naked Economics,* workers are paid less in low- and middle-income countries because their comparative advantage is their cheap labor. Quite frankly, if foreign companies raised their wages to match the rates of high-income countries there would be fewer advantages for them to do business in poorer regions and provide jobs for the supervisors, managers, and factory workers involved. With this

---

372 "The Rana Plaza Accident and Its Aftermath," The Rana Plaza Accident and Its Aftermath, December 21, 2017.

373 Ibid.

374 Ibid.

knowledge in mind, there is little incentive for factory owners in middle- and low-income countries to increase wages to a living wage. Beyond wage increases, there are other ways that garment workers lives could be improved. For example, factories could provide education subsidies for children or offer healthcare services. However, any improvement to quality of life will come at a cost.

Since the Rana Plaza factory collapse, effort has been made by manufactures and by brands to pay closer attention to building standards, wages, and codes of conduct, but progress is still being made to ensure the individuals subjected to these jobs are actually working in better conditions.

Labor inspection systems and enforcement are still developing in low- and middle-income countries. These efforts take time. When problems do arise, there are few systems in place to protect victims. After the Tazreen and Rana Plaza incidents, no compensation was paid to the victims or their families.[375] Some larger fashion buyers and even local companies made a few payments, but those were all voluntary.

Given this context, it is clear some form of benefits or compensation plan for workers in these environments are critical to protect them against the hardships associated with workplace injuries. Financial compensation could be the difference between life at level one and level two for some families. Under current labor codes, compensation is typically low and offered in lump sums, which makes it harder to protect families from poverty in the long run. More work needs to be done in this area to protect workers and their families.[376]

---

375 Ibid.
376 Ibid.

CHILD POVERTY AND EMPOWERING PARENTS

With such a focus on mothers, it is only appropriate a portion of this chapter is dedicated to the children these mothers raise. In 2018, the United Nations Development Program estimated half of all people living in poverty are younger than eighteen years old.[377]

To reduce the number of children living in poverty, more efforts will need to be made to:[378]

- educate parents
- reduce unplanned or unwanted pregnancies
- equip parents to build generational wealth

While parenting decisions are largely personal, rooted in parents' personal experiences, and less likely to be altered by external influence (despite stigma from media and policy makers), community leaders and governments can play a role in empowering parents by addressing the structural inequalities parents face.

Addressing these inequalities starts with empowering parents to support their children. One way to do this is through the creation of programs rooted in expectant giving.

Second Mile, a community development organization that began in 1986, has a program called Pride for Parents that "provides opportunities for families to use the resources they have to get what they need while protecting their pride and dignity."[379]

---

377 "Globally, Youth Are the Largest Poverty-Stricken Group, Says New UN Report | | UN News," United Nations, September 20, 2018.

378 Harrell R. Rodgers, *American Poverty in a New Era of Reform*, (London; New York: Routledge, Taylor et Francis Group, 2015).

379 "Second Mile," n.d. Second Mile Serving Neighborhoods Strengthening Schools Empowering Homes, Accessed July 27, 2020.

They offer significantly reduced prices on items like clothing, school supplies, and holiday toys. Nothing is given away for free. For parents low on cash, they can choose to volunteer with the organization and earn dollars of purchasing power for every hour of volunteer work.

As James L. Payne wrote in *Overcoming Welfare* on children's perceptions of their parents, "when someone else is paying the bills, it undercuts the parent's ability to gain respect and obedience."[380] These types of programs empower parents and strengthen the relationship between children and parents by allowing parents to buy items for their children rather than getting those items from someone who is giving them away.

Another method to empower parents is through expanding affordable, quality childcare services for working parents. Even when childcare is available, it may not address all of parents' needs due to cost or quality or even the hours the care is made available for parents before and after school. With an increase in single-parent families, adequate childcare services have become an even more critical resource.

CULTURE AND TRADITION

More often than not, culture and tradition are used as excuses to justify the dissemination and maintenance of harmful ideas in society, especially when it comes to equal rights. However, culture and tradition are not static. Value systems are constantly changing.

---

380 James L. Payne, *Overcoming Welfare: Expecting More from the Poor—and from Ourselves*, (New York, NY: Basic Books), 1998.

The values keeping women at different levels of advancement and opportunity around the world are not unique to a particular country or region or religious group. The values are patriarchal and are just as subject to change as other values during society's continuous progression. This task cannot be left to women alone. Everyone has to challenge existing gender norms and push boundaries.

While patriarchal values are relatively homogenous, the ways they can be changed globally will not be. Equal rights will look different depending on the context of the transition and the cultures being affected. This is where a community-based approach will be crucial.

Local knowledge and community expertise will play a pivotal role in promoting women's empowerment.

CONCLUSION: WOMEN'S RIGHTS ARE HUMAN RIGHTS

What the statistics in this chapter reveal is though women's rights are improving globally, there is much work to be done. With a focus on equal rights, more people can take control of their lives and take action to address issues impacting them. This focus and perspective can help shift the power dynamic of conversations. If gender discrimination impacts powerful women strong enough to have their voices heard on a global scale, imagine how much more harmful discrimination is for the world's Robins without the tools, resources, or influence to defend themselves. Including individuals impacted by extreme poverty and gender discrimination in decision-making will ensure more decisions benefit the interest of these communities.

Knowledge of our human rights empowers us to claim them. Women's rights are human rights, and a human rights approach to development work is a more effective approach when tackling global issues. Gender equality can be the catalyst for more inclusive, positive change if we are willing to make it a priority and address the data-proven issues facing women and young girls daily.

"Poverty does not prevent births but is unfavorable to the rearing of children, and so restrains multiplication, while the liberal reward of labor encourages it, as the wear and tear of the free man must be paid for just like that of the slave, though not so extravagantly. High wages increase population."

—ADAM SMITH, AUTHOR OF WEALTH OF NATIONS[381]

381 Adam Smith, Edward Cannan, *The Wealth of Nations* (New York: Bantam Classic, 2003)

PEOPLE PROBLEMS

———

Sorry Adam Smith, but poverty doesn't "restrain multiplication," it increases it. In part one, I briefly wrote about why people like Robin have more children. It is precisely because they are poor, the cost of having children is low, and only a few of their children are likely to survive.[382] Having more children is "insurance against child mortality."[383] In fact, when people escape extreme poverty, they often choose to have fewer children.

Why? They receive better educations and want to create more opportunities for their offspring. In fact, the number of babies per woman is decreasing as more women get educated and are allowed access to modern contraceptives. From 1950 until now, the number of babies per woman has decreased from a global average of at or over

382 "Information on Developing Countries—Population, Distribution, Growth and Change—National 5 Geography Revision—BBC Bitesize," n.d. BBC News.

383 Hans Rosling, Ola Rosling, and Rönnlund Anna Rosling, *Factfulness: Ten Reasons Were Wrong about the World—and Why Things, Are Better than You Think*, (London: Scepter, 2019), 95

five children to now less than two-and-a-half children per woman.[384,385]

However, Adam Smith wasn't all wrong. Global population did increase with an increase in wages, but poverty didn't restrain multiplication within families.

Though families are having fewer children, the global population has increased since 200 years ago. In the year 1800, the total human population was one billion, which is about the size of the population of China today.[386] Between 1800 and 1900, the world population grew from one billion to about 1.6 billion.[387] Now, the global population is about 7.7 billion.[388]

So, what happened? If families are having fewer children over time, what caused such a dramatic shift in the rate of global population growth?

Between the twentieth and twenty-first century, an important change occurred. On average, two parents had more than two children who survived long enough to also become parents. As Author Meg Jay wrote in her book *The Defining Decade: Why Your Twenties Matter--And How to Make the Most of Them Now,* "For hundreds of years, twentysomethings moved directly from being sons and daughters to being husbands and wives, but within just a few decades a new developmental period opened up."[389] This transition

384 Max Roser, 2014, "Fertility Rate," Our World in Data, February 19, 2014.
385 Ibid.
386 Max Roser, Hannah Ritchie, and Esteban Ortiz-Ospina, "World Population Growth," Our World in Data, May 9, 2013.
387 "World Population by Year.," Worldometer, Accessed July 27, 2020.
388 Ibid.
389 Meg Jay, *The Defining Decade: What Your Twenties Matter and How to Make the Most of Them Now,* (Edinburgh, United Kingdom: Canongate Books Ltd, 2016).

to a new developmental period is linked to a process called demographic transition.[390]

In this chapter, I will:

- break down the four core stages of demographic transition and how they relate to population size
- describe how Housing First policies have upended traditional homeless policies
- explore shifting perspectives on immigration

DEMOGRAPHIC TRANSITION

Demographic transition can be divided into four core stages:[391]

1. In stage one, there are many births and deaths due to the general bad living conditions of a nation.[392]
2. In stage two, there is explosive population growth and as living conditions improve, there are more births, and fewer deaths.
   a. When the United Kingdom was in stage two between 1750 and 1850, the population doubled.
3. In stage three, explosive population growth slows as fewer babies are conceived, because when the risk of child mortality is lower, parents often choose to have fewer children.
4. In stage four, population becomes more balanced and stable as fewer people die and fewer people are born.

---

390 Kurzgesagt—In a Nutshell, "Overpopulation—The Human Explosion Explained," YouTube video, 6:39, December 22, 2016.

391 Ibid.

392 Think back to the industrial revolution that was discussed in part 1. In the eighteenth century, the entire world, including Europe, was living like Robins. Though many children were born, many died just as fast, which caused population levels to stay stable. The industrial revolution catapulted major world powers into stage 2 as better food, hygiene, and medicine improved life expectancy and decreased child mortality rates.

Most of the world's countries have made it to the fourth stage and in a shorter period of time than major world powers of the eighteenth century. For example, Malaysia and South Africa transitioned in thirty-four years, Bangladesh transitioned in twenty years, and Iran transitioned in ten years. [393,394,395]

According to a Pew Research Center analysis of the UN's 2019 World Population Prospects Report, "By 2100, the world's population is projected to reach approximately 10.9 billion, with annual growth of less than 0.1 percent."[396]

As the child mortality rate continues to decrease around the world, human population growth is also slowing. As parents are better educated, have greater access to contraceptives, and earn more money, their desires start to shift toward having fewer, better educated children. Hans Rosling argued, "the only proven method for curbing population growth is to eradicate extreme poverty and give people better lives, including education and contraceptives."[397]

Discussions surrounding overpopulation have become quite popular in recent decades. Even if the population is predicted to plateau at around ten billion, it doesn't mean that it will be easy to provide resources for all of those people. This is especially important if our goal in this time period

---

393 Kurzgesagt—In a Nutshell, "Overpopulation—The Human Explosion Explained," YouTube video, 6:39, December 22, 2016.

394 Ibid.

395 Ibid.

396 Anthony Cilluffo and Neil G. Ruiz, "World Population Growth Is Expected to Nearly Stop by 2100," Pew Research Center, June 17, 2019.

397 Hans Rosling, Ola Rosling, and Rönnlund Anna Rosling, *Factfulness: Ten Reasons Were Wrong about the World—and Why Things Are Better than You Think*, (London: Scepter, 2019), 101

between now and 2100 is to improve living standards for the world's poorest individuals.

COMBATING OVERPOPULATION THROUGH SEX EDUCATION

One of the best ways to combat overpopulation is through effective sex education. Safe-sex programs teach about the essentials of sexuality, human development, contraception, and fostering positive interactions. They cover how to resist peer pressure over drugs and sex too.[398]

The programs are designed to share the information in a nonjudgmental way that allows young people to ask questions, learn helpful information about health risks such as STDs and AIDS, and make decisions for themselves rather than pressure from other teens or misinformation.

The education typically includes mentors who share information about abstinence along with details about the potential consequences—emotionally and physically—of having sex early in life. Some programs go beyond abstinence training and offer counseling services.[399]

What contributes to young people being left uninformed about sexual health?[400] Obstacles like:

1. fear of judgement from family or friends
2. lack of transportation to clinics
3. lack of information about where to find birth control or contraceptives

This lack of education is dangerous. Harrell Rodgers, Jr. described teen pregnancy as a "superhighway to poverty"

---

398 Harrell R. Rodgers, *American Poverty in a New Era of Reform*, (London; New York: Routledge, Taylor et Francis Group, 2015).

399 Ibid.

400 Ibid.

because the chances the family will end up poor and the children will face many serious problems growing up is high.[401] To reduce the poverty population in future generations, more efforts will need to be made to reduce teen pregnancy rates.

Along with encouraging safer sex, abstinence is also an option. Conversations around abstinence often seems to revolve around religious influence. However, values, even within religious groups, change all of the time. For example, the Roman Catholic Church believes using contraception is morally unacceptable.[402] According to the catechism of the Catholic Church, only "methods of birth regulation based on self-observation and the use of infertile periods, is in conformity with the objective criteria of morality."[403]

Despite this, in a Pew Research Center survey conducted in 2016 among 2,283 respondents—817 of whom were Catholic—8 percent of Catholics said using contraceptives was morally wrong, 41 percent said it was morally acceptable, and 48 percent said it was not a moral issue at all.[404]

Beyond safe-sex programs, hybrid sex education programs try to bridge the gap between abstinence education and safe-sex programs by focusing on the whole person.[405] In hybrid programs, sex education is one part of a comprehensive approach centered on education, self-esteem, career planning, and goal setting.[406]Within hybrid programs, it

401 Ibid.

402 Catechism of the Catholic Church, 2nd ed, (Vatican City: Vatican Press, 1997).

403 Ibid.

404 "Very Few Americans See Contraception as Morally Wrong," Pew Research Center's Religion & Public Life Project, May 30, 2020.

405 Harrell R. Rodgers, American Poverty in a New Era of Reform, (London; New York: Routledge Taylor et Francis Group, 2015).

406 Ibid.

is not uncommon for services like tutoring and counseling to be involved along with formal mentorship components. Hybrid programs require a higher investment of time and resources, which keeps schools and organizations from implementing the strategy.[407]

GIVING THE HOMELESS HOMES: FINLAND

Speaking of investments, finding homes for the increasing global population is already proving to be a challenge.

Between 2017 and 2018, the number of homeless people living in the United Kingdom rose by 7 percent.[408] Between 2016 and 2018, the number of homeless people living in Germany increased by 35 percent.[409] Between 2011 and 2018, the number of homeless people living in France increased by 50 percent.[410]

By contrast, 2017 marked Finland's fifth consecutive year of decreasing its homeless population. According to a 2019 article from the *Guardian* profiling Finland's homeless population, "the number of long-term homeless people in Finland has fallen by more than 35 percent."[411] As of 2019, nationwide about 5,500 people in Finland are classified as homeless out of a national population of over five million.[412]

What is the root of this difference? The Finnish government has radically changed its approach to handling homelessness. The traditional model is to transition homeless

---

407 Ibid.

408 Alex Gray, "Here's How Finland Solved Its Homelessness Problem," World Economic Forum, February 13, 2018.

409 Ibid.

410 Ibid.

411 Jon Henley, "It's a Miracle: Helsinki's Radical Solution to Homelessness," *The Guardian*, Guardian News and Media, June 3, 2019.

412 Ibid.

individuals from the street to night shelters to hostels to transitional housing units and, finally, to independent apartments.

Finland uses a Housing First Model. The solution is exactly what is sounds like: people without homes are given a home first, then supported in addressing the reasons behind why they became homeless in the first place. The strategy was first introduced in 2007 and has turned away from traditional homelessness policies that assume homeless people should work out their problems first before obtaining permanent accommodation.

Within the model, the homeless are given permanent housing on a normal lease with constant support made available. They pay rent, receive housing benefits, and contribute to the cost of their support resources if their income level can support it. The difference is covered by the local government, but the approach requires the support of many partners like volunteers, municipal governments, and NGOs. The individualized support services tenants receive typically involve resources like housing advisors who help the tenants pay rent or apply for government benefits as well as financial and debt counselors.

To address the gap between the homes needed and the supply of housing in the country, Finland also focused on increasing the supply of affordable rentals by using a variety of sources like its pre-existing social housing. In addition, it bought privately owned apartments and built new housing blocks. Now, there are no homeless shelters in Finland. Instead, the shelters are used as supported housing.

Juha Kaakinen, chief executive of the Y-Foundation that also provides housing to Housing First, has admitted to the high costs of the program. However, Kaakinen argues it is "always more cost-effective to aim to end homelessness instead of simply trying to manage it."[413] When compared to the costs associated with a person being homeless, the model saves money. For example, housing one long-term homeless person saves about fifteen thousand euros per year.[414]

The UK-based homelessness charity Crisis conducted a study that found a Housing First policy implemented in the United Kingdom could be more than five times as effectively and nearly five times more cost-effective than current methods.[415]

GIVING THE HOMELESS HOMES: CANADA

The strategy has also been implemented across the Atlantic in Canada as well. In Medicine Hat, Alberta, its sixty thousand residents all have roofs over their heads.[416] The city's policy is within ten days of living in a shelter or on the streets, an individual receives mandated housing. In fact, the city's mayor, Ted Clugston, said ten days is the longest time a person would be left without housing.[417]

Typically, the city finds housing for the homeless faster. In 2009, the city began its efforts to start building homes for the homeless. It costs the city about US$20,000 a year to house a homeless person, but it would cost about US$100,000 a year if they were on the street.[418]

---

413 Alex Gray, "Here's How Finland Solved Its Homelessness Problem," World Economic Forum, February 13, 2018.

414 "Housing First Scheme in Finland: Y-Foundation (Y-Säätiö)," The Y Foundation, August 20, 2018.

415 "Housing First Feasibility Study for Liverpool City Region (2017)," Crisis, November 7, 2017.

416 Terry Turner, "Find Out How This Canadian City Has Eliminated Homelessness," Good News Network, October 7, 2015.

417 Ibid.

418 Ibid.

GIVING THE HOMELESS HOMES: UNITED STATES

The strategy has spread to the United States in Utah, where the Housing First Model has reduced its homelessness by 91 percent in ten years.[419] Currently, Utah is on track to be the first state in the United States to successfully address homelessness all while saving money per homeless person helped.

Right now, there are very few places in the United States where someone earning minimum wage can afford to cover the rent for a one-bedroom apartment. Almost eighteen million households spend more than half of their income on rent.[420] Financial burdens like student loan debt and wage stagnation have kept millions of people from owning homes, which is making it harder for families to build wealth and earn economic security.

To combat this growing trend, Representative Ilhan Omar announced a new plan called the "Homes for All Act" to invest one trillion USD to expand affordable housing.[421] The plan would create twelve million new homes over the next ten years and, notably, invest more into the maintenance of current public housing as well as directing more cash to the Federal Housing Trust Fund.[422] The fund is responsible for building private, affordable housing for low-income individuals. The plan involves building new units to help drive current housing costs down by increasing the housing supply.[423]

---

419 Ibid.

420 "2019 State of the Nation's Housing Report: Lack of Affordable Housing," Cost of Home, 2019.

421 Kriston Capps, "There's a Big Housing Problem. Here's a Huge Plan to Fix It," CityLab, November 21, 2019.

422 Ibid.

423 Ibid.

GIVING THE HOMELESS HOMES: CRITICISMS

The Housing First approach is not without its fair share of criticism. In Finland, many social workers disagreed with the idea the homeless should receive homes without needing to address any of their social, medical, or emotional problems first.

The philosophy of the Housing First Model argues it is much harder to address one's problems without housing security. This idea is similar to Maslow's hierarchy of needs which summarizes five tiers of human needs.[424] From the bottom up the tiers are:

- physiological needs (air, water, food, shelter, sleep, clothing, reproduction)
- safety needs (personal security, employment, resources, health, property)
- love and belonging (friendship, intimacy, family, sense of connection)
- esteem (respect, self-esteem, status, recognition, strength, freedom)
- self-actualization (desire to become the most that one can be)

Maslow argues needs at the bottom of the pyramid, like food and shelter, need to be met before higher needs, like self-esteem, can be met.[425]

Another criticism faced in Finland is in the residential areas where new housing was built for the homeless population. Current residents were unhappy and felt the new tenants would negatively impact their neighborhood. In response, part of the Housing First approach is to collaborate

424 Saul Mcleod, "Maslow's Hierarchy of Needs," *Simply Psychology*, March 20, 2020.
425 Ibid.

with the communities and provide benefits to older residents. For example, there is a focus placed on developing a sense of community through open house events, taking care of green spaces in the area, and picking up litter.[426]

According to the Y-Foundation's "A Home of Your Own" handbook on the Housing First Model's implementation in Finland, it typically takes about two years for areas to adjust to both the new unit and the new residents. It takes about the same time for the residents to get used to the areas.[427]

HOME LESS FREQUENTLY

Among the homeless population, one subsection hard to track is foreign immigrants. In a report on immigration conducted by the Center for Social Justice, it was found "Homelessness among immigrants has been difficult to measure with an increasing number sofa surfing, staying in temporary accommodation and moving regularly."[428] According to the report, recent statistics in the United Kingdom claim "one-third of all rough sleepers are foreign nationals."[429]

Immigrants who do find consistent accommodation are often vulnerable to losing it due to a myriad of factors. However, immigration is not entirely negative despite the vulnerability to poverty immigrant populations face.[430]

In fact, increased immigration could be a crucial component of poverty alleviation in the future. The Center for

---

426 Alex Gray, "Here's How Finland Solved Its Homelessness Problem," World Economic Forum, February 13, 2018.

427 Y-Foundation, "A Home of Your Own," Otava Book Printing Ltd, June 2, 2017.

428 The Center for Social Justice, "Prioritizing Growth: The Future of Immigration Policy," August 2019.

429 Ibid.

430 Ibid.

Global Development economist Michael Clemens described immigration as "the biggest idea in development that no one really tried."[431]

A 2018 report from the Center for Global Development written by Lant Pritchett put it best: "Simply allowing more labor mobility holds vastly more promise for reducing poverty than anything else on the development agenda."[432] In his paper, Pritchett finds the gains from immigrants moving to high-income countries and getting paid their wages are much higher than the gains from a lifetime earnings increase in their home country. His work highlights the importance of shifting away from handouts promoting paternalism and resentment and shifting toward strategies that allow people living in poverty to empower *themselves* through work.

In 2019, Europe had the largest number of international immigrants (eighty-two million), followed by North America (fifty-nine million), and Northern Africa and Western Asia (forty-nine million).[433] Thinking in the millions makes these numbers seem large, but as of 2019, only 3.5 percent of the world's population lives outside their country of birth as immigrants. [434,435]

---

431 Art Carden, "Are We Serious About Reducing Poverty? Then We Need to Welcome Immigrants," *Forbes*, Forbes Magazine, October 19, 2018.

432 Lant Pritchett, "Alleviating Global Poverty: Labor Mobility, Direct Assistance, and Economic Growth," CGD Working Paper 479, Washington, DC: Center for Global Development, 2018.

433 "The Number of International Migrants Reaches 272 Million, Continuing an Upward Trend in All World Regions, Says UN | UN DESA Department of Economic and Social Affairs," United Nations, September 17, 2019.

434 Ibid.

435 By country about half of all international immigrants live in just ten countries (in order by number of international immigrants): United

These statistics are leaving money on the table. According to scientists at the World Bank, if all of the world's middle- and high-income countries let in just 3 percent more immigrants, the world's poorest would have US$305 billion more to spend. Open borders would make the world richer.[436]

In fact, Rutger Bregman argues allowing for open borders is the "single measure that could wipe out all poverty everywhere."[437] Strict border laws lead people to sell their labor for less than they could in high income countries and contribute to unfair discrimination keeping people from the economic and social opportunities they have abroad.

IMMIGRATION AS A GLOBAL THREAT

Arguments against immigration often revolve around its impact on job opportunities. For example, in some cases there is a fear immigration can take jobs away from locals.

The truth is an increased number of workers increases consumption, which increases demand and supports the creation of more jobs. New American Economy (NAE), a bipartisan research and advocacy group focused on immigration policy, found mass deportation in the United States would lead to a US$1.6 trillion reduction in GDP.[438]

Immigrants and undocumented workers often taken the low-skilled jobs citizens don't want. When compared to

States, Germany, Saudi Arabia, the Russian Federation, the UK, the UAE, France, Canada, Australia, and Italy.

436 Terrie L. Walmsley, L. Alan Winters, S. Amer Ahmed, and Christopher R. Parsons, "Measuring the Impact of the Movement of Labor Using a Model of Bilateral Migration Flows," World Bank.

437 Rutger Bregman, Utopia for Realists, (London: Bloomsbury), 2018, 181

438 Daniel Kurt, "Assessing the Pros & Cons of Immigration Reform," Investopedia, May 12, 2020.

US-born citizens, the NAE found low-skilled immigrants are 18 percent more likely to take unfavorable jobs requiring inconvenient hours.

As birthrates drop in the United States, immigration can also fill gaps in the labor market because immigrants often start companies. In the United States, immigrants are twice as likely to start businesses compared to US-born citizens.[439] In states with increased immigrant populations, there are often trends of lower unemployment rates, too.

Another fear is cheaper immigrant labor will drive down local wages for vulnerable populations and low-skilled workers. A number of studies have shown wage impact among low-skilled workers is less than 1 percent.[440]

What about the immigrants who are too lazy to work and living on public assistance?

In the United States, undocumented immigrants take less advantage of public assistance than native citizens. According to a 2018 study by the Cato Institute, eligible immigrants use 27 percent fewer benefits compared to US natives of similar incomes and ages.[441] Undocumented immigrants, with only a few exceptions, are not eligible for public benefits like Social Security, Medicaid, Medicare, or food stamps.

Undocumented immigrants nationwide pay an estimated 8 percent of their income in state and local taxes and, collectively, immigrants pay between ninety 140 billion USD in taxes each year.[442] Of that amount, roughly

439 "Myths and Facts About Immigrants and Immigration," Anti-Defamation League.

440 Daniel Kurt, "Assessing the Pros & Cons of Immigration Reform," Investopedia, May 12, 2020.

441 "Myths and Facts About Immigrants and Immigration," Anti-Defamation League.

442 Ibid.

11.64 billion is paid by undocumented citizens.[443] Despite the fact Social Security is deducted from their paychecks, undocumented immigrants have no way of accessing the benefits.

Immigrants are not as dangerous as people are led to believe, either. Regardless of where they come from, what their immigration status is, or how educated they are, immigrants are less likely than native-born citizens to commit crimes or become incarcerated.[444] Between 1990 and 2017, the amount of immigrants in the United States increased from 7.9 percent of the total population (19.8 million) to 13.7 percent of the total population (44.5 million).[445,446] During this time period, the violent crime rate in the United States decreased from 731.8 violent crimes per one hundred thousand people to 394.9 violent crimes per one hundred thousand people—a 46 percent decrease.[447]

IMMIGRATION AS A POLITICAL TOOL

In a 2017 study by Beth Elise Whitaker entitled "Migration within Africa and Beyond," Whitaker outlined the current international refugee system and highlighted the use of immigration policy as a political tool.[448]

---

443 Ibid.

444 Ibid.

445 Steven A. Camarota, "A Record-Setting Decade of Immigration: 2000-2010," Center for Immigration Studies, October 5, 2011.

446 Steven A. Camarota, Karen Zeigler, "Record 44.5 Million Immigrants in 2017: Non-Mexico Latin American, Asian, and African populations grew most," Center for Immigration Studies, September 15, 2018.

447 United States Crime Rates 1960–2018.

448 The terms immigrants (i.e., migrants) and refugees refer to different groups of people. According to the UN, a refugee is a person outside of their home country due to any circumstance that has disturbed public order. In contrast a migrant is someone who changes their country of

The current refugee system consists of wealthy donor governments paying to keep millions of refugees in Africa and Asia and resettling less than 0.5 percent in Europe and North America.[449] Basically, wealthy countries are paying poorer ones to decrease immigration. Despite this, larger governments are now reducing funding for good governance and democracy programs. This system barely addresses the root causes of migration, but it does provide an opportunity for recipient governments to solicit donor funds.[450]

When countries threaten to close their refugee camps due to a lack of funding, the threat often inspires increased funding. Rather than face the political problems leading people to migrate, the countries highlight their economic troubles to attract aid and avoid taking responsibility.[451]

Recently, Beth Whitaker and Jason Giersch conducted research on eleven African countries to support the idea anti-immigration rhetoric is being used as a political tool. When political party ideologies become too similar, the two researchers noted, politicians build up support by scapegoating immigrants and refugees as the blame for structural problems ranging from crime to unemployment.[452] This strategy legitimizes and strengthens xenophobia in the area, and democracy is used as a tool to spread harmful ideas.

---

residence. The term is common when referring to individuals who move for work or in search of better living conditions. While being a refugee is often political, being a migrant is typically economic.

449 Beth Elise Whitaker, "Migration within Africa and Beyond" African Studies Review, Volume 60, No. 2 (September 2017), p. 209–220

450 Ibid.

451 Ibid.

452 Beth Elise Whitaker and Jason Giersch, 2015, "Political Competition and Attitudes towards Immigration in Africa," Journal of Ethnic and Migration Studies 41 (10):1536–57.

Essentially, as elections become increasingly competitive, hostility surrounding immigration increases.[453]

CONCLUSION

As the global population increases, conversations surrounding the quality of sex education for young people, the provision of adequate housing for homeless populations, and the role of immigration in shaping both cultures and workspaces will all become increasingly relevant. Understanding some of the ideas and data surrounding these topics will lead to more effective policies.

I am a child of immigrants. Nearly my entire family left Liberia to escape as the country they knew and loved slowly became a war zone. Decades later, the countries we live in now have become our homes, yet our connection to our roots remains strong. I have seen firsthand the positive impact immigration can have on families, so I struggled with trying to find an objective way to describe immigration and its impacts on the globe.

In the end, I sided with data. I sought out statistics about immigration. I searched for articles speaking out against it to develop a more well-rounded perspective. I ended up finding information I already suspected but couldn't prove before: immigrants aren't dangerous, lazy, or exploitative as many people are led to believe. Immigration certainly should not be considered a global threat.

What could be a global threat, on the other hand, is over-population. As data predictions change, only time will tell.

Uplifting and empowering people can take many forms:

---

453 Ibid.

- To both combat the threat of overpopulation and empower families—especially mothers— promoting sex education and contraception is a hopefully way forward.
- To beat homelessness, we can start by looking at the word itself and giving the homeless what they need most—a home.
- To make the world richer, to provide more opportunities for jobs and skills exchange, and, more broadly, to eradicate extreme poverty, we can open borders globally.

To put it simply, people-centered problems require people-centered solutions. To make substantive change, we have to start by centering our actions on the people who need to be helped.

"I have spent more energy on poverty alleviation than on anything else."

—PRESIDENT XI JINPING, PRESIDENT OF THE
PEOPLE'S REPUBLIC OF CHINA[454]

---

454 Voices on the Frontline, Directed by Peter Getzels, Written by Robert
Lawrence Kuhn, 2019.

CASE STUDY: CHINA

––––

China's success in alleviating poverty at a national scale is an incredible feat with global implications for how extreme poverty is addressed moving forward.

In this chapter, I will explain:

- the historical context for China's focus on poverty alleviation
- China's poverty alleviation strategy
- the core criticisms of its programs
- the political factors at play in making the plan successful in China specifically

With this information, we can begin to understand what specific elements of the approach can be applied elsewhere.

HISTORICAL CONTEXT

In the past forty-one years, nearly 850 million Chinese people have been lifted out of extreme poverty.[455] When China first began implementing its poverty alleviation strategies, it focused on economic development that lifted people out

––––––––––––

455 Huifeng He, "China's subsidies lifting rural villages out of poverty, but is Xi Jinping's plan sustainable?" November 3, 2019.

of poverty naturally and transitioned China from a poor country to an upper middle-income country.

Despite this progress, there were pockets of poverty throughout the country that did not improve. In 2012, when President Xi Jinping came to power, there were over one hundred million rural Chinese people living in extreme poverty.[456] As a quick reminder, that number was not static; people were falling into poverty while others were lifted out. The last one hundred million were primarily "the poor" who lived in remote areas, were sick or elderly, or had no education or jobs.

President Xi believes for China to be considered a moderately prosperous society, none of its citizens can live below the extreme poverty threshold. Rather than giving away money, the government focuses on giving animals to raise, food, education, and other forms of support.

In November of 2013, President Xi first proposed the concept of "targeted" or "precision" poverty alleviation.[457] By 2017, China's total expenditure on poverty alleviation was over seventy-two billion USD.[458] President Xi's goal is to eliminate extreme poverty in China by the end of 2020, and the focus is treated like a military order. Officials working toward poverty alleviation can't leave their posts or be promoted unless they fulfill the specific goals for their assigned village or town.

Why does all of this need to happen by the end of 2020?

---

456 *Voices on the Frontline,* Directed by Peter Getzels, Written by Robert Lawrence Kuhn, 2019.

457 The use of the word "targeted" and "precision" were in reference to the creation of more individualized procedures and programs.

458 *Voices on the Frontline,* Directed by Peter Getzels, Written by Robert Lawrence Kuhn, 2019.

Aside from being committed to poverty alleviation, the year aligns with the country's two centenary goals.[459] The Communist Party of China was founded in 1921. In 2021, it will be celebrating its one hundredth anniversary where it hopes to share its status as "moderately prosperous society" with no residents living in extreme poverty. Beyond this, China hopes to become a modernized socialist country by 2050, at the one hundredth anniversary of New China in 2049.[460]

CHINA'S PLAN

What is China's plan exactly?

The government's approach is to identify the country's poorest communities and families through a mix of standardized methods, analysis of annual income, and tests of healthcare standards, education, and sanitation. Beyond this, China is focused on connecting "the poor" to the rest of the country by improving the national road network and expanding internet coverage across the country. The five core tenets of China's plan are:[461]

- education
- industry
- ecological compensation
- social security
- relocation

459 Robert Lawrence Kuhn, 2019, *China Daily*, October 11.
460 Ibid.
461 *Voices on the Frontline*, Directed by Peter Getzels, Written by Robert Lawrence Kuhn, 2019.

A hallmark of the plan is its individualized approach for every family below the poverty line. Families are divided into four types of households:[462]

- those that don't qualify for poverty relief
- those that have fallen back into poverty
- those that are newly poor
- those that have been lifted out of poverty

Each family's plan is tracked individually on an interactive map that spans all of China and is updated regularly.

This level of precision would not be possible without numerous, dedicated staff. There are five levels of local party secretaries—provincial, municipal, county, township, village—who coordinate their efforts along with third-party evaluations conducted at random to support accuracy and honesty. Every month, on-the-ground staff visit impoverished families and help them develop strategies to increase their income. These staff members often work for two years or more in the same area.

To understand China's poverty plan beyond articles and research papers, I watched a documentary called *China's War on Poverty: Voices from the Frontlines* hosted and written by Robert Kuhn. He is an investment banker, expert on China, and the author of books such as *How China's Leaders Think*, and bestseller *The Man Who Changed China: The Life and Legacy of Jiang Zemin*. He also received China's highest international honor, the China Reform and Friendship Medal, which has been awarded to ten foreigners in four decades.

In the documentary, Kuhn features Lingmen Village's first party secretary, Huang Haijun, among other families and staff. Like other first party secretaries, Huang Haijun

---

462 Ibid.

is responsible for creating personalized mobility plans for poor families. A featured interaction between Huang Haijun and a local villager gave a clearer picture of what this work looks like daily.

Huang Haijun had been observing a villager's planting habits over time before noting, "I think your ten mu of paddy rice can be better used if you grow mulberry and rear silkworms. It's quite lucrative to do sericulture these days." The villager replied, "The problem is that we have to cross a creek. Maybe the government can help us build a bridge." Huang Haijun ensured her he would write a report.[463]

Stories like these highlight how specific this work gets. At a national level, it could take months, if not years, to ascertain the reason a village farmer isn't planting more lucrative crops is because they need a bridge to cross a creek and maintain regular access to specific areas of their fields. At a precision poverty level, it takes one conversation.

Since it began, China's precision poverty alleviation program has brought out ten to fourteen million people per year out of extreme poverty.[464] As of 2018, there were thirty million people living in extreme poverty, and by 2019, the number was down to 16.6 million.[465,466] China is on track to accomplish its goal of eliminating extreme poverty in the country by the end of 2020.

While China is at the last lap of its *national* poverty alleviation efforts, the world is at the last lap of its *global* poverty

463 *Voices on the Frontline*, Directed by Peter Getzels, Written by Robert Lawrence Kuhn, 2019.

464 Robert Lawrence Kuhn, *China Daily*, October 11, 2019.

465 CGTN America, "Sourabh Gupta has more on poverty alleviation in China," YouTube video, 2:34, July 8, 2019,

466 Ibid.

alleviation efforts. However, the last lap is always the hardest. Impoverished households are often poorly educated and cut off from the outside world.

First Party Secretary Huang Haijun summarized it well when he shared, "People want a better life but don't always know what a better life could be."[467] For the world's Robins, many elements of the world's Camerons lives are beyond imagination. This divide is part of what is driving China's efforts to expand its program beyond housing and subsidies to also introduce more technology and innovation.

Now, let's delve into the five core tenets of China's plan to increase our understanding of what happens on the ground:

1. Education
2. Ecological Compensation
3. Industry
4. Social Security
5. Relocation

THE FIVE CORE TENANTS: EDUCATION AND ECOLOGICAL COMPENSATION

China has made education free for its poorest children. To incentivize teachers, it has provided new benefits like living expense grants and special subsidies. For young children living in the rural mountainside, schools are small, poorly, funded and not as advanced as city schools. Furthermore, enrollment trends decrease overtime, especially in the countryside.[468]

Zhou Jing, a student from Huanxian County working in Lanzhou City, was featured in Kuhn's documentary and

---

467 *Voices on the Frontline*, Directed by Peter Getzels, Written by Robert Lawrence Kuhn, 2019.
468 Ibid.

highlighted this unfortunate pattern: "In junior high, there were around sixty students in my class. By the time we took the high school entrance exam, there were only about forty. From those forty, only five of us enrolled in college."[469]

For adults, migrant workers can receive financial assistance to pursue vocational training. At the village level, poverty alleviation staff members can lead workshops on how to plant trees or raise silkworms.

The ecological compensation tenant is primarily focused on improving the environment and encouraging tourism. If individuals are living in environmentally vulnerable locations, the government provides them with compensation in the form of subsidies.

THE FIVE CORE TENANTS: INDUSTRY

China's industrial development is focused on creating sustainable micro-businesses through pairing. In the pairing process, communities and organizations in wealthier parts of the country collaborate with impoverished communities to help improve their financial well-being. The richer partner shares its experts, knowledge, and wealth with the poorer partner.

One helpful example of this approach can be found in Fuhai County within the Xinjiang Uyghur Autonomous Region, where a small company called Wang Yung Co. has partnered with local farmers to provide jobs and financial support in the countryside.[470] In 2008, a representative from Wang Yung Co. traveled to Fuhai County from Zhejiang and built a factory to collect camel milk. The company was

---

469 Ibid.

470 CGTN, "China's War on Poverty: Getting rich by raising camels," YouTube video, 2:15, August 3, 2019.

willing to pay ten yuan (around US$1.43) per kilo for the milk.[471] One camel could make the camel herders up to thirty yuan and with the factory as a buyer, it would be easy to sell. As of 2008, the local camel herders started buying more camels increased from ten camels to more than two hundred by 2019.[472] There's no coddling either—if the inspected milk isn't up to standards, then it gets rejected.

Though the herders wanted to expand their production, it is getting harder to do because of their limited access to bank loans. Many have already borrowed a lot of money. In response, Wang Yung Co. secures bank loans on behalf of the herders, which helps the herders help themselves while the company makes larger profits.

Industrial development in China is a helpful example of the importance of partnership over paternalism in poverty alleviation efforts. Though the company benefits from the fulfillment of helping others and assisting in alleviating poverty, it also gains a new supplier for its business. *It is an exchange rather than a gift.*

THE FIVE CORE TENANTS: SOCIAL SECURITY

To prevent China's impoverished from slipping back into poverty, the government provides social and medical insurance to villagers along with subsidies for education, microloans, medical insurance, and home restoration. For those who can't work, it also provides direct payments. Beyond the level of extreme poverty, families can reach out to civil affairs offices for more suitable forms of assistance.

---

471 Ibid.
472 Ibid.

To ensure the families who receive benefits need them, the village first party secretaries host democratic evaluation meetings where villagers vote on where each family should be categorized based on the four household statuses.[473] While officials may not always understand the full picture, the villagers are well-aware of how their neighbors live and have a deeper understanding of the social context of the neighborhood. Initial investigations are done door-to-door and involve local leaders. These evaluations are a part of the last step in determining who is and is not considered poor at a local level.

THE FIVE CORE TENANTS: RELOCATION

Relocation is one of the most unique elements of China's poverty alleviation efforts. Because it is so different, I am going to spend more time describing its history and impact.

Rather than focusing on specific individuals and families, relocation moves entire villages into suburban and urban communities within China.

In his documentary, Kuhn identified the four requirements needing to be met before a village becomes eligible for relocation:[474]

- land conditions must be unsuitable for farming
- the environment must be degraded or at risk of natural disaster
- a priority must be placed on people who are enthusiastic about moving
- living conditions must be below standards

---

473 *Voices on the Frontline*, Directed by Peter Getzels, Written by Robert Lawrence Kuhn, 2019.
474 Ibid.

This approach was developed by President Xi Jinping in 1997 when he was serving as the deputy provincial party secretary of Fujian. He was assigned as part of the "Pairing Up" scheme, similar to the pairing processes conducted today to coordinate efforts, between the impoverished Ningxia region and the affluent Fujian province.[475] He encouraged businesses to work in Ningxia and partner with local firms. Beyond that, he proposed a resettlement program where entire communities would move to more fertile land near the Yellow River. This particular project will be explained with more depth later in this chapter.

Before I made sense of this method, I had to stop and ask myself, *why would anyone want to stay in a failing area?*[476]

- For many, the costs of moving all of a family's personal belongings are too high to bear, both financially and emotionally—often generations of history can be associated with a particular house or region.
- City life is expensive, and the cost of living is higher. While in villages, people have their own homes and grow their food. In the city, renting is quite common and there is not enough land available to grow large amounts of food, which makes families dependent on local markets and expensive stores.
- Job insecurity is a major risk for low-skilled workers.
- The decision to relocate can divide families. If young people decide to move to the city for work or school, it can strain their relationships with their parents and other relatives.

---

475 CGTN, "Inside China's 'model town' for poverty alleviation," YouTube video, 6:18, February 26, 2018.

476 *Voices on the Frontline*, Directed by Peter Getzels, Written by Robert Lawrence Kuhn, 2019.

- Though the countryside makes for a challenging living environment, it is beautiful. Some people stay for the simple pleasure of being surrounded by nature, peace, and relative solitude.

When individuals and families relocate, they are placed in new communities filled with other relocated residents.

First party secretaries are also assigned to these regions to help with relocation. For those who move, there are many perks:[477]

- housing is free
- the government provides basic amenities like sofas, beds, kitchenware, and TVs
- for some families, small food rations of food are provided

The biggest logistical challenge for the first party secretaries is helping to combat unemployment among the relocated. In response, the government provides training to help residents find work.

The biggest personal challenge is adjusting to the move. There is no going back—literally.

As soon as villagers move, the government begins demolishing their old homes and focusing on efforts to restore the ecosystem of the land. The villagers lose the land they have subsisted on all of their lives. Many of the people moving worry about how they can survive without it. This is challenging for the elderly villagers who only know rural village life. It involves a change of identity, thought, and approach to life. The government's goal with relocation efforts is for young children and teens who relocate to be integrated into urban life by the time they reach adulthood.[478]

---

477 Ibid.
478 Ibid.

RELOCATION: A MODEL CITY

As I mentioned earlier, President Xi Jinping setup a poverty alleviation program when he was the deputy party chief of Fujian Province. His work led to the development of Minning, the "model city" of relocation programs.[479] The story of the town's relationship to the relocation program begins in the Ningxia region, designated as the least habitable region in 1972 by the World Food Program.[480]

Initially, the region suffered from:[481]

- poor roads
- frequent natural disasters
- severe soil erosion
- no electricity
- no drinking water nearby
- nearly impassable mountain paths during heavy rains

Generations living in Ningxia wanted to escape their unbearable poverty. Thousands of Ningxia residents have now been relocated to a new town called Minning that is paired with the prosperous province Fujian. Before, Ningxia residents could hardly afford food each month. Now, they can buy food at markets, walk or transport themselves along roads, use consistent electricity, and shower with running water.

With assistance from Fujian, infrastructure like roads, water cellars, schools, healthcare facilities, and other model communities have been built in Ningxia over the past twenty years.[482] As a symbol of gratitude, Minning's name is related to Fujian. It is the combination of "Min," the nickname of

---

479 CGTN, "Inside China's 'model town' for poverty alleviation," YouTube video, 6:18, February 26, 2018.
480 Ibid.
481 Ibid.
482 Ibid.

Fujian, and "Ning" for Ningxia.[483]Fujian experts have shared new farming techniques with Minning residents to help increase their incomes.

For example, the village has built three hundred greenhouses for growing mushrooms. Each greenhouse can earn over eight thousand yuan a year.[484,485] Minning has inspired its residents to broaden their perspectives. Now, they are no longer reliant on harvests as their primary sources of income and sustenance.

The partnership between Fujian and Ningxia has gone on for more than twenty years.[486] Since then, over sixty thousand people have relocated to Minning and across Ningxia, and 1.6 million people have benefitted from relocation.[487,488]

WHERE THE PROGRAM FALLS SHORT

Though the benefits of China's poverty alleviation program are life-changing for its recipients, the methods are not without their fair share of criticism. Robert Kuhn outlined four core challenges of the program he observed when making his documentary, outlined below:

1. The first major challenge of the program is its data collection methods.[489]

The officials who lead the poverty alleviation work also lead the assessments, which reflects a clear conflict of interest.

---

483 Ibid.
484 Ibid.
485 Ibid.
486 Ibid.
487 Ibid.
488 Ibid.
489 Robert Lawrence Kuhn, "The Multiple Meanings of Xi's Targeted Poverty Alleviation," (English Translation), South China Morning Post, August 5, 2019.

With the pressure of career destruction if goals are not met, local officials are under a lot of pressure and corruption is an easy trap to fall into.

According to the Communist Party of China's top anti-corruption body, there were nearly forty-nine thousand cases of corruption related to poverty alleviation work in 2017 alone. However, there are third-party investigations and surprise audits. These assessments are a core part of controlling for any fraud or falsification of information by officials, especially within a one-party authoritarian system.

2. The second major challenge is the misalignment of incentives between officials and the populations being helped.[490]

The officials working to end extreme poverty have the opportunity to propel their careers if they succeed in lifting their communities out of poverty. Meanwhile, some villagers want to maintain their "poor" status for government benefits. The opposite problem also persists. Some people lie about their living standards to avoid being labeled as poverty-stricken. This is where village democratic evaluation meetings become a helpful tool to determine general standards of living in an area or for specific households.

3. The third major challenge is ensuring these poverty alleviation tactics help people maintain their status of living above the extreme poverty threshold indefinitely.[491]

The year 2020 can't be the end of the push toward a future without extreme poverty in China. Programs like relocation ensure the impoverished don't look and feel poor anymore,

---

490 Ibid.
491 Ibid.

but many of them struggle to cover their expenses after they've gotten past the extreme poverty threshold.

4. The fourth major challenge is being barely above extreme poverty is not enough.[492]

It may not help China accomplish its goal of becoming a moderately prosperous society because their living standards will be far below China's middle class. The job support and training provided through its relocation efforts won't guarantee the jobs residents work will earn them enough money to live comfortably.

I propose there is a fifth and final major challenge: whether or not this solution is applicable on a global scale.

IS THIS SOLUTION APPLICABLE GLOBALLY?

One of the major advantages China has had in being able to implement such a far-reaching and detailed poverty alleviation program is its one-party-leadership rule and top-down political system. Without this strong authority, along with the threat of career destruction if efforts fail, it would not be possible for China to reach its aggressive poverty alleviation goals.[493]

What is working in China would not necessarily work elsewhere, particularly because cultural sensitivities would also present a major obstacle. For example, one could argue the policy of relocation takes away an individual's freedom to choose where and how they live. Though villagers' lives are nowhere near the opulence seen in China's major cities, some take solace in the fact they have shelters made of brick with solid roofs in areas suitable enough for them

---

492 Ibid.
493 Ibid.

to grow crops, though it is challenging and irregular in many cases. If they are happy there, would it be unfair to let them stay?

Another cultural sensitivity to be mindful of is a country's mindset toward national improvement. China's poverty alleviation efforts are about the prosperity of the nation as a whole with less regard to individual reactions to the methods used for achieving that prosperity. In this case of the disgruntled villagers, why stop relocating communities in response to a few cases of complaints if the work gives the majority of people who may have never had an opportunity to move prior the chance to do so?

The last cultural sensitivity aspect to consider is the concern of these efforts becoming an infringement on privacy. In the case of China's impoverished populations, the government has unrestricted access to everything about their living situation. From the food they eat to the money they save, poverty alleviation staff refer to literal files on each family and track program progress.

Advocating for this kind of access in other countries could present major challenges. As more technology is incorporated into how this data is collected and used, older generations of Robins and Drews, who are distrusting of technology in any context, may be hesitant to allow it in their personal lives.

CONCLUSION

It is undeniable China's strategies have had unparalleled success, but this has occurred at the cost of personal freedom and privacy which could be seen as uncomfortable at best and unacceptable at worst. However, if the rest of the world is ready to get serious about poverty alleviation, new considerations need to be made about how different value systems—both of nations and individuals—would react to methods that result in more personalized and effective methods of impact.

China is a model for how personalized poverty alleviation work can look in the future. The country has invested in the success of its impoverished population, not simply through handouts but through education, skill sharing, and partnerships. As China moves closer to its goal of eradicating extreme poverty in the nation, I am encouraged because I see a detailed working model centered around the needs of Robins.

In part three, I will be sharing a framework for what a new poverty alleviation system could look like. Community-based efforts like China's precision poverty plan are some of the strategies that inspired me. Here, we see a system in place that is working incredibly well. Though global application would require wrestling with philosophical questions surrounding personal freedom and privacy, we need to open up this dialogue sooner rather than later.

Ultimately, it's most important to remember poverty alleviation strategies shouldn't be centered on what the world's Camerons think or feel about poverty. In fact, even the policies that would need to be created surrounding freedom and privacy should be created in collaboration with the world's Robins.

One of the most impactful elements of China's plan is the role of its first party secretaries. They bridge the gap between the haves and the have-nots with detailed reports based on problems China's Robins identify themselves. The process starts with one conversation sparked by a person fully invested in the success of another.

Taking the time to listen can make the difference between impactful policy and failed policy. Anyone can take the time to listen carefully if they choose. These conservations break down the assumptions and biases clouding our judgement.

Seek out the voices of those who need to be heard and enter the conversation prepared to learn. Precise and impactful change starts with an open mind, a caring heart, and a listening ear.

"In the immediate aftermath of war [in Liberia], it was sensible to build the hardware—tangible goods, such as roads, schools, and clinics—before tackling the software—deeper societal rifts. The basics were badly needed and provided the war-scarred populace with visible progress. But now is the time to focus on the software."

— BENJAMIN J. SPATZ, FELLOW AT THE TRUMAN NATIONAL SECURITY PROJECT, FORMER CONSULTANT WITH THE UN PANEL OF EXPERTS ON LIBERIA, SPECIAL ADVISER TO THE GOVERNMENT OF LIBERIA, AND WITH THE UN IN LIBERIA[494]

---

494 Benjamin J. Spatz, "Liberia, a remarkable African success story, still needs help," September 23, 2013.

CASE STUDY: LIBERIA

———

Food is one of my grandma's primary love languages, which is why when I spent my final months of university with her in London, we chatted over Liberian staples like rice and palava sauce, fried fish, toborgee, and, for a British twist, biscuits with tea.

Most people know Liberia for its hardships like the Ebola virus disease that destabilized the country from 2014 to 2016, or its fourteen-year-long civil war, but I know Liberia as my family's country of origin.

Through my mom's stories from growing up in the country's capital city Monrovia, I learned about a side to Africa many don't hear about, a place filled to the brim with delicious fresh fruits, vegetables, and flavors, people always willing to share giggle-inducing stories, and enough soulful singing to fill a church for hours. The harsh reality is the Liberia of my mother's childhood and the Liberia of today are vastly different places.

Liberia is the second poorest country in Africa and the fourth poorest country in the world. [495,496] The economy is still recovering after shrinking by 90 percent during its civil war.[497]

Monrovia's mayor Jefferson Koijee highlighted at a conference related to Climate-Smart Cities in February 2020 that "Monrovia is facing a series of challenges," which include [498]

- inadequate urban legal framework
- inadequate livelihood opportunities for youth
- unsafe neighborhoods with increasing gang activity and drug abuse
- cost-intensive, unregulated solid waste management
- congested and unsafe transport
- greatest of all the threats of climate change.

Why is this relevant? Because if the country's capital is suffering, then its rural areas are certainly suffering as much, if not more so. I'm getting ahead of myself though. Liberia is a small country, and you may not have heard of it! For this reason, I will be spending a lot more time on the history and context of Liberia than I did for China. While China has grown into a world superpower, Liberia is relatively unknown and conversations about its history tend to center around slavery despite starting centuries before.

---

495 Liberian Economy Group, "Liberia's Economic Problems: Longstanding and Widespread Poverty," Unbearably High Foreign exchange rate, November 3, 2019.

496 Ibid.

497 Benjamin J. Spatz, "Liberia, a remarkable African success story, still needs help," September 23, 2013.

498 Front Page Africa, "Liberia: Mayor Koijee Presents Monrovia's Case At the Ongoing," Technical Deep Dive On Climate-Smart Cities, February 20, 2020.

In this chapter, I will be providing some historical context for Liberia's development, a brief introduction to its political and social structure, and dive into its poverty alleviation efforts in the aftermath of a civil war filled with vast amounts of destruction. Lastly, I will share insights from Liberian economists into what the future of the nation could look like and shed some light on how and why a new, stronger national identity can form among its citizens in the near future.

Let's begin.

HISTORICAL BACKGROUND

FAST FACTS

Liberia is on the West Coast of Africa bordering Guinea, Sierra Leone, Côte d'Ivoire, and the Atlantic Ocean. The country is 111,369 square kilometers and is divided into fifteen counties that are further divided into districts and clans.[499] The fifteen counties are:

- Bomi
- Bong
- Gbarpolu
- Grand Bassa
- Grand Cape Mount
- Grand Gedeh
- Grand Kru
- Lofa
- Margibi
- Maryland
- Montserrado

---

499 Africa.com, 2019, Liberia.

- Nimba
- River Cess
- River Gee
- Sinoe.

The county my grandmother is from is Lofa county located on the Northwestern border. The county my mother was born in is Montserrado near the southeast portion of the country.

As of 2019, the country has a population of 5,015,574 and the population is divided into sixteen indigenous ethnic groups and foreign minorities.[500,501] Ninety-five percent of the population are indigenous, 2.5 percent are Americo-Liberians, and another 2.5 percent are Congo people.[502,503,504,505] Within the business community, Indians, Lebanese, Europeans, and other West African nations form a significant part of the population as well. The population is also quite young; half of the population is under eighteen.[506]

How does Liberia fair on the poverty front? The numbers aren't great.

According to the latest Household Income and Expenditure Survey from 2016, roughly 50.9 percent of Liberia's population is living in poverty.[507] Based on the International

---

500 Worldometer, 2020, *Liberia Population (Live)*.

501 Africa.com, 2019, *Liberia*.

502 Ibid.

503 Ibid.

504 Ibid.

505 The Congo people descend from repatriated Afro-Caribbean and Congo slaves.

506 Ibid.

507 Alejandro De la Fuente, World Bank using Global Monitoring Database, Poverty & Equity Brief, World Bank, 2019.

Poverty Line—Liberia's Robins—the number is 40.9 percent.[508]

The impoverished make up 68 percent of the country's rural population.[509] In urban areas, about 690 thousand are considered poor.[510] Proportionally, poverty is also more than two times higher in rural areas: 71.6 percent versus 31.5 percent in cities.[511,512] According to the World Bank, urban poverty in Liberia is primarily due to high costs of living.[513] After covering expenses like housing and utilities, many urban households do not have enough money to afford food.

However, things aren't all negative. From the end of Liberia's civil war in 2005 to 2018:

- life expectancy at birth has increased from 55.4 years to 63.7 years[514,515]
- the mean years of schooling increased from 3.8[516,517] years to 4.7 years
- as of 2019, 65 percent of those primary school aged and 24 percent secondary school aged are enrolled in school[518,519]

---

508 Ibid.

509 Ibid.

510 Ibid.

511 Ibid.

512 Ibid.

513 Front Page Africa, "Liberia Poverty Rate Stands at 54 Percent—World Bank Report," October 19, 2016.

514 UNDP, "Inequalities in Human Development in the 21st Century: Briefing note for countries on the 2019 Human Development Report," 2019 Human Development Report.

515 Ibid.

516 Ibid.

517 Ibid.

518 Africa.com, 2019, Liberia

519 Ibid.

HISTORY BEFORE NEOCOLONIALISM

Now that all of those numbers are out of the way and you have some broad context, we can move on to a brief summary of Liberia's history.

Why is this brief summary important? Liberia's history paints a clear picture of *why* the country is low-income today. From ethnic conflict to civil war to disease, Liberia's circumstances have made it more than challenging for it to succeed economically, socially, and politically. It is through this lens a more objective look at the reasoning behind Liberia's poverty alleviation efforts can be developed.

Evidence has shown the land making up modern-day Liberia was inhabited as far back as the 1100s.[520,521] The earliest ethnic groups to arrive in the region were the Bassa, Days, Gola, Kru, and Kissi, who were pushed toward the Atlantic Ocean when the Mende-speaking people began their westward expansion.

A combination of desertification, the decline of the Sudanic Mali Empire in 1375, and the decline of Songhai Empire in 1591 pushed ethnic groups closer to the coast. Between 1461 and the late 1600s, the Portuguese, British, and Dutch constructed trading posts in what is now known as Liberia.[522]

Prior to the fall of the Mali Empire, the Vai people also migrated to the region after the Manes conquered it.[523] When the Vai migrated, the ethnic Krus fought back, joining forces with the Manes to do so, but the Vai prevailed.

---

520 Ibid.

521 Ibid.

522 During the spice trade, the region was known by Europeans as the melegueta Coast or the Pepper Coast due to the melegueta pepper in its rural areas. The pepper was very rare, and Europeans called it "the grains of paradise."

523 The Vai people were part of the Mali Empire.

Coastal populations built canoes and traded commodities with other West Africa regions and Europeans. Later, the Kru left the region and worked as paid laborers. They even worked on the Panama and Suez canals!

US INVOLVEMENT

By 1822, Black American settlers were taken to Cape Mesurado where Monrovia, Liberia is today. The United States gave the American Colonization Society (ACS) a US$100,000 grant to settle the colony. The American reverend Jehundi Ashman led the effort, and local chiefs were coerced at gunpoint by an agent of the ACS and a US naval lieutenant to sell the Cape.[524] The chiefs sold the land for less than US$300 worth of things like muskets, beads, tobacco, gunpowder, iron, and silverware.[525]

What was the ACS and why was the group so interested in the region?

The ACS, formed in 1816, was a society of white philanthropists and slaveholders who, in an attempt to avoid the complications of integrating Black and white people, took land in West Africa after the American Civil War and urged African Americans to settle there instead of staying in the States.[526] Many African Americans moved there until World War I. The society included members such as James Monroe, Andrew Jackson, Daniel Webster, and Francis Scott Key.[527]

---

524 Stanley Meisler, *Liberia,* March 1973.

525 Ibid.

526 US Embassy & Consulate in the Repulic of Korea, *Liberia: From Colony to Country,* 2020.

527 In 1821, the ACS arrived on the Mesurado River for the first time. The River is near modern-day Monrovia. Before the capital city was called Monrovia, it was called Christopolis; but in 1824 it was renamed

Rather than sending former slaves and freemen back to their countries of origin, the ACS sent all of them to Liberia without thinking about how the involuntary merging would impact local populations. This flagrant oversight had negative social and cultural implications felt in Liberia to this day. The conflict between the descendants of African Americans and indigenous tribes in Liberia will be discussed later in this chapter.

The idea of colonizing for African Americans instead of integrating them into general society was very controversial at the time for Americans who opposed slavery.

Some abolitionists, like William Lloyd Garrison, argued creating Liberia was just a way to ease white minds without handling the issue slavery presented in the United States. Because of the controversy, the ACS lost support and never fully accomplished its goal.[528]

MAJOR EVENTS ON THE HISTORICAL TIMELINE

In 1822, the indigenous populations surrounding Monrovia started attacking the city, angered it was built on stolen land. They continued to attack at random until the mid-nineteenth century.[529]

Liberia was one of two countries, Ethiopia being the other, that were not part of the Scramble for Africa.[530] It did lose territory that was ultimately annexed by France and Britain,

---

"Monrovia" after James Munroe who was president at the time and supported the ACS.

528 By the end of the Civil War, the ACS had settled around thirteen thousand freedman and six thousand recaptured blacks from slave ships. Only about half of the original settlers survived the tropical diseases during their first twenty-five years in Liberia.

529 David Lewis, 2014, *MONROVIA, LIBERIA (1822-)*.

530 Africa.com, 2019, Liberia

but Liberia maintained its overall independence. About thirty years earlier in 1847, Liberia was declared an independent republic by a young African American man from Virginia named Joseph Jenkins Roberts.[531]

In 1971, William Tubman, Liberia's president of twenty-seven years, died while in office.[532,533] His presidency marked a period of Liberian history where the divide between Americo-Liberians and indigenous populations got wider. His welcoming economic policies had attracted a lot of foreign investment that benefitted the Americo-Liberians. Following his death, Vice President William Tolbert took over and became the first president who spoke an indigenous language. He also promoted a program to bring more indigenous people into the government.

In 1980, a coup lead by Samuel Doe overthrew William Tolbert and instability began.[534] Tolbert was killed during a late-night raid on his Monrovia mansion.

Between 1980 and 1984, Samuel Doe, who was an ethnic Krahn, led Liberia.[535] He headed a governmental body called the People's Redemption Council that ended Africa's first republic and suspended the country's constitution. Doe was the first leader in Liberia who was not an Americo-Liberian.[536] He had no political or leadership experience and is believed to have been illiterate when he became president.[537] Concerns about his subordinates in government plotting to

---

531 Ibid.

532 Peter Dennis, *A Brief History of Liberia,* The International Center for Transitional Justice, 2006.

533 Ibid.

534 Ibid.

535 Ibid.

536 Ibid.

537 Ibid.

overthrow him led him to execute his vice head of state. After the execution, he began filling his cabinet with people within his Krahn ethnic group.

In 1985, the first open elections after Doe's coup were held.[538] Even though external, international observers believe an opposing candidate from the Liberia Action Party won the election, Doe ensured his victory by replacing election officials within his own special committee.

Between 1989 to 2003, Liberia suffered a civil war so destabilizing it warrants its own section of this chapter.[539] Within this time period, the civil war grew to include seven major factions of fighters, and power shifted hands to Charles Taylor. After the war, Charles Taylor was convicted of crimes against humanity by the UN. A presiding judge at his trial said, "The accused [Charles Taylor] has been found responsible for aiding and abetting as well as planning some of the most heinous and brutal crimes in recorded human history." [540, 541]

In 2003, the Liberian civil war ended with Charles Taylor accepting a peace deal put together by Economic Community of West African States (ECOWAS) that offered him asylum in Nigeria.[542] Toward the end of that year in October, the UN established the UN Mission in Liberia to promote active disarmament, demobilization, and rebuilding efforts. Fourteen

---

538 Ibid.

539 Ibid.

540 Jurjen van de Pol, *Ex-Liberia Leader Taylor Sentenced 50 Years for War Crime,* 2012.

541 Given Liberia's close roots to the horrors of slavery, Taylor's crimes served to continue an infamous legacy of human mistreatment rather than setting a new standard.

542 Peter Dennis, *A Brief History of Liberia,* The International Center for Transitional Justice, 2006.

years of civil war ended with a peace agreement in June 2003 and the implementation of the National Transitional Government of Liberia (NTGL) for two years.[543,544,545]

In 2005, presidential and legislative elections took place.[546] While the United States has faced its second election weighing the pros and cons of having a qualified, well-educated female president running the country, Liberia has already accomplished this milestone in electing Ellen Johnson-Sirleaf. Former president Sirleaf was the first elected female president in Africa. Prior to her presidency, she worked in various government positions and at the World Bank as an economist. She won re-election in 2011, and the UN Security Council set a deadline of 2015 to reduce the number of US troops in Liberia by half.

In 2018, when President George Weah and Vice President Jewel Taylor (the ex-wife of Charles Taylor referenced above) were elected, it marked the first peaceful and democratic transition of power in seventy-three years.[547,548,549]

THE FOURTEEN-YEAR WAR

As I mentioned earlier, Liberia's civil war was incredibly destructive. The civil war in Liberia destabilized the entire nation and is a core historical factor for why over half of the nation's population is living in poverty. Ten percent of the

---

543 Government of the Republic of Liberia and the European Commission. 2008–2013. "Country Strategy Paper and Indicative Program."

544 Ibid.

545 Ibid.

546 Ibid.

547 Republic of Liberia, "Pro-Poor Agenda for Prosperity and Development (PAPD)," Liberia: UNDP Liberia, 2018.

548 Ibid.

549 Ibid.

population of Liberia, nearly three hundred thousand people, died and more people were injured.[550,551]

Benjamin Spatz described the war as one of "the most brutal chapters in human history."[552] Some generals involved in the fighting were known to sacrifice people and participate in instances of cannibalism.

More than half of the population became refugees. Take, for example, my own grandmother. She left Liberia in the 1980s to go to my mom's university graduation in England, only to find she would be unable to safely return to Liberia for decades.

The war devastated the economy and the nation's basic services. For example, the health sector lost more than 60 percent of health care workers who decided to resettle in other countries due to the war.[553] Amenities like running water, electricity, and oxygen for unstable patients were all more readily available in mission-sponsored centers than in government-sponsored centers.[554]

The war changed the demographics of the nation. Women now comprise the majority of the population between the ages of twenty and forty because of the war's

550 Liberian Economy Group, "Liberia's Economic Problems: Longstanding and Widespread Poverty," Unbearably High Foreign exchange rate, November 3, 2019.

551 Ibid.

552 Benjamin J Spatz, 2013, Liberia, a remarkable African success story, still needs help, September 23.

553 Lawrence Sherman, Peter T. Clement, Meena N. Cherian, et al., "Implementing Liberia's Poverty Reduction Strategy: An Assessment of Emergency and Essential Surgical Care," American Medical Association, January 2011.

554 Ibid.

impact on the male population.[555] As I discussed in earlier chapters, women are especially vulnerable to poverty because of their lack of access to both jobs and services like health and education. This impact is worse for women in rural areas.

After the war, the country's infrastructure was destroyed. The government lacked both the financial and human capital to support the population. Roads, telecommunication, water and sanitation systems, and transportation were all either ruined or left in need of major repairs. Beyond physical infrastructure, the institutions that built and maintained these resources were also destroyed.

POLITICAL STRUCTURE

Liberia's political system is modeled after the United States' system with three equal branches of government: the executive branch, the legislative branch, and the judicial branch. The country honors two codes of law: statutory law for urban communities and unwritten tribal law for rural communities.

Despite these structures, 75 percent of Liberians admitted to paying a bribe to an official over the past twelve months in 2013.[556,557] For those with the right connections, the government is the primary source for a stable job with reliable income, not a supportive, transparent institution.

For public officials, their primary concern tends to focus more on supporting extended family members and providing them with jobs than on qualifications or having long-term

---

555 International Monetary Fund, 2008, "Liberia: Poverty Reduction Strategy Paper," Washington DC.

556 Benjamin J. Spatz, Liberia, a remarkable African success story, still needs help, September 23, 2013.

557 Ibid.

goals for the country. It is considered "'common street wisdom" that the elite in Monrovia use their connections and positions of power in government to exploit the indigenous population in Liberia.[558] Whether in peace or conflict, the elites benefit while the impoverished stay in poverty and are left powerless.

Nepotism, in this way, can restrict the government from finding qualified people to work and serves as a form of corruption. This is not a phenomenon unique to Africa.[559]

Beyond political favoritism, Monrovia's needs take precedence over the rest of the country's needs more often than not. This relationship makes it harder for rural citizens to trust the motivations and incentives of the inner-city elite.

SOCIAL STRUCTURE

Liberia's history and social structure are unique because of the country's relationship with the United States. Though Liberia was never formally colonized, the United States has been an indirect colonial ruler of Liberia. In this way, the United States has been able to glean some of the benefits of colonialism without needing to manage any of the responsibilities.

The United States' strong influence on Liberia is not entirely positive. Notably, when making national decisions specific to Liberia, the final decision is often made based on American values rather than Liberian values, which can make conditions in Liberia worse. Solving Liberia's problems is especially hard when people are more interested in American solutions than Liberian solutions.

---

558 Ibid.

559 Even the US has its share of political dynasties and opportunities rooted in nepotism.

Do you remember the earlier discussion of the tensions between America-Liberian and indigenous people? The Americo-Liberians were the Black settlers from the United States. After arriving on Liberian soil, they begin to politically and culturally dominate the country.[560]

The lighter-skinned settlers kept their names from America and copied the culture and lifestyle of the antebellum South, choosing to dominate the darker-skinned indigenous Liberians rather than learning their ways. The Black settlers in Liberia behaved similarly to the white settlers in other parts of Africa. They stayed by the coast and occasionally sent out troops to contain raucous tribes.

This quote from an *Atlantic* article about Liberia published in 1973 provides a helpful glimpse at the types of interactions, or lack thereof, sustained between the indigenous populations and the Americo-Liberians: "The Americo-Liberians were so different from the aborigines, as they liked to call the others, that Liberian history records a Black explorer, Benjamin Anderson, who, just like David Livingstone and Henry M. Stanley and Sir Richard Burton, set off into the interior in 1868 to see what darkest Liberia was like."[561,562]

The Americo-Liberian elite didn't stop at treating the indigenous populations like outsiders. They also:

- denied citizenship to indigenous Liberians until 1904[563]

---

560 The Americo-Liberians had so much influence that in 1854, a few years after Liberia officially became a republic, a school called the Ashmun Institute was founded in Pennsylvania with the primary goal of preparing Americo-Liberians for leadership in Liberia.

561 Stanley Meisler, Liberia, March 1973.

562 Ibid.

563 TheGrio, *Former American slaves played oppressive role in Liberia's past*, February 1, 2010.

- denied full voting rights until the twentieth century when President William Tubman was elected in 1944
- restricted property rights[564]
- enforced a one-party oligarchic rule for 133 years[565]

The country's motto hints at the exclusionary power dynamics of the republic: "The Love of Liberty Brought Us Here."

Today, the divide between Americo-Liberians and indigenous populations is still felt. In 2012, the divide was referenced in a poverty alleviation briefing that described the need for the "tendency to bifurcate the Liberian identity into an Americo-Liberian vs. Indigenes cleavage" to end in order for political, social, and economic development to be successful.[566]

Now, there are divides between those who left Liberia and those who stayed, those who were victims and those who were perpetrators. These "new Americos" are making strict divisions between Americo-Liberians and indigenous populations a lot more flexible, but the civil war has brought up new divisions.[567]

As new lines form within the Liberian population, it will take the combined effort of the government and of individuals to heal the wounds.

---

564 Ibid.

565 Ibid.

566 Republic of Liberia, Pro-Poor Agenda for Prosperity and Development (PAPD), Liberia: UNDP Liberia, 2018.

567 TheGrio, *Former American slaves played oppressive role in Liberia's past*, February 1, 2010.

EDUCATION AND THE BRAIN DRAIN

The "lucky" Liberians were the ones who could afford to leave when the country got too dangerous. After Samuel Doe's government coup in the 1980s, a lot of the Americo-Liberian population fled to the United States and other countries to seek a better life.

This "brain drain" caused a serious problem, as the most educated in the population either left or moved toward cities in hopes of being recruited for high-paying jobs. Some left Africa entirely.

The war halted opportunities to build human capital in the nation as the conflict led to a mass exodus of the majority of skilled workers. It resulted in a struggling Liberian public sector due to:[568]

- the staff's lack of technical training
- small budget
- lack of coordination across departments
- high turnover

Over a decade later, these populations are beginning to return to Liberia, which is causing additional resentment from the indigenous populations who don't wanted to be overshadowed by the "new Americos."[569,570] The "Americos" return with foreign money, better education, and western-ized behavior. Some major organizations, like the World Health Organization, have recently argued it is this very population of returned Liberians who have the skills to

---

568 International Monetary Fund, 2008, "Liberia: Poverty Reduction Strategy Paper," Washington D.C.

569 Lawrence Sherman, Peter T. Clement, Meena N. Cherian, et al., "Implementing Liberia's Poverty Reduction Strategy: An Assessment of Emergency and Essential Surgical Care." American Medical Association, January 2011.

570 Ibid.

create jobs, decrease unemployment, and support national development.[571]

For the Liberians who stayed, there is a shortage of young people with enough education and job skills to increase Liberia's productivity growth.

As of 2017, two-thirds of the children who should be in school in Liberia were not in school and large swathes of the population have not had the opportunity to learn through formal education.[572] Education is required by law but is not enforced very strictly. More than half of the labor force hasn't finished primary school, and only 47.6 percent of the country's population is considered literate.[573,574]

Those in school learn very Eurocentric material. Children know more about waterways in the United States or Europe than local waterways, and learning materials are based on European standards. This detachment from the material makes it harder for students to learn.

POVERTY ALLEVIATION PLANS

POVERTY ALLEVIATION: POVERTY REDUCTION STRATEGY (2008–2011)

After the civil war, the Liberian government placed more focus on addressing poverty nationally. Efforts started with

---

571 Ibid.

572 Liberian Economy Group, "Liberia's Economic Problems: Longstanding and Widespread Poverty," Unbearably High Foreign exchange rate, November 3, 2019.

573 International Fund for Agricultural Development, Republic of Liberia: Country Strategic Opportunities Program, 2019, (EB 2019/128/R.17).

574 United Nations Department of Economic and Social Affairs Division: Population, Liberia Population., September 6, 2020.

the Interim Poverty Reduction Strategy in 2007. This strategy was implemented for a twenty-four-month period starting July 2006 and centered on maintaining national peace and establishing a pathway toward sustainable poverty reduction.[575]

In 2008, President Sirleaf introduced her Poverty Reduction Strategy (PRS) from 2008 to 2011. Sirleaf's focus on conducting county consultations across all fifteen counties to break out of the Monrovia-dominated government were unprecedented.

The central objectives of the three-year period for the plan were to:[576]

- establish a more secure environment in the nation
- promote sustainable growth and development
- rebuild human capital and increase opportunities for Liberians
- strengthen its institutions

The plan was separated into four core pillars to represent the strategic areas for sustainable growth described at length in the Interim Poverty Reduction Strategy Paper.[577]

The first pillar of the plan was to consolidate peace and security. Security forces perpetuated the harmful institutions concentrating power among the elite and left indigenous Liberians feeling unprotected. These issues were, of course, exacerbated by the civil war.

The second pillar of the plan was to revitalize the economy. This pillar of the plan was focused on:

---

575 Government of the Republic of Liberia and the European Commission, 2008–2013, "Country Strategy Paper and Indicative Program."

576 International Monetary Fund, "Liberia: Poverty Reduction Strategy Paper," Washington DC, 2008.

577 Ibid.

- building up the private sector
- strengthening local markets
- rebuilding the local financial services industry

Through this pillar, the goal was to encourage local entrepreneurs to start businesses and create jobs to increase the size of the middle class, with a particular focus on agriculture, forestry, and mining.

The third pillar of the plan was to strengthen governance and rule of law. This pillar was focused on rebuilding the broken-down institutions the civil war left behind. The aim was to:

- increase local citizen participation in government
- build up institutions in the legal and judicial system
- create a more equal and just system of law to defend Liberians' human rights

The fourth and final pillar of the plan was to rebuild infrastructure and deliver basic services to Liberians. This pillar of the plan involved core infrastructure like roads, bridges, and transportation.

How did the plan ultimately fare?

In implementing the plan, President Sirleaf made important progress in reducing poverty—incomes grew, more children were in school, more healthcare services were made available, and infant mortality rates fell. However, poverty was far from eradicated. As there was more work to be done, the following president, George Weah, came up with his own plan as well.

President Weah was an internationally famous soccer player and UNICEF goodwill ambassador before becoming president of Liberia. He was born in a slum in Monrovia and called attention to his humble upbringing when running for president. Weah was the first African to be crowned FIFA World Player of the Year in 1995.[578]

POVERTY ALLEVIATION: PRO-POOR AGENDA FOR PROSPERITY AND DEVELOPMENT (2018–2023)

The current poverty alleviation strategy in place in Liberia is the Pro-Poor Agenda for Prosperity and Development.[579] It is the second part in a series of five-year national development plans for the Liberia Vision 2030 framework.

According to the report, the fundamentals underpinning the PAPD are:[580]

1. Liberia is rich in human and natural resources, but
2. is deprived of development largely because its human capital lacks the knowledge to transform the natural resources into wealth.

With these underpinnings in mind, the primary objectives of the plan are to build up Liberia's institutions, increase income stability, and reduce absolute poverty across the nation. President Weah's plan has four pillars as well.

The first pillar is empowering the people by:

- providing equal opportunities for Liberians in education, health, youth development, and social protection
- building up human capital among Liberians
- reducing the maternal mortality rate
- reducing gender inequality
- increasing the social protection of investments

---

578 Jonathan Paye-Layleh, *Thousands march in Liberia to protest falling economy,* January 6, 2020.

579 Republic of Liberia, Pro-Poor Agenda for Prosperity and Development (PAPD), Liberia: UNDP Liberia, 2018.

580 Ibid.

The second pillar is stabilizing the economy and creating jobs. Within this pillar, the government hopes to create a more inclusive, more business-friendly economy.

The third pillar is developing a more cohesive society to support sustainable development. Under the pillar, the key focus points will be on addressing the root causes of conflicts to:

- reduce fragile social systems
- strengthen the justice system and human rights
- build up national security

The fourth pillar is focused on governance and treasury. This pillar ensures the public sector is held accountable for creating shared prosperity and sustainable development across social classes, while reducing corruption. The central outcomes for this pillar are:

- shifting the concentration of economic and political power in the country away from Monrovia
- improving natural resource governance

So far, President Weah's plan is not, well, going according to plan.

Based on a recent report from *The Associate Press*, "The Liberian economy has declined so dramatically during President Weah's two years in power that banks are unable to pay depositors, salaries are delayed, and the prices of basic commodities have skyrocketed."[581]

In January 2020, thousands of Liberians marched in protest of Liberia's failing economy under President Weah's leadership. The demonstrators want President Weah to get a new economic management team. President Weah's response

---

581 Jonathan Paye-Layleh, *Thousands march in Liberia to protest falling economy*, January 6, 2020.

has been to encourage citizens and opposing government officials—who he believes are responsible for the riots—to focus on creating jobs.

LIBERIA LOOKING FORWARD

THREE CORE AREAS OF GROWTH: ELECTRICITY, AGRICULTURE, AND FINANCE

While there are many areas for growth and development to focus on within Liberia's poverty alleviation plan, three core areas stood out as common threads throughout the sources I read:

- electricity access
- agriculture
- financial inclusion

Placing an intense focus on these areas would push Liberia's development efforts toward a more equitable future.

As of November 2019, 5 percent of Liberia's total population has access to electricity, approximately 250 thousand people out of millions.[582] Having access to stable and affordable electricity makes fighting poverty easier and assists in promoting economic development.

According to the Mines and Energy Ministry, in early 2020 a new plan called the West Africa Power Pool (WAPP) Project will change Liberia's electric system. Currently, Liberia lacks the resources to cover the entire country with electricity without external support in the form of technical and financial investments from external partners.

---

582 Obediah Johnson, *Only 5% of Liberia's 4.5 Million People Have Access to Electricity*, November 26, 2019.

Agriculture is a primary source of livelihood for rural populations in Liberia and employs about 80 percent of Liberians, with women making up more than half of the agricultural labor force.[583] Despite this, it receives 2 percent of the national budget.[584]

Growth in the sector is slowed by setbacks like regulatory delays and a lack of infrastructure. President Weah's PAPD strategy has recognized the importance of agriculture to economic growth in Liberia and, as a result, has included a push away from subsistence farming toward commercial farming. This development is not without its challenges.

The International Fund for Agricultural Development identified six major challenges to agricultural development in their report focused on country strategic opportunities in Liberia.[585]

1. inadequate infrastructure
2. limited access to funding
3. low agriculture research
4. weak extension systems
5. weak land rights systems
6. limited human technical capacities

The implications of the work in this area are far-reaching and overcoming these challenges would result in nationwide change, impacting both rural and urban populations. On the topic of agricultural development in Liberia, World Bank economist Daniel K. Boakye advised during a World Poverty Event in 2016, "If we were to improve the productivity in the agriculture sector, there would be enough food to sell in the

---

583 International Fund for Agricultural Development, Republic of Liberia: Country Strategic Opportunities Program, 2019, (EB 2019/128/R.17).
584 Ibid.
585 Ibid.

urban sector and there will be enough income from the sale of agriculture products in the urban center, and rural farmers will have enough income to purchase their nonfood items."[586]

Providing farmers with modern equipment, better roads, and suitable markets would change lives.

Lastly, financial inclusion is another major area of growth that, if focused on, would have far reaching implications. In July 2019, the Central Bank of Liberia launched a National Financial Inclusion Strategy that aimed to use digital financial services to make finance in the nation more inclusive.

As their press release for the effort said, "Ultimately, this will enable Liberians from all walks of Liberia to borrow, save, make payments, insure against risk, plan for retirement and, in the process, contribute to poverty alleviation."[587]

The Central Bank of Liberia's strategy hopes to bring 50 percent of adult Liberians into the mainstream of the financial sector by 2024.[588] While this plan sounds great in theory, it may not work out in practice. In that same month of the announcement, the Central Bank ran out of money, which has caused a shortage of banknotes nationwide.[589]

Right now, a core issue facing Liberians in rural areas is the lack of availability of financial services and a limited access to credit. Currently, 35.7 percent of adult Liberians have accounts with a financial institution.[590]

---

586 Front Page Africa, *Liberia Poverty Rate Stands at 54 Percent—World Bank Report*, 2016.

587 Central Bank of Liberia, *CBL Concludes National Financial Inclusion Strategy*, July 1, 2019.

588 Ibid.

589 Isaac Kaledzi, *Liberia: Banknotes in short supply, banks run-out of cash*, November 5, 2019.

590 Central Bank of Liberia, *CBL Concludes National Financial Inclusion Strategy*, July 1, 2019.

The Central Bank of Liberia claims part of the problem is people are keeping their money at home and in general have a negative view of the local economy and currency.[591] Liberia's Ministry of Finance shared there is not sufficient money to meet demand in the vaults of commercial banks. Now, customers are left to form long lines at ATM machines.

INEQUALITY AND DISCRIMINATION

According to the 2019 World Bank Poverty & Equity Brief, "Poverty in Liberia is projected to continue increasing over the next few years, driven by increasing food prices, lower commodity prices for minerals, and the aftermath of the Ebola epidemic."[592]

The inequalities between regions, genders, ages, and ethnic groups continue to contribute to Liberia's fragile social status. Ninety percent of the population is under thirty-five years of age and 52.6 percent is within the working age range (fifteen to sixty-four years old).[593] This young, working-age population is increasing the demand for jobs, but their demands change with age. In addition to jobs, young people also want farmland, infrastructure, and public services.

The issue of discrimination is particularly difficult for women. Women in Liberia have lower access to education and are overlooked for work, despite playing a major role in the country's largest sector of industry and serving as primary caretakers for their children.[594] A woman having

591 Isaac Kaledzi, *Liberia: Banknotes in short supply, banks run-out of cash,* November 5, 2019.

592 Alejandro De la Fuente, World Bank using Global Monitoring Database, Poverty & Equity Brief, World Bank, 2019.

593 International Fund for Agricultural Development, Republic of Liberia: Country Strategic Opportunities Program, 2019, (EB 2019/128/R.17).

594 Ibid.

less influence in decision-making within the household or the community at large is very common.

Without targeting segments of the population who are systematically overlooked (e.g. women, youth, disabled people, etcetera) those populations will continue to slip through the cracks and have limited opportunities in areas where able-bodied men control the community.

Another major point to address in the future is poverty rates are higher in rural areas than in urban areas. This discrimination impacts the ease of access people have to public services between rural and urban areas.

Wealthy, urban areas have more access to water, sanitation, and electric services. Liberia's rural areas are rife with potential and opportunity but, despite this, remain underdeveloped and hard to access due to Liberia's poor-quality roads in remote areas.

WILL LIBERIA MEET THE UN'S SUSTAINABLE DEVELOPMENT GOAL BY 2030?

At its current rate, no.

However, a group of seven Liberian economists who call themselves the Liberia Economy Group might just be able to change things. In November 2019, the group published a report outlining some problem-solving steps to help Liberia alleviate poverty, and the plan sounds promising.[595]

The economists argue a core problem-solving action that needs to occur is raising awareness throughout all of Liberian society about the nature of poverty and steps they can take to solve it.

---

595 Liberian Economy Group, "Liberia's Economic Problems: Longstanding and Widespread Poverty," Unbearably High Foreign exchange rate, November 3, 2019.

They highlighted "families, communities, schools, civil society, including religious houses and political parties, government and private businesses" as core facets of society to communicate with via meetings, radios, newspapers, and social media.[596] They also advocated for the importance of fair elections to select government leaders.

Their plan highlights three core "approaches," serving as a helpful course of action for Liberians and their government officials.

The first approach is the "value addition approach."[597] This strategy focuses on the ways value can be added to human resources; one primary way of doing this is through education. Not the same Eurocentric education dominating current curriculums, but education based on Liberian culture.

The economists advocate for Liberia to take their raw materials exports one step further and add value through manufacturing, with the goal being to support local consumption first before sending out the excess as exports.

The second approach is the "local purchasing approach."[598] The economists are adamant Liberians should not import products that can be produced in Liberia and they should buy products with Liberian dollars as well, rather than preferring American dollars over local currency. Additionally, the group calls for the Central Bank of Liberia to stop giving commercial bank loans primarily to foreign businesses rather than local ones.

---

596 Ibid.
597 Ibid.
598 Ibid.

The third approach is the "savings generation approach."[599] The report advocates for Liberians to continue building up private savings while using public funds to finance activities Liberians could do themselves but instead have foreigners doing.

The economists break down areas within the government of Liberia's current budget that could be decreased; for example, government officials' salaries and travel expenses.[600] The report also broke down how to redirect those savings into other areas of the national budget like:

- food reproduction and distribution
- hiring locals to build and renovate schools using local materials
- regulating teacher and health worker salaries
- road construction or maintenance

CONCLUSION: COUNTY BY COUNTY. REGION BY REGION. STEP BY STEP.

As I researched and read reports outlining Liberia's history in preparation for writing this chapter, I realized something both significant and sad about Liberia's history: Liberia may have been made a republic in July of 1847, marking over 172 years as a sovereign nation, but the country has really only had twelve years (2006–2014; 2016–2020) under a democracy making an effort to listen to the voices of both indigenous people and Americo-Liberians without being plagued by war or disease.

That's less than the time it takes for the average American student to finish primary and secondary school.

---

599 Ibid.
600 Ibid.

Extreme poverty is a global issue, and Liberia has more than its fair share to eradicate. Liberia has a total population that is less than 2 percent (approximately 1.5 percent) of the population of the United States (five million versus three hundred thirty million). Larger nations have lifted more people out of poverty. It's only a matter of time before Liberia lifts its population out of poverty too. County by county, region by region, and step by step. Liberia's 40 percent in extreme poverty can be reduced to zero, and the standard of living for the entire country can be increased.

Right now, Liberia is managing a large population lacking trust—in its institutions, in its leadership, and in its own citizens. Understandably, after years of war and mistreatment both from foreigners and Liberians themselves, these relationships have been shattered. Why put money in a bank if you can't trust the banking system? Why trust your neighbor if you witnessed them committing crimes during the war? Why stay in Liberia if you don't trust your government to uplift and empower you?

Development work needs to start with rebuilding trust before substantive solutions can rise up. There is still work to be done, but I am confident in Liberia's potential to lift its Robins out of extreme poverty. As the government's plans indicate, attempts to make progress are already underway.

In a 1995 interview with an independent international news organization, wealthy Liberian businessman William Cox noted, "Liberia will be Liberia one day...'We will call ourselves Liberians. Just like the Americans say, 'I'm proud to be an American,' I want to say, 'I'm proud to be a Liberian.'"[601]

I would like to believe the day Cox referred to has already come and Liberians all over the world are proud of their roots, if only because of how much those before us have survived.

I am proud to be a Liberian now. I will be even prouder when Liberia's Robins are all able to not only survive but thrive.

---

601 Cindy Shiner, *Roots of Ex-US Slaves Still Run Deep In Liberia*, October 26, 1995.

PART 3

SOLUTIONS

"If we're only satisfied with quick and easy solutions, that's an indicator that we might be more interested in our own sense of satisfaction than we are in actual progress."

—MARK WEBER, POVERTY, INC. DOCUMENTARY PRODUCER, STRATEGY & OPERATIONS LEAD AT THE MIT-IBM WATSON AI LAB[602]

---

602 Kris Mauren, James F. Fitzgerald, Michael Matheson Miller, Jonathan Witt, Simon Scionka, Tom Small, Magatte Wade, et al. 2015, Poverty, Inc.

A HOUSE BUILT
ON A ROCK

———

During one of my last interviews for my research, I realized I was looking at poverty alleviation efforts in the past and present all wrong. Rather than asking questions like "how has no one found a catch-all solution yet?" or "if we have been working on this problem for decades, why are people still poor?" I should have been looking at the historical context of our efforts.

Instead of looking at the six hundred million-plus people living in extreme poverty as a problem, I should have considered it a signal of progress. We have spent millennia trying to understand the root causes and consequences of poverty in society, and it has led us to a world where less than 10 percent of our global population is living on less than US$2 a day.

We are closer than ever before to eradicating extreme poverty precisely because of the research groups, international organizations, local non-profits, and sympathetic individuals who have donated and worked toward solutions to this problem. Rather than focusing on past failures or missteps,

I should have been focusing on the evidence showing every misstep is still a step of some sort toward working solutions.

Our generation is standing on the shoulders of giants who have, through a long process of trial and error, led us to a point where we have incredible amount of information on what modern poverty alleviation efforts should, and in some cases do, look like today. Yes, poverty still exists but, as I mentioned in part one, poverty is relative.

Aiming to eradicate *all poverty* would mean aiming to eradicate people comparing themselves and their circumstances to those of people around them. I will leave it up to philosophers, psychologists, and sociologists to decide whether that will ever be possible. In a way, inequality functions as form of incentive or motivation for people to work, to improve, and to aim for larger goals.

Aiming to eradicate *extreme poverty* in particular would mean aiming to ensure every person on this planet now replete with resources has access to the basic essentials they need to survive day-to-day, escape the scarcity mindset, and empower themselves. It would mean every person on this planet would have access to necessities like food, water, clothing, and health care.

I am not advocating for a global get-rich-quick scheme to help everyone live in a utopia of equal opulence and wealth. Rather, I am advocating for a future where the quality of life, even at the lowest end of the socioeconomic spectrum, is improved to a level more accurately reflective of human progress.

This can be our stage one.

Take a look at your daily life. Your basic needs are likely met. You have completed enough of your education to confidently read and write. If you are reading this book, you likely have enough free time to believe that you can solve not only your problems, but the problems of others as well. With all of this in mind, ask yourself: how can I make a difference?

Or, rather, ask yourself: How can I start to make a difference?

In this chapter, I will introduce a starting point for action by proposing a method to problem-solving at any scale. I will be shaping my chapter based on the five stages as an example of how I've gone about understanding the problem of poverty.

What are the five stages?

1. Define the Problem
2. Select the Solution
3. Implement the Plan
4. Test the Results
5. Iterate and Improve

With the five-stage process I am outlining, I hope to streamline and simplify an approach that can feel overwhelming at times.

STAGE ONE: DEFINE THE PROBLEM

I have spent the majority of my time in this book focused on this stage. I wanted to understand poverty at in its basic form and develop a clearer picture of the historical context that defines it.

From wars to theory to psychology, poverty is significantly more complex than I could have ever imagined. Without diving headfirst into my problem, I could have never envisioned what potential solutions could look like.

It's important here to emphasize the plural, *solutions,* as well. As I have said a few times now, poverty has no one-size-fits-all solution. We need to embrace complexity in our solutions, combine our ideas, compromise, and solve on a case-by-case basis. We need a multipronged approach to poverty alleviation. It will take the combined forces of many movements allied together for improvement.

Our best hope for understanding humanity's issues is to continue pushing to understand the root causes. With these causes outlined, it easier for people to identify incentives and goals to galvanize people toward action.

Sometimes the solutions are simple and right under our noses. A simple example that stood out to me was one brought up in *Factfulness*: "All that's needed to stop a child from accidentally drinking her neighbor's still-lukewarm poo is a few plastic pipes, a water pump, some soap, and a basic sewage system."[603]

STAGE TWO: SELECT THE SOLUTION

How can we go about selecting a solution, or multiple solutions, to address extreme poverty?

A helpful starting point would be to reshape the current system in a simpler way. The funnel system makes it hard to communicate between key players, creates bureaucratic systems of power, and can alienate the world's Robins. As a quick refresher, in the funnel system, influential powers like the UN, the World Bank, the IMF, and governments support the majority of research and provide the lion's share of funding for projects. This money gets funneled to aid agencies, NGOs, and recipient governments and ultimately gets funneled to "the poor."

Rather than a funnel system with centralized sources of power, I propose a system shaped closer to a pentagon-shaped

---

603 Hans Rosling, Ola Rosling, and Rönnlund Anna Rosling, *Factfulness: Ten Reasons Were Wrong about the World—and Why Things Are Better than You Think*, (London: Sceptre, 2019), 121.

house—a system where there are fewer concentrations of power or resources and focus is placed on providing the world's Robins with not only money, but critical resources to improve living standards.

I've named this approach the "Money Plus Method" to represent the shift away from a focus on money toward a focus on solutions beyond it. The method is community-based and centered on the self-identified needs of the world's Robins. It flips the current system on its head by leading with Robins' needs and incorporating external players afterwards.

So, what does this simple, five-node house look like? Let's start with the foundation and "build" our way up.

The foundation of the house is comprised of the "Big Guys" (e.g. the UN, IMF, World Bank, foundations, philanthropic organizations, corporations, and other large funding sources) on one side and middle- and high-income country governments on the other. As the primary source of funds for efforts surrounding a lot of the world's social problems, it makes the most sense these core figures would form the foundation of the house.

These big organizations set international standards, influence policy, and are a primary source of funding for international development work. Donations from individuals are helpful, but without the monetary and in-kind donations of these large organizations, it would be harder to move forward with efforts and research in less lucrative areas.

Above the foundation of the house and working upward, there are two more nodes: "The Biz" and the "People's Champions." "The Biz" represents the middlemen: the NGOs, aid agencies, think tanks, and other similar organizations on the ground doing research and galvanizing local efforts with their expertise.

What are "People's Champions?" To start, I'll have to go back in time to my study abroad experience in Dakar, Senegal. One of my class's first projects was to complete a family tree based on my host family. With my broken French, I was able to navigate through a few questions about my host family and their relatives.

Their background—though interesting—paled in comparison to the presentation given by one of my fellow classmates about her charismatic host brother. He described himself as aspiring to become a "People's Champion," or rather, an advocate for himself and his community. I laughed at the time, but the self-given title stuck. The role is an accurate and critical component of the Money Plus Method.

"People's Champions" are individuals who serve as ambassadors for their local communities. They are the leaders on the ground who are well-known and well-versed enough in their community's history and culture to communicate its interests and needs while ensuring the voices of those they represent are both heard and considered.

Why does this role exist? Precisely because when groups of people gather together, it is easy to succumb to the pitfalls of groupthink, coercion, conflicting ideas, feedback loops, corruption, and dominating voices. With a "People's Champion" to filter through any conflicts and come to a common consensus before sharing ideas with the other nodes of the house, the process can mitigate some of these issues. Also, because there is no centralized unit of power, there's nothing stopping the Robins from directly engaging with other figures on different nodes if the "People's Champion" doesn't communicate important information.

Lastly, the house is complete with the addition of a roof, which in this context is the world's Robins. By now, you are likely very familiar with the individuals at this income level. The Robins in this "house" are organized based in community groups like clubs, churches, or any area where there are large groups with common interests congregating regularly. With Robins as the roof, a core component of the home, it is natural their needs and opinions will be seriously considered.

This new system forces communication along with checks and balances between nodes, because there is no core government power to blame or criticize. Instead, there is a constant push and pull between nodes as the problem-solving process is carried out.

Innovation is needed to combat poverty, but not so much we forget the past.

Rather than repeating old mistakes and assumptions, it's more effective to look at ways previous plans have failed and iterate based on those failures instead of constantly trying to develop new ideas. The Money Plus Method isn't a new concept. It's simply reframing the current approach to poverty alleviation in a simpler way that's fully centered on the world's Robins—their needs, their wants, their opportunities, their empowerment—rather than the world's money.

After centuries of effort, we know what needs to be done, and there are clear themes of what solutions have been working consistently—solutions like:

- education
- inclusive institutions in government
- shelter
- electricity
- nutritious food and potable water
- contraceptives

- sanitation
- peace
- security

There are even more. We just need to prioritize these things, not just as an ethical issue or a humanitarian issue or a political issue. Rather, we need to prioritize these things as an investment into humanity's collective future.

We can improve the quality of life for Robins once and for all. Right now, we are close, but not quite there. The critical ideas are available, but individuals and organizations are repeating the same harmful cycles of sympathetic giving in the interim while simultaneously complaining about an "unchanging system." Yet, we are part of the system and are complicit in maintaining its flaws. Who is stopping us from progressing in this area other than ourselves?

Now, you may be wondering after all of my writing about how harmful money can be when used as a blanket solution to this problem, why is my core solution called the *Money Plus Method*? Shouldn't we be reducing the amount of money thrown into this problem? Why is there money involved at all?

This relates back to earlier points about embracing complexity in solutions. Money isn't the *only* solution to poverty. It's *one part* of a more complex solution. At the end of the day, a major contributing factor to why the world's Robins are poor is a lack of money.

Giving Robins money isn't inherently a bad thing, but money alone will not address the structural factors that have made and kept Robins poor over time. While money will reduce Robins' problems in the short term, money will not address all of Robins' problems in the long term.

SELECT THE SOLUTION: WHO AM I?

Do you remember the poverty theories introduced in part one?

As we explore a solution framework for poverty, let's not forget the importance of considering the cultural and behavioral elements of solutions as well.

While providing for the three dimensions of needs within health, education, and living standards is fundamental, work needs to be done to undo the negative psychological impact of living in poverty.

The word "poverty" is often defined by what individuals lack. However, individuals living in poverty should not be defined by what they lack or allow others to define them such a way.

Eradicating poverty at a cultural and behavioral level will need to involve encouraging the world's Robins to set expectations for themselves and for their communities. As discussed in part two, it will require increasing hope. When the world's Robins are stuck in poverty traps and grow accustomed to receiving handouts, the relationship doesn't just impact the donors. The paternalist system creates *parents* out of donors and *children* out of recipients. That is a hard mindset and expectation to break. The relationship could lead anyone to begin to doubt their capacity to support themselves.

Yet, any emotion in excess can become negative. Being too prideful and self-confident can lead Robins to reject jobs and support that could build their human capital. This is where "People's Champions" can serve as role models. Seeing familiar individuals who have succeeded, made use of local resources to improve their lives, or simply found work they are proud of can make a huge difference. Where local role models are few and far between, work can be done to encourage new role models to rise up.

STAGE THREE: IMPLEMENT YOUR PLAN

The importance of community has been highlighted throughout this work. Successfully implementing the Money Plus Method requires having a clear understanding of the communities forming the core of the approach.

What defines a community?

University of Chicago Booth School of Business Professor Raghuram Rajan—well-known for predicting the 2008 financial collapse years before it happened—argues the community, along with the state and the markets, are the three pillars in our society. He refers to his focus on the community and its empowerment as "inclusive localism."[604]

He understands the community to mean different things within different contexts—for example professional and religious communities—but pays closest attention to communities, or rather neighborhoods, where people live. To further prove his point, he draws attention to the fact that in the United Kingdom, 70 percent of people identify with their neighborhood as their primary source of identity.[605]

The most essential element of his definition of community is his focus on the community as "the place where people get capabilities," particularly as a result of how the surrounding people influence a person's life chances as they develop, and the place where a person is able to "build a sense of identity"

---

604 UChicago, "How the Loss of Community Threatens Society with Raghuram Rajan (Ep. 26)," UChicago Big Brains, Podcast audio, June 3, 2019.

605 Ibid.

and solidarity among others.[606] As I mentioned in part two, community trust influences how severe financial needs feel to individuals.

If a community breaks down, the opportunities for social mobility break down along with the community institutions. More often than not, the most talented people within the community leave and take their families with them, which decreases the quality of the community and leads to the disintegration of strong community units. Do you remember the "brain drain" discussed in the Liberia case study? "Brain drain" is a helpful illustration of this impact.

Leadership and influence are based on trust and credibility developed over long periods of time. To develop strong community leaders, incentives need to be created to keep talented, influential leaders in their communities. One example Professor Raghuram Rajan proposes is the development of incentive schemes like paying off student loans for people who work in their communities for a set period of time.[607]

A strong sense of community and leaders to bring communities together will need to become the root of our social and economic interactions in the future as we push away from traditional work and begin to find more value in attributes like empathy, creativity, and morality.

With stronger, more powerful communities and recognized leaders within them, the government would have an easier time collaborating with and supporting smaller locales as well. First, we need to determine what we want communities to be responsible for doing. Then, we can determine

---

606 Ibid.
607 Ibid.

what tools can be used before concerns about privacy can come to the forefront.

Can community-focused policies be successfully implemented at the scale of entire nations? The honest answer is likely no. That's part of the point. A community-focused approach to problem-solving will involve implementing policies and plans so specifically related to individual community groups that trying to expand them beyond those locales could cause more harm than good.

In this way, poverty alleviation would transition from having several tiers of central governing bodies to a more decentralized system focused on meeting specific needs, whether immediate or long-term.

IMPLEMENT YOUR PLAN: SHOW ME THE MONEY

So where is the money part of the Money Plus Method going to come from?

One option presented by Dambisa Moyo in her book *Dead Aid* is "conditional cash transfers." The reasoning behind conditional cash transfers was to distribute money equally throughout a population rather than depending on the government to equally distribute funds and base the payments on actions taken to escape poverty.[608] Moyo provides three core reasons to support conditional cash transfers:[609]

1. They enable donors to circumvent potential corruption.
2. The payments are a form of expectant giving because action is required from the recipient.
3. The money ends up with people who need it.

---

608 Dambisa Moyo, "Dead Aid: Why Aid Is Not Working and How There Is a Better Way for Africa," 1st American ed, (New York: Farrar, Straus and Giroux), 2009.
609 Ibid.

Another approach is savings clubs. A savings club is "a group of people who pool their savings by making regular contributions–weekly, biweekly, monthly–to a fund which is then paid out to each member of the group according to an agreed upon schedule."[610]

The 2013 documentary *Living on One Dollar* provides a great illustration of how these clubs work. The documentary follows the story of four young friends who live on less than one USD a day in rural Guatemala. One of the local friends they made, Anthony, saves the equivalent of twelve USD with twelve of his friends every month.[611]

At the end of each month, the money is randomly distributed to one person. This process continues over and over again until each person in the club benefits from a large sum of money at a single time. The large sum of money can be used on big ticket items. This ingenious approach provides financing opportunities for individuals who may not have access to traditional banks, and the practice can be found—under different names—globally.

The last option I will share details on is establishing a universal basic income (UBI). The idea has gained a lot of traction and was a leading policy for former candidate for the Democratic presidential nomination Andrew Yang.

Within the context of the world's Robins, the effort is more centered on how Robins know their situations best and will make the best decisions about what to buy with their money.

With additional income, discretionary spending can increase, which supports the creation of new jobs and

---

610 Ventures Nonprofit, 2017, *What is a Savings Club?*, November 30.

611 *Living on One Dollar*, Directed by Zach Ingrasci, Sean Leonard, Ryan Christofferson, and Chris Temple, 2013.

businesses within communities. UBI could also be considered a form of compensation for unpaid stay-at-home moms as well.

How does UBI work in practice? GiveDirectly is a helpful example. The charity was founded by four economics graduate students who have been advocating for cash aid since the early 2010s.[612] Starting in the fall of 2016, GiveDirectly announced it would give every adult in a small, unnamed village in Kenya an extra twenty-two USD per month for twelve years.[613] Due to the length of the project, it will take a significant amount of time to measure the true impact. The money gets wired to bank accounts linked to the villagers' phones.

In an NPR article about the experiment, a handful of recipients were highlighted.[614] The two who stood out for representing both sides of the spectrum were Denis Otieno and Dancan Odero.

Denis Otieno has four children and decided to use the additional money he receives to plant tree saplings as his children's "bank account," with a plan to sell them for lumber after they grow and use the money to fund his children's education. Now with extra money to work with, he and his wife can budget without the stress putting a strain on their marriage. They have also developed a long-term plan for the time after the twelve years when the study stops, and they stop receiving the funding.[615]

---

612 Nurith Aizenman, 2017, *How To Fix Poverty: Why Not Just Give People Money?*, August 7.

613 Ibid.

614 Ibid.

615 Ibid.

Dancan Odero is single and has epilepsy. His personal experiences struggling with epilepsy made it hard for him to work, and he lives a life dependent on his mother and family. His condition has made it harder for him to fit into his village socially. Before the money from GiveDirectly, he could not afford any seats for people to sit in if they came to visit.

With the additional money from GiveDirectly, he bought a couch set that allowed him to invite people over to his home. Now, he has reclaimed his dignity and feels more independent in the village. Unlike Denis Otieno, Dancan Odero has no longer term plans for how to survive and permanently escape from life under the poverty line after the money runs out when the twelve-year experiment is complete.[616]

Is Dancan Odero's lack of long-term planning an indication the plan is a failure? Not quite, though the answer is not black and white. In the short term, the money GiveDirectly provides to the villagers is lifting them out of poverty which is empowering in and of itself. In the long term, even the charity's chairman Michael Faye admits the direct cash benefits are another version of the billions in relief aid the world spends on poverty and is not a permanent solution. He argues "it would be enough for [the] experiment to show that just giving poor people cash is more efficient and effective."[617]

Only giving people money doesn't work in the long run for the same reason a football player that grows up poor can end up with a multimillion-dollar contract and die poor. If you don't address all of the moving components related to poverty, you're just addressing one part of the problem. Money is one solution to one part of poverty.

---

616 Ibid.
617 Ibid.

One question running through my mind as I considered the potential implication of UBI was if the price of goods would just increase and erase any sort of benefit people would receive from the additional income. Luckily, Andrew Yang included a section of his campaign website dedicated to addressing the potential for UBI to cause rampant inflation.

With regards to the relationship between UBI and inflation, if companies were to increase their prices, the general counterargument is competitions between firms will help to keep prices in check. For industries and goods where technology has influenced pricing, it has typically pushed the pricing of goods down. Rather than being concerned about the impact of UBI on inflation, it is more helpful to consider whether or not, and to what extent, technology will influence pricing in the future.[618]

A major criticism is on the impact that UBI could have on people's attitudes toward unemployment and income differences between jobs. For example, some critics of UBI argue having a baseline income would lead people to apply for jobs for enjoyment or personal interest instead of necessity. When more people are taking on jobs for leisure or indulging in less:

- fewer goods are required and unskilled workers have less work to do
- with fewer people working, quotas aren't met
- when quotas aren't met, those who are working are at risk of losing their jobs

This job insecurity works against low-income individuals.

In a world with UBI, why work when we can just make free money?

---

618 Andrew Yang, *Move Humanity Forward,* 2020.

This is one of the major arguments against a UBI where, as a result of UBI, recipients will not look for work. The role of the workplace, and of work more broadly, has changed over time and made this complete disregard for formal work less likely. How so?

In our modern times, the workplace has become a place to build social capital. Having a job adds order and structure to our daily lives and promotes the development of both personal and professional relationships. Work also creates an opportunity for social mobility as incomes increase. Some scholars like Oren Cass, a senior fellow at the Manhattan Institute for Policy Research, have claimed "work is the cornerstone of meaning, family relations, and social capital."[619]

Another popular reason why people don't support UBI is because of the risk that people, when given the freedom additional income provides, will move. That hypothetical reaction does not match up to the reality. Moving is more than packing up and leaving a place. Moving also means leaving friends, family, connections, familiarity, social status, and a person's *community*. Making such a big change and personal sacrifice would require more than just some additional money for most people.

The opinions on both sides of the argument for UBI were scattered across spectrums of enthusiastic agreement and complete disdain. I encourage you to continue reading about the implications of UBI beyond this short section because it is a topic that will continue to gain influence and popularity over time as the nature of when, how, and where we work changes.

---

619 Oren Cass, *The Working Hypothesis*, 2018.

STAGE FOUR: TEST THE RESULTS

With such high stakes—people's lives—how can you skip to the working ideas? In other words, given so much historical context, could we skip from the trial-and-error stage directly to the proven solutions?

While it's hard to skip trial-and-error stages, especially as new methods are introduced, there are encouraging stories of progress being made that combine prior knowledge and modern technology.

TEST THE RESULTS: EDUCATION

For example, strengthening the quality of education among the world's poorest is always highlighted as an impactful way to address poverty. However, it's hard to learn when you are hungry or suffering under the worrisome weight of food insecurity. In Kenya alone, one in four children are stunted due to chronic undernutrition. To help combat this problem, founder Wawira Njiru started a company called Food4Education in 2012.[620]

Food4Education provides meals for primary school children to improve both nutrition and educational outcomes. They source their food from local farmers to boost local markets and prepare high quality food themselves. The core of their solution is their advanced Tap2Eat technology. Tap2Eat is a digital mobile platform that allows parents to pay for the subsidized lunches Food4Education provides through mobile money. Unlike mobile banking, mobile money is available to anyone who has a mobile phone and enables an individual to receive, store, and send money *without a formal bank account*. The amount a parent loads into Tap2Eat

---

620 Food4Education, n.d.

is credited to a virtual wallet for their student, and the students are able to pay for their lunches with a wristband that connects with the wallet.

Since the company was founded, they have delivered over one million meals to students, which has helped improve students' nutrition, attendance, performance, and pursuit of higher levels of education.[621]

While food insecurity has a major impact on performance, students have no chance of learning or improving if they can't get to school in the first place. In Mali, the distance students travel to get to class can sometimes be enough to deter them from attending school, and the problem is exacerbated by gender.

The secondary school attendance rate is 47.8 percent. By gender, it is 52.9 percent for boys and 42.8 percent for girls, which is particularly harmful for students who live in rural areas and depend on their education as a primary tool to help their family escape poverty.[622] In response, the Sahel Women's Empowerment and Demographic Dividend (SWEDD) Project, an initiative funded by the World Bank, has provided bikes for twenty-eight young girls living in Mali in hopes of contributing to an effort to increase the girls' chances of staying in school and decrease their chances of dropping out.[623]

Beyond bikes, the program also offers school kits with items like books, notebooks, and bags to three thousand girls, sanitary kits with soap and sanitary pads, provides grains and other food for the nine hundred parents or host parents,

---

621 Ibid.

622 World Bank, *Mali: Using Bikes to Get to School and Stay in* School, July 25, 2018.

623 Ibid.

and trained 238 teachers and school counselors about children's and women's rights.[624,625]

Now that we've explored the primary- and secondary-school levels, we can explore college-level education solutions as well. For example, the state of Tennessee is pioneering efforts to increase educational equity. Tennessee is the first state in the United States to offer tuition-free community or technical college for every graduating high school senior starting in 2014 through a "last-dollar" program called Tennessee Promise.

The "last-dollar" refers to the fact the state government covers the cost of tuition not already covered by federal Pell grants, state awards, or scholarships—making the program cheaper for the state government. The program started a means of promoting workforce development early and encouraging employers to move to the state.

The results of the program so far have been positive, with the state's rate of high school students going to college increasing from 58.1 percent in 2014 to 64 percent in 2015.[626,627]

The number of students applying for the program has increased every year since it started thanks to promotion of the program by teachers and counselors. Now, about four-fifths of high school seniors in the state apply for the program yearly.

For low-income students, expenses like textbooks, car repairs, childcare, transportation, and long workweeks are

---

624 Ibid.

625 Ibid.

626 Reade Pickert, *Is This Free College Program a Model for the Nation?*, December 4, 2019.

627 Ibid.

all roadblocks when trying to make ends meet for the costs not covered after tuition fees are paid. These struggles tie into the social and emotional factors of attending college as a low-income student that the financial aid program doesn't address. To combat these issues, students in the program get paired with a volunteer mentor who is able to help them apply for financial aid, remember important deadlines, or check in about graduation requirements.

Not even free tuition is a quick-fix solution for educational inequality. According to David Deming, the director of the Malcolm Wiener Center for Social Policy at Harvard, there is no one-size-fits-all approach to attain educational equity. He advocates for a solution where "the federal government provides the money and then a very basic framework that gives states flexibility to enact programs that work best for their populations,"[628] which sounds like advocating for community-based solutions to me.

On that note, let's move forward to an illustrative example of how education fits into the grand scheme of poverty alleviation at a national scale.

TEST THE RESULTS: SINGAPORE'S SUCCESS

Countries focusing on creating prosperity rather than eradicating poverty analyze poverty data differently.

The best way to illustrate this difference is through the story of Singapore's success.

A few decades ago, Singapore was poor and behind in global development. With a focus on prosperity over poverty, the Singaporean government was able to ask different questions, create more unique solutions, and emphasize data

---

628 Ibid.

application to their situation. One of the government's top priorities was improving its education system.

In the short-term, the goal was to get students through primary and secondary school. Singapore thought more about its long-term goal: understanding what the job market would look like for all of the educated students who would be entering it and how the economy would be able to create and sustain jobs for the students.

With this long-term focus in mind, Singapore prioritized investments and attracting companies willing to create jobs rather than building schools, and this influx of companies is what increased the need for education. Today, Singapore is one of the richest countries in the world and approximately 99 percent of the population attend secondary school, with more than half going on to post-secondary education as well.[629]

Singapore's story shows that while data is helpful, it's hard to make any substantial, long-lasting change without a focus on the causes and trends. Beyond this, it is an example of the positive role governments can take in planning and setting goals as opposed to creating systems benefitting only Camerons.

STAGE FIVE: ITERATE AND IMPROVE

The last stage to problem solving is to iterate and improve based on things already being done. The final question then becomes: *how can we harness our current resources to make sure we are helping the people who know the best ways to solve their problems?*

---

629 Clayton Christensen, Efosa Ojomo, and Karen Dillion, "Poverty data never tells the whole story," 2019.

A new class of researchers called the "randomistas," led by the Nobel Prize winning economists Abhijit Banerjee, Esther Duflo and Michael Kremer, are leading the global charge in changing the general approach toward the world's Camerons helping the world's Robins.

Rather than theorizing and philosophizing about "the poor," they've decided to go out into the world and do research predominantly rooted in randomized control trials (RCT), which are more objective and simpler for the general public to understand. What makes RCTs so exciting is how broadly applicable they are. The methodology can be used to understand how different factors maintain and sustain poverty globally.

Aside from changing our general approach toward research and experimentation, how else can solutions be improved?

Another way to improve is through the use of social media and modern communication channels to increase interactions between the various "nodes" of the Money Plus Method. We have a plethora of almost universally-available communication channels that allow for clear and quick communication between key players on a regular basis.

Even in rural areas and among the world's poorest, people either own or have access to some form of a communication device. For example, people who may not have sim cards in their phones can use them as a music player for entertainment or as a flashlight during a power outage. By harnessing this technology, we can more accurately understand who and how to help.

CONCLUSION

We can move closer to eradicating extreme poverty by:

1. improving our data
2. focusing on analysis that creates prosperity
3. exploring various solutions and iterating based on prior efforts
4. implementing the ideas that we are passion about
5. being unafraid to adjust when things go wrong or there are better ways to accomplish a goal

Let's stop our armchair activism and start taking action. The future is now!

"What does it mean for a poor person not to need you anymore?"

—IAN ROSENBERGER, FOUNDER OF
TEAM TASSY AND THREAD[630]

---

630 Ian Rosenberger, "Why poverty has nothing to do with money," Filmed
June 2014 at Grandview Ave, TED video, 9:18 - 9:23.

TAKING CARE OF
BUSINESS

———

After visiting Haiti in 2010, shortly after the country survived a catastrophic earthquake earlier in the year, Ian Rosenberger decided to start a company called Team Tassy in hopes of answering that question. Prior to starting Team Tassy, Rosenberger was a contestant on *Survivor: Palau*. He is an ultramarathon runner and has been featured in publications such as *Fast Company*, *The Atlantic*, *The Guardian*, CNN, and the *Huffington Post* for his work. His company provides jobs for Haitian families by shipping recycled plastic out of Haiti to be processed into fabric and turned into finished products.

In his experience, Rosenberger realized alleviating poverty in Haiti has less to do with money and more to do with resources. He found the way people could support themselves and "not need you anymore" would be through finding jobs and earning their own money.[631] Jobs are what empower

---

631 Ian Rosenberger, "Why poverty has nothing to do with money," Filmed June 2014 at Grandview Ave, TED video, 19:24.

people to create wealth, but to obtain those jobs they need the appropriate skills.

Rosenberger took cues from organizations in the United States when organizing Team Tassy. For example, his decision to start his work in one specific neighborhood was based on The Harlem Children's Zone, and his decision to focus on job training and creation was influenced by Bill Strickland's Manchester Bidwell Corporation.[632]

One of their Haitian partners Marc Noel highlighted the difference between Team Tassy and other organizations coming and going to Haiti with resources in the short-term: "Many organizations come. The organizations change. Haitian people stay the same. They gave you some food, and they finish. They leave. Other organization, they just food. Not jobs. Give you some money. He forget you. Give you some food. He forget you. Give you some medicine. He forget you. They don't care what we do after. They don't care. You are different. Team Tassy is very different. You sit with our families. Others don't. You respect your promise."[633]

Team Tassy is able to make a difference, not just because it provides jobs, but because it works with its families to make a long-term, sustainable investment in their futures. This kind of effort is easier and more personalized first at the neighborhood level.

Jobs are critical, especially in the case of individuals living in extreme poverty, because jobs give people a sense of accomplishment and raise self-esteem. Jobs have ripple effects as well. With a job, there is a higher chance of escaping

---

632 Ibid.
633 Ibid.

poverty. For low-income people with children, the amount of resources made available to their children increases, and the likelihood of future generations living in poverty decreases.

With a job, a person is able to provide for themselves and maintain both their pride and dignity, all while gaining useful life skills applicable inside and outside of work contexts.

However, they are not the *only* way to alleviate poverty. As with most solutions, they have to be more multifaceted and sensitive to individual needs.

In this chapter, I will:

- provide details on how twenty-first century careers will be different from careers of the past
- shed light on how automation will re-shape the future of work
- emphasize the importance of skills training in a rapidly advancing world
- underscore why job creation alone is not enough to support the world's Robins

THE TWENTY-FIRST CENTURY CAREER

The job market is changing and making it harder, even for the highly skilled, to find and keep jobs. David Deming, the director of the Malcolm Wiener Center for Social Policy at Harvard, has found through his research that within the United States, though more traditional industries like manufacturing may grow, they won't grow at the same rate they did in the early twentieth century when they helped build up modern ideas of the middle class.[634]

Current ideas of what makes up a career are also changing.

---

634 Simon Torkington, "The jobs of the future—and two skills you need to get them," World Economic Forum, September 2, 2016.

Josh Bersin, founder and principal at Deloitte, organized the idea of a traditional career into three parts within his article titled "Catch the wave: The 21st-century career".[635]

1. The first component of a career is its importance as an element defining who we are and what we do. He argues a career "represents our expertise, our profession, and ultimately our identity."

2. The second component is its role as something individuals can build, grow, and improve over time.

3. The third component is the financial and psychological rewards received from our work and how they contribute to our lives having meaning and purpose.

In the past, it was normal—if not expected—for college graduates to start working for a company and stay there throughout their entire careers. Some companies have job models so strict promotions are unlikely unless someone in a position of authority dies or quits. Now, all three of these elements have been disrupted as expertise, duration, and rewards within work have shifted to reflect the changing skills, attitudes, and opinions on work in the twenty-first century.

As of 2017, only 19 percent of companies had traditional career models, and that number will continue to decrease.[636] In contrast to the straightforward career paths of the past, today a college graduate could work for four to five companies within the first ten years of their careers.[637]

It is becoming more common for companies to have flatter structures with less traditional climbing of the career

---

635 Josh Bersin, *Catch the wave: The 21st-century career,* July 31, 2017.
636 Ibid.
637 Ibid.

ladder, especially when young people sometimes enter jobs with less experience but more skills than experienced staff. This divide has increased as rapid technological advancement makes it all too easy for skills to become obsolete.

Why have young people's attitudes toward work changed? Many factors are responsible, but one in particular highlighted in Bersin's article was increasing life expectancies. He argues with life expectancies for millennials expected to reach an average of ninety years, not only are governments pushing to increase the retirement age to reduce the burden of retirement benefit payouts, but fewer people are able to retire after the traditional thirty years of work.[638]

Bersin argues young people now will likely be working for half a century or longer. With such a long time spent working, cycling through different stages of learning and working within different careers paths is a natural response.

Luckily, even in the face of automation, technology's influence on the job market in the long run will not be the catastrophic issue many fear. In fact, that idea is rooted in what Charles Wheelan describes in his work *Naked Economics* as the "lump of labor fallacy."[639] The fallacy describes the belief that the amount of work available in an economy is fixed, so new jobs are created as other jobs are destroyed.

The reality is jobs are continuously created as individuals provide new goods and services or an improvement on methods of providing older ones. In the short run, technology will take away some unskilled jobs and will require a focus on new training, new skills, new positions, and new investments by employers as the future of work is reshaped.

---

638 Ibid.

639 Charles J Wheelan, *Naked Economics: Undressing the Dismal Science: Fully Revised and Updated,* (New York: W.W. Norton & Company), 2019.

AUTOMATION AND THE FUTURE OF WORK

According to the World Economic Forum, 42 percent of core skills required to perform existing jobs will change by 2022 as we live through what is now more commonly being defined as the Fourth Industrial Revolution.[640] Do you remember the details shared about this new era in part one?

This change isn't just referring to high-tech skills, either. Managing Director at the World Economic Forum Saadia Zahidi believes, "specialized interpersonal skills will be in high demand, including skills related to sales, human resources, care and education."[641]

If workers are willing and able to adopt advanced technology to assist with their work, it will make them more efficient in their jobs. Bersin described this effect as the "machine augmentation of work."[642]

What will the future of work look like then?

For starters, it will involve a lot more math, science, and data analytics. Anyone without these skills will have limited career prospects in the future.

If you haven't already, start building up your math intuition and break out your math workbooks because by 2039, approximately 4.5 million new STEM-enabled job are expected to be created.[643]

Computers are better and faster with numbers and data than most humans. Those kinds of jobs are more vulnerable to automation than jobs related to the arts. In fact, as more and more people develop high-demand tech skills, the value

640 Saadia Zahidi, 2020, *We need a global reskilling revolution—here's why*, January 22.
641 Ibid.
642 Josh Bersin, "Catch the wave: The 21st-century career," July 31, 2017.
643 Ibid.

of those skills declines.[644] This relates back to Zahidi's points on the importance of interpersonal skills.

It is important to complement STEM skills with soft skills like communication, design, creativity, and collaboration—from a STEM focus to a STEAM focus.[645] New soft skills in research, writing, problem-solving, and teamwork will also become important in the workplace.

Some of the future's best jobs will require *both* technical and social skills. Whereas many technical jobs required continuous training before, today's job market and the job market of the future will require continuous learning of new skills, tools, and systems, especially for "renaissance jobs" which are roles combining technical and creative skills with industry experience—roles like user experience designers and project managers.[646]

I have referenced college graduates getting jobs more than once now, which is an important distinction to make. However, why limit the solution to jobs requiring degrees? As Sean Malone wrote in a 2017 article for the Foundation for Economic Education, "everyone needs an education, but not everyone needs to get a four-year degree."[647] Higher education is expensive and not always a good fit for everyone. Instead, a new emphasis on opportunities like apprenticeships, trade schools, and certificate courses should be highlighted as well.

To address everyone's needs, we will need to be open-minded about the routes people take to success.

---

644 Ibid.
645 STEAM is referring to science, technology, engineering, arts, and math.
646 Ibid.
647 Sean Malone, 2017, *10 Solutions to Intergenerational Poverty,* August 29.

Now more than ever before, and certainly in the future, it will be challenging for the world's Robins and under-skilled populations at Drew, Taylor, and Cameron's levels to find and keep jobs. Simple tasks and low-skilled work will be overtaken by automation.

Making requirements like college degrees a necessity for every job increases barriers for people who are already struggling.

Humanity has to think long and hard about two inevitable elements of the future:

1. teaching everyone, regardless of income, how to work in machine augmented job environments
2. providing skills and education for the world's poorest in a variety of formats

COMPLEMENTS, NOT SUBSTITUTES

Machine-augmented jobs are the way of the future, but that growing trend does not mean machines will replace humans in *every* element of work. In fact, as Peter Thiel describes in his book *Zero to One,* "computers are complements for humans, not substitutes."[648] Thiel highlights some important differences between humans and computers. For instance, while computers are faster and more efficient with data processing, they can't make decisions in complicated situations or make basic judgements as instinctively as humans.[649]

This is not to say that computers are completely inept in this area. Computers are able to find patterns in data, but it is more of a challenge to compare patterns and interpret complex behaviors. That work—creating meaning out of

---

648 Peter Thiel, *Zero to One,* Crown Business, 2014.
649 Ibid.

patterns and trends—is where the valuable role of a human analyst fits in.

Computers *help* humans to solve hard problems, but they can't always find answers. With more machines helping with problem solving, things are done faster and more effectively without the competition for resources created when multiple people are working together. Computers don't like luxury goods. They don't need vacation time or groceries or apartment space in ever-filling urban cities. Computers can help to reduce competition between individuals while increasing efficiency in the workplace.[650]

A SKILLS REVOLUTION

Now that the traditional career model is becoming more and more obsolete as new workers enter the market, there is an opportunity available to help people build on skills they already have and use them to obtain new jobs or find new work at their existing companies.

Helping the world's Robins build critical job skills will be a key component of improving global social mobility and reducing inequality in the future. Improving social mobility will benefit everyone too; the World Economic Forum's Global Social Mobility Index for 2020 indicates a mere 10 percent improvement in global social mobility would boost economic growth by nearly 5 percent over the next decade.[651]

Are companies willing to train—or re-train—current and future employees with the skills of the future? Right now, it seems we are in a period of transition with many training

---

650 Ibid.
651 World Economic Forum, "Global Social Mobility Index 2020: why economies benefit from fixing inequality," January 19, 2020.

departments relying on online courses and programs for people to teach themselves.

That's not to say the importance is not noted by companies. The market for education, professional skills, and corporate training is worth over US$400 billion.[652] Large companies are now investing in internally developed content. Learning and development (LD) has become the fastest-growing segment of the HR technology market.[653] A recent Deloitte Global Human Capital Trends report noted LD had increased from being the fifth most important issue for business and HR leaders in 2016 to the second most important issue in 2017.[654]

Employers of the future need to be aware that as the pressure to advance at technology's pace increases, employees are seeking out opportunities for professional development as they work for longer portions of their lives in more varied places.

To make things easier, companies can help their staff by creating or supporting opportunities to gain new skills and plan out their career development strategies. Companies not keeping up will lose out on talent.

JOB CREATION PROGRAMS

What does this new focus on training workers look like? Potentially, something similar to the Future Jobs Fund in the United Kingdom. The Future Jobs Fund (FJF) was a one billion GBP fund that supported job creation for young and

---

652 Josh Bersin, Catch the wave: The 21st-century career, July 31, 2017.
653 Ibid.
654 Ibid.

disadvantaged job seekers from October 2009 to March 2011.[655]

It assisted them in gaining long-term unsubsidized jobs. Each participant was in their fund-sponsored job for six months, or longer, if employers were able to combine FJF funding with other sources.

Jobs within FJF were regular jobs with employee rights, meaning employees were paid a wage (at least minimum wage) but many did not receive employee benefits. They did receive rights to vacation time and had a maximum working time set.

To incentivize employers, the government provided subsidies to employers. The program was announced as a key component of a broader jobs program called the Young Person's Guarantee (YPG).

The YPG was targeted toward eighteen to twenty-four-year-olds reaching twelve months of unemployment. The program included either:[656]

- one of ten thousand jobs in key sectors
- six months of job training and a place on a Community Task Force working on valuable community projects
- a job from the FJF

Involvement in either the training or a job was required to continue receiving government benefits like the Jobseeker's Allowance.[657]

---

655 Department for Work and Pensions, 2011, "Early Analysis of Future Jobs Fund participant outcomes—Update."

656 Ibid.

657 Jobseeker's Allowance (JSA) is a benefit for people who are not in full-time employment (work less than sixteen hours per week), are capable of working and are looking for work.

The FJF marked a significant shift away from supply-side employment policies that didn't create jobs. These policies focused more on job training to help unemployed people from underprivileged groups become more competitive applicants in the general labor market. The program was not without its challenges.[658] For example, the short-term form of employment for those in the program put them at risk of being exploited. Further, the program put existing workers of participating employers at risk. Local labor unions pushed to be involved in the program to minimize these risks and guard against employers firing employees and taking on FJF staff to do the same work.

CONCLUSION: BEYOND JOBS

Prioritizing jobs in poverty alleviation efforts is not a new strategy. However, there are exceptions to this. Notably, for people who can't work or people who have mental or physical disabilities restricting their abilities to work, new and more specialized approaches to job training and support are necessary. As a new focus on mental health makes waves globally, more efforts in this area are beginning to take shape, but there is a lot of work and progress to be made.

Beyond this, efforts to support those living in poverty can't stop with jobs. An approach with more long-term impact will require job training, placement, childcare, and also support low-income workers while they work. This support could take the form of education and skills training to promote advancement within their roles or competitive qualities for future work opportunities.

---

658 Department for Work and Pensions, "Early Analysis of Future Jobs Fund participant outcomes—Update," 2011.

The skills holding low-income workers back are not always job related, either. Sometimes attitudes and general work habits like arriving on time and following instructions aren't well-established, which requires development and time to instill. This approach is more substantive and more expensive, but it is also, most importantly, more effective.

As Valerie Jarrett wrote in her New York Times Bestseller *Finding My Voice,* "Creating jobs is vital, but without affordable housing, good schools, paved streets, safe parks, and places to shop, people can't live and raise their families with grace." [659]

Jobs are one piece of a larger solution to extreme poverty involving uplifting and empowering people to help themselves.

---

659 Valerie Jarrett, *Finding My Voice,* (New York City: Viking Press, 2019).

"Resist blaming any one individual or group of individuals for anything. Because the problem is that when we identify the bad guy, we are done thinking. And it's almost always more complicated than that. It's almost always about multiple interacting causes—a system."

—HANS ROSLING, SWEDISH PHYSICIAN, CO-AUTHOR OF FACTFULNESS[660]

660 Hans Rosling, Ola Rosling, and Rönnlund Anna Rosling, *Factfulness: Ten Reasons Were Wrong about the World—and Why Things Are Better Than You Think*, (London: Sceptre, 2019), 226

DON'T EAT THE
RICH. FEED THEM.

———

Are Camerons obligated to help Robins?

Beyond this, is it ethical for Camerons and their families to spend their wealth on designer clothes, multiple homes, and flashy vacations while Robins struggle to make ends meet?

While I can't influence what Camerons spend their money on, I can address the types of incentives that can encourage people of the world to spend more of their money on eradicating poverty. It all starts with a shift of focus from eradicating poverty to creating prosperity for all individuals, high and low income. Prosperity occurs when more people are able to improve their general well-being. Rather than focusing solely on what makes people poor, we should aim to understand what helps people become wealthy, not just earn more money: creating and exchanging goods and services with people.

How does this fit into the context of interactions between Robins and Camerons? It all relates back to our earlier discussions of paternalism versus partnerships in part one. Instead of enabling a system that discourages the world's Robins from taking responsibility for their lives, they could be partnering with each other.

A successful partnership-based approach to poverty alleviation depends on trusting people who make up the large corporations many outsiders deride and can play an active role in helping to end extreme poverty. How? By making a genuine, long-term effort to get involved, create jobs, support innovation, and fund new businesses.

In this chapter, I will:

- address the "money" part of the Money Plus Method in more depth
- highlight the importance of connections and opportunity for empowering the world's Robins
- explain the role of innovation in modern poverty alleviation strategies.

SHOW ME THE MONEY

Self-interest is a core part of human behavior, which is why determining what could incentivize Camerons to contribute is helpful for developing successful programs and opportunities to help the world's Robins. Effective programs and opportunities for low-income communities require money. Whether that money comes from the government through the tax revenues of those making enough to pay or from private businesses with corporate social responsibility goals to meet, funding is a key driver of change-making action.

Combining public and private funding would help to combat the bureaucracy often accompanying the excess regulation and complex processes created to handle government programs. The combination would help decision-makers, whether politicians or otherwise, focus on actions to improve things for the greater good rather than just providing short-term benefits for a single individual.

Businesspeople and politicians are not inherently Robins' enemies. Through business and effective policy, Robins can be provided jobs, goods, and services they need to uplift, not only their life circumstances, but their family's as well.

Encouraging businesspeople and politicians to engage with poverty alleviation efforts starts with making an effort to see where businesses can fit into the poverty alleviation puzzle and gaining a better understanding of how governments can effectively react to the needs of "the poor."

CONNECTIONS AND OPPORTUNITY

The Merriam-Webster dictionary defines charity as "generosity and helpfulness especially toward the needy or suffering."[661] More often than not, charity falls into the realm of sympathetic giving. In contrast, philanthropy is often expectant giving.

Bill and Melinda Gates outline some key factors of philanthropy making it so impactful in their 2020 annual letter. In particular, they call attention to the differences between government funds and philanthropic funds.

While governments focus on solutions that they are certain of, donors are able to take and support risks "governments can't, and corporations won't" through philanthropy.[662] Foundations and other philanthropic funds have more freedom to try riskier solutions to problems and help small ideas grow. Within this realm of giving, it is important

---

661 Merriam-Webster Dictionary, Online Version, s.v. "Charity."
662 Bill and Melinda Gates, *Why we swing for the fences*, February 10, 2020.

donors focus on supporting the implementation of ideas centered on those in need, rather than relying on their perceptions of what impactful solutions would be.

Aside from funding, how else can Camerons contribute to uplifting and empowering the world's Robins? As I wrote in part one, transferring skills and knowledge can be just as valuable, if not more so, than money. The world's Robins lack access and opportunities more than any innate talent or ability.

While the existence of millionaires and billionaires can be either a source of motivation or envy, educating the world's Robins on the value of setting and accomplishing attainable financial goals can help create sustainable solutions to poverty alleviation as well. For Robins, the issue typically isn't financial irresponsibility so much as it is an inability to save money, cover their bills, *and* afford essentials like food and water due to lack of income and expenses extending beyond their means.

Connecting the world's Robins with community leaders, influential connections, educational opportunities, and jobs can be more life-changing than a blank check. The money also doesn't have to come solely from the distantly wealthy. Remittances are also an impactful way to relieve poverty and involves a transfer of wealth within familial or social circles.

Evidence from the World Bank suggests a 10 percent increase in per capita remittances leads to a 3.5 percent decline in the proportion of poor people.[663] As FinTech proliferates financial markets, it is becoming easier, faster, and cheaper for people to send and receive money digitally.

---

663 World Bank, Remittances, Households, and Poverty. Global Economic Prospects, World Bank, 2006.

In 2018, remittances to low- and middle-income countries were US$529 billion, a 9.6 percent increase compared to 2017.[664] Global remittances are expected to reach over seven hundred billion by the end of 2020.[665]

Remittances diversify and increase household incomes, which is crucial for low-income households needing the additional funds for investments into education and homes. With the support of remittances, people are able to protect themselves from general economic instability, market downturns, or insufficient government support like a lack of state-provided social security. At scale, remittances have also begun to serve as a source of foreign currency for governments as well.[666]

A SHIFT IN PERSPECTIVE

If the fulfillment of sharing connections and skills, which costs nothing but time from the donor's side, isn't a strong enough incentive, maybe money is.

In *Factfulness,* the Roslings highlight the importance of making better decisions about the world by understanding how populations are spread out now and how they will be spread out in the future. The authors call attention to some helpful forecasts that provide a profit-centered incentive for collaboration:

"If the UN forecasts for population growth are correct, and if incomes in Asia and Africa keep growing as now, then the center of gravity of the world market will shift over

---

664 Sudhesh Giriyan, *Outlook 2020: Digital trends that will shape the remittance industry,* February 3, 2020
665 Ibid.
666 The Conversation, "We asked Senegalese migrants why they leave home. Here's what they told us," March, 2019.

the next 20 years from the Atlantic to the Indian Ocean."[667] To be more precise, the book forecasts by 2100, "more than 80 percent of the world's population will live in Africa and Asia."[668]

This change has large implications for where, how, and even when business will take place in the future. As of 2018, "the people living in rich countries around the North Atlantic, who represent 11 percent of the world population, make up 60 percent of the Level 4 consumer market."[669] However, that figure is predicted to shrink to 50 percent by 2027. By 2040, "60 percent of Level 4 consumers will live outside the West."[670]

The middle-income consumer market, predominantly found in Africa and Asia, is expanding. While local brands expand their reach and grow their customer bases on these continents, foreign businesses are playing catch up. There is profit to be made in markets within Asia and Africa, but many business professionals are stuck operating under the false pretense "the West" will continue to dominate indefinitely.

This mindset is especially pervasive with regards to Africa. For many, Africa is a continent that will never improve or develop. That mindset is not only harmful, inaccurate, and outdated, but it is also leaving money on the table and costing businesses potential customers.

As Rosling notes in *Factfulness,* "The majority of the world population is steadily moving up the levels. The

---

667 Hans Rosling, Ola Rosling, and Rönnlund Anna Rosling, *Factfulness: Ten Reasons Were Wrong about the World—and Why Things Are Better Than You Think*, (London: Sceptre, 2019), 146

668 Ibid.

669 Ibid.

670 Ibid.

number of people on Level 3 will increase from two billion to four billion between now and 2040. Almost everyone in the world is becoming a consumer."[671] The vast majority of the world is advancing through income levels and seeking out products matching their fluctuating price points, preferences, and budgets.

Looking forward, businesses have a choice to make. They can either continue to predominantly serve Camerons in an increasingly competitive marketplace where they are forced to create demand for individuals who have all of their basic needs met, or they can expand their perspective beyond Camerons to the billions of consumers like the world's Robins, Drews, and Taylors looking for ways to improve their low-to-middle-income lives.

Alleviating poverty can increase profits when businesses expand to underserved markets, create jobs, improve local economies, and fulfill the needs of their consumers. Robins, Drews, and Taylors have money to spend, and there is money to be made creating affordable products to meet their needs.

Rosling drew attention to a shocking but helpful example that ties together poverty alleviation and profit in *Factfulness,* as well. He highlighted every pregnancy results in approximately two years of lost menstruation.[672] If you recall from the chapter on overpopulation, the number of babies per woman is actually decreasing over time. This is not only good for combating overpopulation but is also good for feminine hygiene product manufacturers who are now able to sell more of their products.

---

671 Hans Rosling, Ola Rosling, and Rönnlund Anna Rosling, *Factfulness: Ten Reasons Were Wrong about the World—and Why Things Are Better than You Think,* (London: Sceptre, 2019), 157

672 Ibid.

Another boost for their business is the increase in educated and working women. Women with higher levels of education and women who work are more likely to have fewer children. Fewer pregnancies lead to more periods, which leads to more sales. Businesses can benefit from improvements in global development.

Why are these big market opportunities not attracting large swathes of entrepreneurs looking to make money in relatively new markets? Primarily because operating in economies catering to consumers like Robins, Drews, and Taylors takes more effort and time compared to building businesses for Camerons in level four. For example, businesses sometimes have to navigate complex regulation, licensing, or zoning laws of a particular country (or across countries for international companies.)

The challenges facing large companies should not be transferred to smaller ones. Micro-entrepreneurs, local or otherwise, are not solely responsible for addressing poverty and, in fact, have been proven *not* to address the structural causes of poverty in their work.[673]

Rather, a collaborative effort between businesses of all sizes and consumers is what helps to create new markets, institutions, and organizations.

TECHNOLOGY AND INNOVATION

Do you remember the concept of leapfrogging introduced in the Industrial Revolution chapter? Let's revisit it again in our discussion of technology and innovation within poverty alleviation. Leapfrogging helps explain why and how Robins

---

673 Thilde Langevang, "Fashioning the future: Entrepreneuring in Africa's emerging fashion industry," Working Paper, Copenhagen: Center for Business and Development Studies: Copenhagen Business School, 2016.

will be able to use twenty-first century tools to solve their nineteenth century problems. An accelerated path of development is essentially required for people living like Robins because the "development" stage of a lot of technology is already complete.

Why bother teaching Robins how to use the telegram when smartphones have already been invented?

With this context in mind, how can individuals create prosperity within their families, their communities, their nations, and beyond instead of focusing on the elements of their lives that are lacking? Through innovation.

But what is innovation? Efosa Ojomo of the Christensen Institute defines innovation as "practical solutions to real problems."[674]

The solution and the infrastructure in place to enact it don't need to be developed at the same time. For example, he argues sometimes "innovation comes before the infrastructure"[675]

He also argues prosperity is able to take root when organizations invest in what he calls "market-creating innovation."[676] Instead of relying on donor support, this kind of innovation provides affordable products customers need.

MARKET-CREATING INNOVATIONS

Market-creating innovations are what push companies to create things that are simple, affordable, and accessible rather than aiming for complex and expensive products for

---

674 Efosa Ojomo, "The Poverty Paradox: Why Most Poverty Programs Fail and How to Fix Them," Filmed August 14, 2017 at Gaborone, TED video, 15:26.

675 Ibid.

676 Ibid.

Camerons only. This innovation is so critical because it leads to *sustainable* economic development and increased living standards that lift large groups of people out of poverty—creating prosperity rather than simply alleviating poverty.

Market-creating innovation usually starts at the simplest form of a product and moves upmarket until it is able to displace established competitors, or it maintains its lower quality and avoids direct competition with industry leaders. They don't make products any better, they make products more affordable.[677]

Ojomo identified five core reasons why market-creating innovations are able to make a serious impact on local communities:[678]

1. They create jobs by encouraging local producers to hire local talent and to make, distribute, sell, and service their products locally.

2. They promote the development of sustainable infrastructure because the development of the new market pushes business leaders to fill in the gaps with their own infrastructure.

   a. Their ties to market needs also make them more usable than government-sponsored projects that often miss the mark on where infrastructure investments need to be made.

3. The innovations strengthen institutions by promoting the creation of legal systems, regulations, and education to sustain and support the market.

---

677 Efosa Ojomo, 5 Reasons Why These Powerful Innovations Might Be Our Best Shot At Solving Poverty, August 6, 2019.

678 Ibid.

4. They create revenue for governments and introduce individuals who may have been considered non-consumers in the past to the formal market.

   a. This transition turns these former non-consumers into tax revenue sources for governments who can then use those funds to strengthen communities and institutions while also providing better social services.

5. They combat crime and corruption by changing incentive structures for people who often have very few options to make ends meet.

   a. Through creating more opportunities to build wealth and strengthen corruption fighting institutions, corruption ends up being a less appealing option for personal progression and the punishments are stricter when an individual is caught.

Market-creating innovations aren't perfect, but they are a helpful starting point and more useful than focusing purely on what people living in poverty lack. They focus on how to make use of the resources and skills available for effective solutions.

SUSTAINABLE SOLUTIONS

Right now, poverty alleviation is suffering from the "broken well problem." What is that exactly? Efosa Ojomo discussed the issue in his popular Ted Talk and book "The Poverty Paradox."[679]

The problem is related to the hundreds of thousands of broken wells that can be found all over Africa today. The wells are built by volunteer groups, religious organizations,

---

679 Efosa Ojomo, "The Poverty Paradox: Why Most Poverty Programs Fail and How to Fix Them," Filmed August 14, 2017 at Gaborone, TED video, 15:26.

and others who have traveled to Africa in a well-intentioned effort to make a difference.

Building wells is addressing a symptom of poverty, not a cause. To make matters worse, many volunteers never teach local residents how to repair or maintain the well over time, which means as soon as the well breaks or malfunctions, they are left with a defunct relic of a volunteer project gone wrong. Years go by and, if that particular neighborhood or village is no longer "popular" with organizations, they are left with only part of a solution to their problem. It is much easier to build a well than it is to address structural deficiencies in communities.

Building wells is a great example of a surface level solution to a problem that is encouraging for volunteers to contribute to, produces a tangible product, increases optimism, and makes it easier for many people to engage in problem-solving together. The problem is that type of problem solving is often self-centered at its core. It's easy and encouraging for volunteers, not for Drews, and certainly not for Robins.

It doesn't take community-specific knowledge to build a well, but it does take community-specific knowledge to know *where* to build one, how often it will be used, and most importantly, whether that well is addressing a pressing need the community faces.

Poverty alleviation efforts are cyclical in nature. New organizations and individuals are constantly introducing new ideas, watching them succeed or fail, and working from there to continue the same cycle of trial and error until something works. There's always a next big thing to focus on and in this phase of poverty alleviation "innovation" is the new buzzword.

CONCLUSION

A focus on innovation to fight poverty is a helpful and modern approach to discussions about poverty alleviation, but what does investing in *innovation* look like for the world's extreme poor? Startup competitions and business incubators aren't necessarily relevant for populations of people who can't afford a roof over their heads. Time to be thoughtful about business strategies is a luxury of its own. A fight for survival does not leave much time to be imaginative beyond meeting basic needs, and many living in extreme poverty don't have enough influence to speak up for themselves.

Many living in extreme poverty are unable to read or write. Community leaders would need to be willing and able to translate ideas in a way clearly communicable to investors or create solutions that work around that knowledge gap. If only the ivory tower voices of C-suite executives and academics are paid any mind, then it will be impossible to make real progress. This is why it's so important for the world's Robins to be a part of the conversation.

While the partnership model is a crucial next step toward funding ideas and solutions that matter to reshaping the relationship between the haves and the have-nots, sustainable solutions can't stop with funding. Measures of how effective poverty alleviation strategies are should be based on whether or not they create long-term, sustainable growth and whether or not they encourage prosperity by shifting the largest amount of people out of poverty.

There needs to be a balance between coming up with new buzzwords just to introduce something new and deciding to iterate on past efforts. A lot of effort, money, and time have already been spent on eradicating poverty. Now, the amount of time and resources all of us, not just the individuals already fighting and working on poverty alleviation, are willing to dedicate to alleviating poverty matters more than ever before.

Businesses are beginning to pay closer attention to developing corporate social responsibility initiatives, social impact investing is a growing field within finance, and taking sides on all social issues has become all too easy through social media. While not everyone is directly exposed to individuals living in extreme poverty, relative poverty can be found everywhere. Extreme poverty is not an issue to file away under problems out of sight and out of mind.

We have to choose to care about eradicating extreme poverty and improving global living standards. Those goals need to be a top priority for real change to happen. Beyond choosing to care, we need to make choices reflecting our dedication in everything from volunteering to voting. To put it simply, **we need to ensure our actions related to poverty alleviation speak louder than words.**

PART 4

THE LAST LAP

HELLO, MY NAME
IS ROBIN

———

In this chapter, I am changing things up. One helpful way to understand extreme poverty is to hear from people who live through it daily. To aid in this understanding, I will be sharing a series of "interviews" conducted in Liberia and Nigeria.

The three conversations below were inspired by:

1. consolidated responses from nine individuals living in extreme poverty
2. a series of conversations with my grandmother who lived in Liberia for the majority of her life

I added details to the responses by consolidating some of my interview questions. For example, "If you are sick, how do you handle it?" and "How do you maintain your personal hygiene?" were originally separate questions.

Many answers to my interview questions received repeat responses. The answers from the three "individuals" in this chapter represent the core themes of the responses I received. I also used cultural references from my grandmother to add more illustrative detail in some responses.

For example, my grandmother raised her children and children from low-income families within her community. This was a common choice made by families in Liberia who did not have the money or resources to care for their children. This detail was added to Yara's story to represent that experience.

If you would like to read the interview responses I received and the full list of questions without any consolidation, you can view the material in the appendix.

PROFILE #1: YARA

Yara is a seventeen-year-old female living in Monrovia, Liberia. She hopes to one day own a big, successful business. At seventeen years old, she is the average age of a Liberian citizen.[680] That average age makes Liberia one of the youngest countries in the world. In her interview she refers to things like petty goods, which are basically any small, inexpensive items. Examples of food such as fufu (a doughy food) and coconut came up during the interviews.

She also references using iron soap. For context, the civil war in Liberia drove many soap companies away. To address the need for soap, NGOs introduced an "emergency soap" known to local Liberians as "iron soap" because of its appearance.[681] The soap is used for bathing and laundry despite being very rough on the skin and damaging clothing with continued use.[682]

---

680 Oliver Smith, "15 curious things you might not have known about Liberia," July 26, 2018.

681 Vermont Soap, 2013, *Improving the Productivity and Profitability of Artisanal Soap Making in Liberia*, March 26.

682 Ibid.

Though a specific industry is never specified, Yara's interest in business was based on the many interview respondents who expressed a passion for gaining financial independence and general success.

DAILY LIFE

- **What is a typical day like for you? How do you pay for your living expenses?**

A typical day for me starts with preparing my petty goods to be sold at the market. One of my uncles is a fisherman. Every day, he gives me fish to sell. As long as I give him a portion of my earnings, I can use the rest of the money to pay for things like food, water, and new petty goods.

My uncle also has a farm. I sell most of his produce and cook the leftovers for him and his family. I pay for all of my living expenses by selling petty goods, fish, or produce from my uncle's farm.

- **Are you renting your home, or do you own it? How many people live with you?**

I live with seven other people: my uncle, his wife, and their four children. My mother has a hard life. My father died during the Ebola crisis, and since then she had to provide for me and my three younger siblings. To relieve some of her burden, I live with my uncle and his family now. They provide for my needs, and I contribute as much as I can to the family's expenses by selling. I am always well fed, and I have a roof over my head.

Once a few months ago, I injured my arm while I was at the market. My aunt took me to the hospital. I am very lucky and grateful God has provided for me here. Not everyone in my community is as fortunate.

- **If you are sick, how do you handle it? How do you maintain your personal hygiene?**

If I am sick, I usually ask my uncle or aunt for any medicine they may already have at home. If I am sicker or more injured than their medicine can help with, I go to the government hospital, but the standards are not very high.

I keep myself clean by taking a bath outside either at night or very early in the morning when everyone is sleeping. We have a trench toilet outside as well. I bathe with iron soap and use local oil as lotion because it is cheaper than the imported goods they sell at the market. It's enough to feel clean even though the soap makes my skin feel dry. I can't afford anything different.

- **Did you go to school? How long?**

I graduated from grade six, but I did not go any further in school. I didn't have high enough grades, and my mom could not afford to keep me and my siblings in school anyway. I have always liked selling, and I would like to start my own business one day. It was easier on my family to leave school and focus on selling petty goods instead.

Now, on a good day, I can send a bit of my daily earnings to my mom and occasionally treat my younger siblings to treats like hard candy.

- **Do you have children? Do they go to school? If so, how do you pay for their school fees?**

I don't have any children yet. When I do, I will send them to government school. I don't know how I will be able to cover the costs for the supplies yet. The money I make now wouldn't support it. Hopefully, my husband or his family will be able to help.

- **How do you manage your money, pay off your debts, and plan for big financial goals? When you have financial problems, who do you go to for help and support?**

My uncle helps me manage my money. Sometimes, I can save money through mobile money as well. I use the money I save to buy petty goods, and I sell just to turn the money around quickly. I am not in any debt, but I would like to take out a loan to start my own business someday. I don't meet all of the requirements yet. My uncle and aunt think I am too young and inexperienced to start a business right now, so they won't co-sign my application for a loan even if I went to the bank.

If I have financial problems, I can help myself by selling more petty goods, produce, or fish.

- **What do you think you can do to improve your life financially in the long-term? What would be your dream solution to improve your life financially?**

I can sell and farm, and I am willing to do either of those things to improve my life. My dream is to have a big and successful business—something better than my small work selling petty goods. I am practicing and building up my skills right now, but I want to expand and sell more goods. When times are slow on market days, I chat with the elders to get advice for how to increase my sales and build my business. They always share great advice.

- **If you were the president of your country, how would you improve things for your community specifically, and for your country more broadly?**

President? There are so many things that could be improved here. I just want to focus on my business, but if I had the chance, I could do a lot. When I go to the interior to visit my mom and siblings, the roads are always really bad. It takes days to go home. I usually stay in the city because I can't afford to miss so many days of selling.

Once, my mom gave me crops from her garden to sell, but the roads were so bad the crops spoiled on my way back to the city. Many of the roads aren't paved and those being built aren't finished. I would start with the roads. I would improve the roads to make it easier for people in the village to get to the city.

For my community, I would build indoor toilets and bathrooms, hand pumps, and help to clean up. For my country, I would make education and medication free, promote agriculture, increase security, and improve the lives of people who have a hard life like my mom.

UPLIFT AND EMPOWER

- **What about your life makes you happy? What about your life makes you hopeful for the future?**

When I make a lot of money selling, I am very happy, and I feel like my business is improving. It gives me hope one day I really can have my own big business. I want to be able to take care of myself without any help. I want to sell enough to be able to take care of my mom and siblings too.

- **What is your biggest goal or desire for yourself (and for your children) in the future?**

My biggest goal is to be a big, successful businesswoman in the future. Hopefully, I make enough money to afford my own land and farm in the future, too. Beyond my business, I want to find a good husband who will help me and my children have a better life. I want my children to go to school for longer than I did. If they do, they can take over my business and make it grow even more for their families.

Yara's story is compelling because she represents many of the young adults living in extreme poverty in Liberia. She is hardworking, ambitious, and business savvy. What would uplifting and empowering someone like Yara look like?

Remember, money is not the only answer. While donating to Yara would make you feel good, once your money ran out, she would still have to fend for herself. Yara would like to start a business, but she isn't sure of the industry yet, and her only concrete experience is selling petty goods. Uplifting and empowering Yara could look like someone with an MBA teaching her the fundamentals of entrepreneurship, business management, and accounting so she can start a successful business one day. However, any effort would need to start with listening to Yara's needs and solutions first. In a partnership, all sides are heard and respected equally.

While you may not know someone living in extreme poverty like Yara, maybe there is a seventeen-year-old in your community who is low-income and just as driven as Yara to create a better life. Could you commit to mentoring or supporting a young person near you?

PROFILE #2: MARY

Mary is a thirty-four-year-old teacher living in Monrovia, Liberia. She hopes to one day buy land and a home for her family. As a teacher, Mary experienced the dismal state of Liberia's education system firsthand. According to UNICEF, the Liberian civil war "destroyed or damaged close to 60 percent of school buildings, including water and sanitation facilities which are key to keeping children, especially girls, in school."[683] Only 54 percent of Liberian children complete primary school.[684]

When teachers like Mary emphasize the importance of education, it is because they see the dire need for improvement in their communities. Many schools lack the resources and funding to support students, whether public or private. For families that can afford private schools, the fees are high compared to local incomes. Some faith-based school charge as much as US$1,000 per year and uniforms cost between seventy-five to one hundred dollars.[685] For context, a recent World Bank Macro Poverty Outlook focused on Liberia stated that "the proportion of poor households living below the international poverty line of US$1.9/day (2011 PPP) is projected to increase further to 45.4 percent in 2020."[686] This trend indicates the vast majority of families simply cannot afford to cover the costs of items like school supplies, let alone private school fees.

Mary also brings up squatting in her interview. In Liberia, "public and abandoned buildings, garages, improvised structures on vacant lots, and even wetlands are occupied by squatters lacking formal claim to the property."[687] In the aftermath of the civil war, hundreds of thousands of people were displaced. Many Liberians formed informal settlements.[688]

---

683 UNICEF, *Basic Education*, 2020.

684 Primary school in Liberia covers grades 1–6. Middle school covers grades 7–9. Secondary school covers grades 10–12.

685 Henry Karmo, *Liberia: Hike in Tuition Draws Attention of Senator, Poised to Hold Discussion with Education Minister*, September 11, 2019.

686 World Bank, "World Bank Poverty & Equity and Macroeconomics," Trade & Investment Global Practices Report, 2020.

687 Ailey Kaiser Hughes, *Brief: Using Land Policy in Liberia to Improve Life for The Urban Poor*, 2020.

688 Ibid.

- **What is a typical day like for you? How do you pay for your living expenses?**

I recently changed jobs, so my typical day has changed. I used to clean homes and cut grass in my neighborhood to cover my living expenses. I would start my day early in the morning and clean the house of whoever opened their door and was willing to pay. I worked until sunset. My income was never consistent, but I could afford food. I was fine. If cleaning and cutting grass wasn't successful, I offered to do laundry.

Recently, one of the teachers at my community school left her job. I showed interest in teaching before, and I completed high school. With my qualifications and connection to the school's administrators, I was selected to fill her role. It is a small private school, and the pay is very low compared to the tuition the school charges. Most teachers earn extra income by tutoring families who can afford to pay for it.

- **Are you renting your home, or do you own it? How many people live with you?**

Before I got married, I used to squat on the Alay. The Alay is a road passing through my community. The government is not ready to build it yet. Squatting gave me a place to stay, but I was always scared the government would come and force me and my community members to leave. We didn't have any documents to prove we could be there. Now that I am married, I rent a home with my husband. We live with our two daughters.

- **If you are sick, how do you handle it? How do you maintain your personal hygiene?**

If I am sick, I go to the government hospital because the treatment is free. The standards are low, but I can't afford private care for myself or my family.

I keep myself clean by taking baths. Our home has a bathroom outside that I use. I take my baths at night. Lotion and soap are expensive here, so I only use local soap for my baths. It makes my skin very dry. My neighbor said she could teach me how to make soap from grass. We are going to meet soon so she can show me. For lotion, I have cream, but I only use small amounts. I share with my children and my husband. It is very expensive.

- **Did you go to school? How long?**

I am a high school graduate. I have always enjoyed school, though I couldn't afford university. I wanted to become a teacher to improve my student's lives.

- **Do you have children? Do they go to school? If so, how do you pay for their school fees?**

Yes, I have two daughters. They go to government school now, but they are much older than their classmates. My husband and I couldn't afford the fees. They are just now starting year one a few years after the standard age. My husband and I pay their annual fees of 11,000 Liberian dollars with our salaries.[689]

LONG TERM GOALS

- **How do you manage your money, pay off your debts, and plan for big financial goals? When you have financial problems who do you go to for help and support?**

I save my money with my susu (savings club). The susu makes it easier to cover any big problems that come up. I have a little bit of debt because my husband and I did not have enough money to pay our rent last month. Our landlord is a family friend, so they have been kind to us.

---

689 11,000 Liberian dollars is approximately 55 US Dollars.

If I am having a problem, I go to my friends or family members. They are the only people who can help me with everything. If I am having a financial problem, I can get credit from my susu, but there is interest. For spiritual matters, I ask the church to help me as I am a Christian and a member of the church.

- **What do you think you can do to improve your life financially in the long-term? What would be your dream solution to improve your life financially?**

I am able to teach, and I think my teaching job will improve my life financially in the long-term. I would like to save money and pay my daughters school fees. I want them to go to private school next year, but the fees are very expensive. I don't know if my husband and I will be able to save enough.

My dream solution is to buy land, build a house, and own my own home. If we were not familiar with our landlord, we could have lost our home. I would like my husband and I to own land and property so we can pass it on to our daughters one day. My husband and I are also thinking about having another child, hopefully a son. We will need the extra room.

- **If you were the president of your country, how would you improve things for your community specifically and for your country more broadly?**

My hope for the future of Liberia comes from my students. A lot of my students would not be educated without government schools. Many lost one or both of their parents during the Ebola crisis. I have had to send children home when they didn't have books or pencils to do their work. If I was the president, I would improve education.

For my community and my country, I would make education and medication free. I would also improve agriculture, security, and roads. I would aim to empower citizens with business, jobs, and education.

UPLIFT AND EMPOWER

- **What about your life makes you happy? What about your life makes you hopeful for the future?**

When I am healthy, I get really happy, because being in good health gives me hope. I am also happy when I am able to take care of my children and help others in the community.

I am hopeful for the future because my husband and I are saving up to buy land and build our house. I will be most hopeful when we own a farm as well.

- **What is your biggest goal or desire for yourself (and for your children) in the future?**

For my children, my biggest wish is for them to have a good education. I want them to do well in school and have more opportunities than I had.

For myself, my biggest goal is to have property.

Mary is a teacher. Like my mom who has been teaching for over fifteen years, her hope for the future comes from her students and her passion for teaching is rooted in her positive educational experience. I have personally met many teachers who sow good into the world through education. Unfortunately, in Liberia, getting a formal education is challenging. Beyond tuition, affording school supplies like paper, pencils, and books can be a lot of pressure on struggling families.

What would uplifting and empowering Mary look like? Mary would like to buy land, build a house, and educate her children. How you can help Mary in particular may look different depending on your circumstances, but many of us are capable of donating to nonprofits that have boots-on-the ground volunteers working with people like Mary every day. Reaching out to nonprofits is a helpful way to engage with one of the nodes the five-node house I introduced in part three and learn more about who is being helped and how. Through nonprofits, you can learn more about people's specific needs and ask for regular updates about how your donations are making a difference.

You can still start locally, though. As I mentioned, there are pockets of poverty in your city or town, even if you don't see them. Maybe a local teacher in your area needs support filling her classroom with school supplies for low-income students. Could you offer up school supplies? Or even mentor and support one of the low-income students who may need a boost in self-confidence in addition to the supplies themselves?

PROFILE #3: BEN

Ben is a fifty-two-year-old cleaner at a law firm in Lagos, Nigeria. He hopes to one day own a computer or IT firm. Ben's job makes him a more accurate representation of a Drew than a Robin. However, his life is a helpful indicator of what living standards for the world's Robins will look like as they make their first transition from level one to level two.

Ben's desire to work in a formal office job was common among the interview participants. Beyond working in an office, Ben's interest in owning a computer or IT company in particular is a helpful reflection of the rise of Lagos, Nigeria as a technology hub within Africa in recent years. The suburb Yaba, near the University of Lagos, is home to over sixty startups "including businesses like booking site Hotels.ng."[690]

---

690 Yinka Ibukun and Gwen Ackerman, Africa's Technology Hub Rises in a Congested Lagos Neighborhood, June 11, 2019.

Yaba has been described by leaders in the technology community like Bosun Tijani, co-founder of the Co-Creation Hub, as giving "the tech community in Nigeria an identity and making people in every part of the country believe that technology is possible here."[691]

DAILY LIFE

- **What is a typical day like for you? How do you pay for your living expenses?**

I wake up at 5 a.m. every weekday to prepare for work and leave home at 5:45 a.m. to beat the traffic to work. I work as a cleaner at a law firm from 8 a.m. to 5 p.m. At the close of work, I go through a lot of traffic and get home most days at about 7:30 p.m. I pay for my living expenses from the meager salary I earn and a few tips here and there.

- **Are you renting your home, or do you own it? How many people live with you?**

I live in a rented, one-room apartment with my wife and three children.

- **If you are sick, how do you handle it? How do you maintain your personal hygiene?**

If anyone in my family falls sick, we self-medicate with local herbs or buy medicine from our local chemist. We have our own supply of medicines at home. We only go to the hospital for serious emergencies. We keep ourselves clean by bathing with soap and water. We buy local products to save money.

- **Did you go to school? How long?**

I only attended primary school for five years. No one in my family could afford the cost of my fees and supplies. My

---

691 Ibid.

teachers always had to send me home early because I was not prepared for our lessons. I couldn't afford the books to do the homework. I had no paper or pencils at home either. I work hard now to make sure my children stay in school longer than I could.

- **Do you have children? Do they go to school? If so, how do you pay for their school fees?**

  Yes, my kids go to a local school nearby. The tuition is free, but I pay for books and other materials. It is 15,000 Naira per session.[692]

LONG TERM GOALS

- **How do you manage your money, pay off your debts, and plan for big financial goals? When you have financial problems, who do you go to for help and support?**

  I don't earn enough money to save after my expenses, so I can't plan for big financial goals. I also have a few debts to pay off right now. Usually, if I am having financial problems, I ask my employer for help.

- **What do you think you can do to improve your life financially in the long-term? What would be your dream solution to improve your life financially?**

  I can read and write. My work ethic is also really good. I am willing to do any work that will improve my life, but with my skills, I can do any office job. If I can get a better paying job and learn new skills, my financial life will improve a lot. Getting either a scholarship or sponsorship for my children's school fees would also go a long way in improving my life financially in the long run.

---

692 15,000 Naira is approximately 38 US Dollars.

My dream solution to improve my life financially would be to learn computer or IT-related skills and get a better paying job.

- **If you were the president of your country, how would you improve things for your community specifically and for your country more broadly?**

If I were the president of Nigeria, I would empower the youths more by improving the education sector and making education free. I would also make skill acquisition centers where skills can be learned for free. The graduates from these programs would then be placed in various industries in the society. They could work to earn a living through those jobs and gain enough experience to branch off on their own if they wanted to.

Also, I would make a stable power supply available to help small businesses and entrepreneurs grow. Through the Central Bank of Nigeria, I would also make low-interest loans accessible for start-up businesses to encourage self-dependence.

UPLIFT AND EMPOWER

- **What about your life makes you happy? What about your life makes you hopeful for the future?**

I am happy and grateful to God for good health and a stable mind. I get very happy when I hear the word of God. I am also happy when I have a job and can use my money to support my family. I am hopeful for the future because I trust and believe in God to take care of me.

- **What is your biggest goal or desire for yourself (and for your children) in the future?**

In the future, I see myself owning my own computer or IT firm and running it successfully. There is a lot of computer and IT activity in Lagos, and I would like to get involved. With training, I can do well in that sector.

My biggest goals are to succeed in life, be financially independent, and give my children the best education possible up to any level they aspire to complete.

Through Ben, we have met a future computer whiz who is living in a global tech hub. Ben has the ambition and drive to take lessons in technology and even start his own company one day, but does he have a computer? Are there affordable training schools nearby where he can learn those skills? If he does gain the skills, will he have the connections to find a job, build experience, and later start his own company?

One conversation isn't enough time to determine the answers to all of these questions about Ben, but it is a starting point. How many people, regardless of age, in your community want to learn more about coding or AI but don't have the money or resources to learn more? For some, learning through online resources is fine, but not everyone has access to stable internet or a personal computer they can use for hours on end as they debug code. What could helping someone like Ben look like in your community?

You could begin with seeking out community leaders. The process could start as simple as posting a message on social media to find out who in your personal network may know anything or anyone relevant. Are you willing to be someone's bridge to access and opportunity?

CONCLUSION

Humans love connection, feelings of accomplishment, and personal fulfillment. It is these emotions that push us to seek out solutions to problems faster than we stop to understand them in the first place.

Through Yara, we met an ambitious girl who wants to build a business. Through Mary, we met a teacher and mother hoping to build a better life for her family through land, a home, and education. Through Ben, we met a future computer whiz who might only need a computer to reach his potential.

All of them want to be independent. They have personal metrics for success. They want to thrive rather than just survive. With so much nuance in how to help and what to help with, where do you start? Begin at home.

While on the surface you may *think* you know the solutions to the problems of people like Yara, Mary, or Ben, there are many details of their lives you may never find out. Even learning as much about a person as the content of this interview provides would require building trust and a strong relationship first. Building trust takes time and personal investment. Those are elements community involvement can create.

Beyond this community-based approach is the importance of listening to the voices needing to be heard. Even my suggested approaches were just that—suggestions. Any people-problem solved without the input of the person being helped is incomplete. To really make a difference in the lives of people living in extreme poverty, we will need to be willing to learn as much as we believe we can teach.

"...You talked about eradicating extreme poverty, which is a beginning, but you stopped there. Do you think Africans will settle with getting rid of extreme poverty and be happy living in only ordinary poverty? It is going to take a long time, we know that. It is going to take lots of wise decisions and large investments. But my 50-year vision is that Africans will be welcome tourists in Europe and not unwanted refugees."

—NKOSAZANA DLAMINI-ZUMA, THE CHAIRWOMAN OF THE AFRICAN UNION[693]

---

693 Hans Rosling, Ola Rosling, and Rönnlund Anna Rosling, *Factfulness: Ten Reasons Were Wrong about the World—and Why Things, Are Better than You Think*, (London: Scepter, 2019), 189

WHAT'S NEXT?
YOU DECIDE.

———

While studying abroad in Dakar, I saw small children on the street everyday begging for money. I felt guilty about it each time I made eye contact and denied their requests because I didn't want to fall into the trap of sympathetic giving while I was writing against it. Yet, my lack of action was an action. Over-theorizing poverty had led me to neglect people and their basic needs.

This behavior felt incomplete. And this feeling is often hard to ignore. It's the kind of cognitive dissonance leading people to believe "the poor" are just lazy or unintelligent. This belief is easier and more comfortable to accept than the deeper more multi-dimensional truth that, more often than not, the world's Robins are facing pressures and hardships mentally, physically, financially, and emotionally beyond what any Camerons have had to face in their lifetimes.

I was told one day by a professor that if I felt bad, I could buy food for the young boys instead of giving them money outright, but that was a form of sympathetic giving in my mind. Transitioning from sympathetic giving to expectant giving can feel cruel.

Working on issues to alleviate the structural problems facing the world's poor is a lofty and necessary goal. However, it's hard to do as one person with little influence and a limited amount of resources. After my research, the question remained: *what does poverty alleviation look like from a day-to-day, individual-to-individual perspective?*

In this chapter, I will:

- address our current progress in eradicating extreme poverty by 2030
- highlight the importance of community advocates
- provide an illustration of why changing behavior and facing facts will be challenging barriers to overcome
- share a guideline for understanding how you can begin to improve the lives of others

IF POVERTY ERADICATION IS A RACE, THEN WE ARE SLOWING DOWN BEFORE THE FINISH LINE

Let's start with the big picture before we zoom into the details. How is *the world* progressing in the realm of poverty alleviation? We are doing well, but we could be doing better. Even with hundreds of millions lifted out of extreme poverty between the 1990s and now, the world is not on track to eradicate extreme poverty by 2030 as the UN has aimed for in its sustainable development goals.[694] The number of people living in extreme poverty may be declining, but it's declining at a slower pace than in the past.[695]

---

694 Elisabeth Hege, Samien Barchiche, Julien Rochette, Lucien Chabason, and Pierre Barthelemy, *2030 Agenda for Sustainable Development: A first assessment and conditions for success,* October, 2019.

695 Ibid.

If the current pace continues, 6 percent of the global population, over 500 million people, will be living in extreme poverty in 2030, and the goal of eradicating poverty will not be achieved.[696]

Economic development is multifaceted and complex. There is no one-size-fits-all version. General strategies need to be tweaked and adjusted to meet specific issues. The distinguishing features between rich and poor countries are typically the policies put in place to strengthen their economies, open up to foreign trade, and invest in people through education and healthcare.

If we were to globally eradicate extreme poverty by 2030, our work would not be finished. We can't just stop at crossing the boundary line of extreme poverty because living life just above the line leaves you at risk of falling back under the line again very easily. Changes in living standards will require shifts in the legal, regulatory, and political institutions influencing and shaping society.

The private sector will need to grow as well. While collaborations between for-profit and not-for-profit companies are strained by the differences in incentives, for-profit companies are best equipped to scale solutions. This is where the value of the partnership model can again shine. Progress can happen more effectively if people collaborate across business types.

THE WINNER TAKES IT ALL

Now that technology has advanced so much, being just slightly better than the competition is enough to beat the majority. This applies for businesses as well. When businesses

---

696 Ibid.

succeed, fewer people benefit. Economists call this the "win-ner-take-all society."[697]

Small advancements in economic development over time can add up to large changes in living standards and poverty populations. Once these needs are met, economic growth does not guarantee fortune. Social equality is a better sign. If you recall from part one, relative poverty is important to keep in mind. Robins who are barely over the poverty line would still *be* very poor compared to the world's Camerons and would still *feel* very poor if they were sounded by evidence through social media, advertisements, movies, and TV shows depicting hundreds of thousands of people living better lives than them.

For a more concrete example, consider the general quality of life in the United States in contrast to the general quality of life in Europe. The United States is the epitome of a "winner-takes-all society." The country encourages entrepreneurship or employment to encourage people hoping to make money, and taxes and regulations are low to support businesses. As I mentioned in part one, a person living at the poverty line in the United States is considered to be part of the richest 14 percent of the world population. The United States is one of the wealthiest countries in the world. It is also one of the most unequal countries on earth by income.

In contrast, many European nations are more equal. Nine of the top ten most equal countries in the world are in Europe.[698] Europeans have more streamlined health care systems, better educated students, and have more vacation time.

---

697 Rutger Bregman, *Utopia for Realists*, (London: Bloomsbury, 2018) .
698 Benjamin Elisha Sawe, 2018, *The Most Equal Countries in the World*, August 3.

This kind of equality is not free. Many Europeans pay higher taxes than Americans, which indirectly transfers wealth from rich to poor individuals through strongly funded government programs, and regulations are much stricter in many areas for employers. Inequality still exists, but the standard of living for the average European is higher than the average American.

RAWLSIAN VIEW VERSUS UTILITARIAN VIEW

There will always be some form of poverty in the world. Why? Because poverty is relative. In a world where people find reasons to compare each other, someone will always be on the losing side. It's just a matter of figuring out how losing looks and what a fair amount of losing is in the context of winners who win so much. If the standard for what losing looks like is high, things can be better for everyone.

I found two dominant views of how social welfare looks that helped wrap my mind around the issue of aiming for equality within vast amount of inequality: a Rawlsian view versus a utilitarian view.

A Rawlsian view of social welfare emphasizes the importance of maximizing living standards of people at the bottom. Under a Rawlsian system, equal societies are built up by centralizing focus on lifting low-income individuals out of poverty. This view makes an unequal system more equal.

In contrast, a utilitarian view emphasizes every human's life and happiness should be considered equal. By increasing aggregate happiness, individual happiness can be improved also. The implications of this view are everyone receives the same benefits for different amounts of work and needs.

Which view is "right"? Well, it depends. Equity is relative.

A WORLD WITHOUT POVERTY

Before development can lead everyone to a world without poverty, it has to be defined. What would this world look like? What minimum changes would need to occur to accomplish this goal?

- Would a post-poverty world be one where everyone is educated, healthy, and productive?
- Would it be a world with no more diseases?
- Or a world where everything people need or want can be supplied?
- Or, maybe, a world where generational wealth can be built up easily and fairly without discrimination?

Our goal should be to create a better life than our current day to day, but with solutions that take advantage of our advanced resources and technology.

The world's Robins aren't going to stop progressing in their economic and social growth or limit their wants to suit the barriers Camerons place on them. Assisting with poverty alleviation by providing the same resources and technology across the world's total population is one impactful way Camerons can help Robins.

COMMUNITY VOICES

What system is the best for ensuring there are long-term improvements that benefit the majority? Seeking out a larger, more bureaucratic influence to make the decision is often the default for large decisions and large problems. However, as James Payne wrote in *Overcoming Welfare,* "Government officials are not gods with superior mental powers, capable of discerning solutions that evade the rest of us. [The] government is made up of ordinary people who are just as confused and misinformed as the rest of us can be."[699]

To handle the personal problems people face living in poverty, a large governing body would need localized knowledge. Beyond this, the system would need to collect and interpret knowledge correctly and efficiently across all populations.

These larger bodies cannot compete with the more customized and generous systems that could be created by small, local efforts. The new "system" could be composed of multiple, smaller systems with interconnections between them rather than one central source.

One primary method to have your voice heard at varying levels of influence is through voting. Our goals as global citizens should be improving our ability to be active and informed members of the voting process.

CHANGING BEHAVIOR

Getting people to change their beliefs is hard. Getting people to change their behavior is harder. Even with large communities of people, or influential figures alone, believing in the same ideas, it's challenging to transform those beliefs into actions.

I'll give you an example from an experience I had in one of my clubs in university. Soon after becoming president of the organization, I pitched the idea of starting a scholarship fund for our members to pursue unpaid internships. Nearly the entire board was in full support. We hit the ground running by visiting university staff early in the process to get a

---

699 James L Payne, *Overcoming Welfare: Expecting More from the Poor—and from Ourselves*, (New York, NY: Basic Books, 1998).

clearer picture of what regulations we would need to adhere to, reaching out to other clubs on campus with similar initiatives, and had follow up meetings to discuss implementation strategies.

A full year later, and with a board member working on the project as a primary goal for her position, the scholarship fund still hadn't started. There was so much red tape, unforeseen complications, and time required in addition to our schoolwork that it more and more challenging to accomplish the goal before the board changed hands. The fund wasn't stopped by a lack of belief in the idea or a lack of effort. Getting things done is just challenging.

Beyond committing to take action, individuals also need to be open to their prior ideas or beliefs being incorrect. New ideas challenging traditional beliefs are presented all of the time. They will continue to be presented and dismantle the status quo. This process of admitting a downfall—of being wrong—is stifled by the fact it has become easier than ever to solely find evidence proving yourself right.

Why face discomforting facts that will force you to change your activities or question your lifestyle when you can instead focus on evidence telling you everything is okay, everyone else is wrong, and your way of living is the best way of living? If your core beliefs about others were questioned or proven to be incorrect, would you be brave enough to change your mind? Or would you stay within your comfort zone instead?

To move forward in humanity's progress and continue to improve standards of living for everyone, we need to be more willing and open to question our assumptions, look for data that conflict with our points of view, and dig in if we find things that are wrong or uncertain. The world's knowledge is just a mouse click away for most of us. Be bold enough to get things wrong and change your perspective.

NUMBERS MATTER

Convincing arguments these days are replete with data and statistics that can make the most empathetic of arguments seem cold, calculated, and distanced. This blame typically falls on economists who quantify many social issues, put a price on nearly everything, and often find themselves weighing hard questions that impact people's lives.

Katherine Baicker, an economist and current dean of the University of Chicago Harris School of Public Policy, once said, "If you're not willing to put a price on it, you're doing a terrible disservice to the people you are purporting to care about."[700] Without data and quantitative facts, it's harder to determine the tradeoffs that need to be made to help people effectively.

It's easy to push numbers aside and focus on emotion when it's *your* problem on an individual level—when it's your health concern, your rent payment, your family member, or your friend. As the amount of people being helped increases, the numbers, the data, and the general trends are critical.

Consider the following example: It's 2 a.m. and a local hospital is on fire. There are one hundred patients inside. You know for sure your friend has recently had surgery and is inside the building. When firefighters arrive at the scene, they can't just run in, save your individual friend, and call it a job well-done because you are happy. There are at least

---

700 Katherine Baicker, "Can Economics Save the World?" (panel event, Chicago, IL, November 19, 2019).

ninety-nine other patients to be saved. They consider the facts and the variables: how much time they have, how long the fire has been burning, how fast they can navigate the building and save lives. Without thought and care, without knowledge and information, those firefighters won't be able to maximize the amount of people they save.

When people's lives are on the line, precision is key. Within problem-solving, numbers become more important than ever. Not to dehumanize the subject matter, not to make abstract a concrete issue, but because we care; if we care, we should make an effort to do things correctly.

THINK SMALL

Rather than aiming to create the next big idea, it is helpful to think small and to solve where no one else is solving in the context of poverty alleviation. Businesses, both for-profit and not-for-profit, often tend to focus on the same high-recognition areas because that's where the funding is and where attention is placed. Instead of following the crowd, think for yourself and look where no one else is looking, pay attention to what others don't see or don't care to look at, and find a way to become a voice for others. Do what you can to help others, even if it's not big and flashy.

In a world where social media fame is easy to obtain and just as easy to lose, everyone is aiming to gain influence, prestige, and followers. But it's important to favor quality over quantity for impact. It's better for us all to excel in small-scale efforts to address our community's causes of poverty than to aim for the stars and fail, putting the lives of millions at risk. In whatever you do, work with unselfish passion and commitment to action. It may not lead to prestigious awards, but it will lead to impact.

HOW CAN YOU HELP?

You can start by cancelling your flight to Africa.

Extreme poverty isn't just an African issue or an Asian issue or a South American issue. It is a global issue. Before flying overseas to help relieve poverty abroad, consider the poverty in your own backyard.

Every country on every continent has people impacted by poverty—whether it is relative or absolute. Bringing extreme poverty down to zero will take more trial and error, more methods, more innovation, and more communication. Most importantly, it will take more trust—the trust that people are aware of their problems and are creative enough to solve them when given the right resources. People need opportunities, connections, and education to learn more about life's possibilities, not handouts, performative sympathy, and empty promises.

Based on the past, we now know what has worked and what hasn't. As the world continues to advance, we are becoming more aware of what can work in the future, too. Changing our mindset toward poverty can change lives. Don't let the statistics and data overwhelm you.

Look at the three dimensions of poverty. For ease, I will repeat them below:[701]

The first dimension is health which includes:
- nutrition
- child mortality rate

The second dimension is education which includes:
- years of schooling
- school attendance

---

701 Oxford Poverty & Human Development Initiative (OPHI), "Global Multidimensional Poverty Index," UN Development Program (UNDP).

The third dimension is living standards which includes access to:

- cooking fuel
- sanitation
- safe drinking water
- electricity
- flooring
- asset ownership

Choose a dimension you care about, educate yourself, and start helping where you can. In my personal life, I motivate myself by checking The World Poverty Clock, a real-time approximation of how many people are living in extreme poverty.[702] Find numbers and statistics to motivate you to take action.

When volunteering, don't just go to where the first search results take you or where the voices are the loudest. Go to where you are confident your passion and engagement with social problems can ensure your actions matter. The more precise the efforts, the more helpful and structured the programs likely are for volunteers and for the populations they are helping as well.

Getting bogged down by meetings can slow things down. Seek out programs that train volunteers. Follow up that training by encouraging volunteers to work together, and work with people of varied experience levels rather than spending the majority of time in meetings chatting about issues.

CHECK YOUR PRIVILEGE

Job creation sounds great for people who already have skills, but people living in extreme poverty have nothing at all:

---

702 World Poverty Clock, "World Poverty Clock."

no jobs, no education, no connections, and no privileged social network. Education is a good start, but how do you *motivate* people to learn and study when they have no hope or direct point of reference for academic success? Books are great, but what about people who can't read or audiobooks that aren't available in local languages or dialects? Short-term solutions to Robins' problems will likely align with the types of basic necessities often overlooked by the world's Camerons.

How does this apply to your life? You can work toward changing your mindset by checking your privilege. Literally.

List out a typical day for yourself and try to break down what elements of your day are indications of your privilege. From there, you can determine how those privileges can be transferred to the world's poorest and determine where you can make an impact—no matter how small—in helping improve the lives of people with less of life's necessities and conveniences.

I'll start. Below are some things I often take for granted in my life. My list may look similar to yours or completely different:

- Fast and consistent Wi-Fi to do my schoolwork, surf the web, access the world's information, and use the cloud for data storage
- Electricity throughout my home all day, every day
- Hot, running water for my showers
- Quality education and the opportunities I have had through my classes and extracurricular activities
- Free time for entertainment like watching TV, movies, or YouTube videos
- Comfortable, relatively affordable feminine hygiene products to use when I am on my period every month

- Consistent money for public transportation and long-distance travel
- Traveling internationally for vacation, not just for work or school
- Streetlights when I am walking home late from the library
- Convenience apps for food delivery and car rides

Unsure of where or how to start your own list? *A helpful indicator something is a privilege is when it works so well you nearly don't need to think about it.* What conveniences within your life are so embedded into your routine you couldn't imagine your day without them?

CONCLUSION: THERE IS NO ROADMAP

In part three of this work, I created a framework to help reshape how we currently think about poverty alleviation as a system. A five-node house that all aims at the world's Robins. I was surprised when the idea came to my mind because nebulous issues like "how to address poverty" are the kind of questions I usually *don't* like to answer.

First, I shied away from proposing anything new because addressing poverty will take time and, without a global commitment, I may not live to see the impact of anything I share. Second, there can be more than one right answer for the same problem. Ultimately, these reasons were why I pushed forward because, even after writing, I have more questions and more I would like to learn.

The journey to poverty alleviation doesn't have a definitive end point. The appropriate solutions will continue to evolve and change as poverty changes. However, this problem is more than just equations and models. The variables aren't just numbers, they are people's lives.

There's no point in this book where I explicitly state, "This is it. Here's the roadmap. Here's how to end poverty—globally," because *there is no straightforward roadmap.* Every neighborhood, every community, every city, and every country's plan will look different.

Where are the pockets of poverty in your community? Can you think of any resources and systems in place where you live to help those in need? How active are these organizations? How much support do they have—financial or otherwise—to do what they do? Remember there is more than one way to give. Money does not have to be the beginning and end of your engagement with poverty alleviation. Your time, your knowledge, and your skills are valuable too.

My hope is, as you have read, you have been able to apply the facts and figures throughout this book to your own life and determine where the wealth gaps may be in your community and beyond. Filling them will require local expertise and creativity only individuals have the power to provide.

This book is a starting point to engaging more meaningfully in actions and conversations that will help to eradicate extreme poverty globally. What comes next is up to you.

How can you *uplift and empower* someone today?

ACKNOWLEDGEMENT

To my mom, thank you for reading nearly every page of just about everything I've ever written. This book would not have been completed without you. You're my biggest fan, and I am yours.

Grandma Rebecca, thank you for sharing your story, for inspiring me to consider new ideas, and for offering up your heart and home.

Grandma Hawa, thank you for encouraging me to never *just* try and always focus on doing my best.

Fellize, may your life and memory continue to inspire everyone you met in your short time with us.

To My Entire Family, thank you for your unwavering love and support of me and everything I do.

To My Beta Reader Community Superstars:

To my mentors Alita Carbone, Chelsea Fine, Patrick Philips, and Kathryn Volzer: thank you for encouraging me to be the best version of myself both professionally and personally. Your guidance and support have been invaluable. I will forever be grateful. To Juliette Teunissen, thank you for sending so many helpful psychology research papers and for being my *first* book pre-sale. To Katherine Vu, thank you for your unwavering support of my ideas and for calming me down during my rants about school or society. To Jack Balch, thank you for connecting me with Kendra Freeman and believing in my idea even when I wasn't sure if I would finish this book. To Daniela Campillo Valencia and Danielle Zhang, thank you for sharing such incredible feedback and improving my foundational chapters. To Ms. Stephanie DeVilling, thank you for supporting my love of writing in high school and approving my idea to start the Uplift and Empower Scholarship Fund. To the Wright family, thank you for your continued support since kindergarten! I am so grateful to your entire family, and I am looking forward to many more years of friendship. To Sarah Knorst, thank you for believing in me! Your presence in my life is a present. To Ms. Skiba, thank you for cultivating my love of English through your grammar lessons in middle school. The stories I wrote for your class laid the foundation for the writing skills I have now. To the Olorunlogbon family, thank you for taking care of my mom while I am away from home and for always being so supportive. We have shared so many positive memories! To Uncle Micha, no donation is ever too late. Thank you for always sharing a listening ear and a kind heart. To Uncle Sayndee and Aunty Leilani, thank you for believing in me from day one and for spreading the word about *Uplift and Empower* so fervently. You were bold even when I was still worried about sharing the news. Your presence at my live chapter readings was always appreciated. To Uncle Abraham, introverts unite! Thank you for sharing the title of the "quiet one" in the family with me. Every time my mother and I visit you, I know that I can stay indoors and work without judgement. To Uncle Andy, thank you for sharing your wisdom based on years of experience in international development and for inspiring me to write the Liberia case study in this book. Our conversation at Grandma's house sparked months of research I am still learning from. To Uncle Diye, thank you for your excitement and enthusiasm about this project, for sharing so many book recommendations, and for connecting me with Liberians to interview on short notice. This book would not have been the same without your support.

To My Entire Beta Reader Community, my loyal support network, the first people to believe in my dream of creating this book:

Thank you! Thank you! Thank you! I could write paragraphs about each and every one you along with details about the formative roles you have all played in my life, but I will save that for your personal thank you notes and signed copies! Without your help, *Uplift and Empower* would not have come to fruition. My gratitude goes to the following people:

Abraham Ballah, Adam Freindlich, Alita Carbone, The Nicholson Family, Ann Obatomi, Antoinette E Nelson Rodriguez, Ash Mohiuddin, Ashley Boren, Ashley Smith, Audrey Sung, The Olorunlogbon Family, Cammy Dennis, Carlene Garboden, Carolyn Imes, Chelsea D'Agostino, Chelsea Fine, Cheryl Goldner, Christina Flood, Cynthia Assaf, Daisy Zhang, Daniela Campillo Valencia, Danielle Zhang, Dave Joseph, Denise Brown, Digue Guilavogui, Donna Ridge, Dooie Doh, Doubra Wariebi, Dr. Dana Suskind, Edgar Aguado, Elaine E Tang, Elina Ren, Elizabeth Furlong, Emma Weber, Eric Koester, Erica Lin, Esela Segbefiq, Esmeralda Barajas, Gaurav Bhushan, Geeta Minocha, Gianna Sposato, Gillian Shen, Grace Bridges, Hannah Dubinski, Hannah Maluth, Hannah Martin, Hunter Brookman, Irina Bercu, Isabel Wang, Jack Balch, James J Jenkins, James McLellan, Janelle Hartley, Jennifer Zhuo, Jesse Cui, Jessie Cyr, Joshua Wariebi, Juan David Campolargo,

Julie Hensel, Juliette Teunissen, Kacey Marioghae, Kaesha Freyaldenhoven, Kaitlin Gili, Karen Smith, Karina Gandhi, Karina Hooda, Katherine Vu, Kathryn J Volzer, Katie Helsley, The Daley Family, Kristen Jackson, Kristen Joseph, The Phan Family, The Skiba Family, Laurie Stewart, Lawrence Speelman, Lynette Wu, Lynnette Jiang, Madeleine Hoke, Mahesh Bhide, Margaret Dunor-Collins, Maryam Siddique, Matthew Baechle, Melissa Mecca, Micha Williams, Mike and Tina Stelogeannis, Diye Wariebi, Nadeen Issa, Natalia Delery, The Carbonell Family, Nicole Radosti, Olotu J. Wariebi, Pam Lange, Patrick Phillips, Pattie Stanley, Paula Marques, Peggy Lewerenz, Penny Dekker, Quentin Dupouy, Rebecca B Wariebi, Sai Chicka, Sammy Zucker, Sarah Brown, Sarah Knorst, Sayndee Sando, Shannon Hong, Sharon Lopez, Stephanie DeVilling, Stephanie Diaz, The Wright Family, Tonya Ashley, Veronica Lubofsky, Victoria Constant, Vincent Po, Wavian Li, Wilson Wang, Woods Wiser, Yerkezhan Kassenova, Zené Mizaan Sekou, and Zihan Xiong.

I'd also like to gratefully acknowledge:

My New Degree Press team—Eric Koester, Jordan Waterwash, Ryan Porter, Brian Bies, Jennifer Candiotti, Lyn S, Heather Gomez, Mackenzie Finklea, Chanda Elaine Spurlock, Leila Summers, and the team behind-the-scenes encouraging students and young professionals to write books— thank you! Your efforts, encouragement, and enthusiasm turned me into an author. You all believed in me before I believed in myself.

My Dakar winter 2020 study abroad cohort Jennifer Zhou, thank you for being my first college-aged reader and providing such helpful comments despite your responsibilities. To Grace and Ann for reminding me to sleep on days when I'd stay up all night researching and writing. Also, of course, thank you to Olivia for telling a story that ended up becoming a node of the *Uplift and Empower* house. These names just brush the surface! Every day of that experience, every class, every "quarter," every teacher influenced me, and I am eternally grateful to both the UChicago study abroad team and the Odyssey Scholarship for making that opportunity possible. Thank you to Eric Benjaminson, in particular, for allowing me to interview you. Your perspective pushed me to view the facts and figures surrounding poverty as motivation to continue working toward poverty eradication rather than feel overwhelmed.

My Social Media Warriors—Thank you to everyone who liked, commented, and shared my pre-sale campaign posts. Thank you especially to everyone who replied to my messages and spoke with me about this book. Without your support and engagement, I would not have made it to this point!

Lastly, I'd like to acknowledge a source of my inspiration and the guiding lights of my research process:

Thank you to the thought leaders, business owners, and industry experts who allowed me to interview them: Ashleyn Przedwiecki, Mathilde Charpail, Kathy Booton Wilson, Sara Wasserteil, Mark Loranger, Andy Nicholson, Diye Wariebi, Jorge Arteaga, Kori Hale, Kendra Freeman, Eric Benjaminson, Andy Coxall, Amit Varshneya, and T. Debey Sayndee. Thank you, especially, to George Ndebeh for connecting me with the nine individuals who inspired my interviews with Robins.

With lists like these, names are always forgotten. My writing process may have started in October 2019, but the community of support that got me here has been forming for much longer. Thank you to every single one of you for making me feel supported, seen, and heard. It truly takes a village!

GLOSSARY

———

PART 1

WHERE WE ARE

Equality
Equal access to opportunities that build wealth.

Extreme poverty
Living on less than US$1.90 per day.

Sustainable Development
Development that uplifts and empowers individuals to solve their own problems and, ultimately, address their challenges independently in the future.

A WAR, A PLAN, AND A NOT-SO-SILVER BULLET

The Marshall Plan
A core component of the modern-day concept of international development. Through the plan, countries in need after World War II received aid from the US government. The plan was an extension of the US government's goal to keep communism from spreading.

Corruption

Dishonest or fraudulent behavior done with the intention of receiving some form of personal gain. In the context of this work, it is considered a constant within global development.

WHAT IS POVERTY?

Foreign Aid

The money, services, or physical goods one country sends to another to help it in some way.

Poverty

A state of being where your resources and possessions do not adequately address your needs.

Relative Poverty

This type of poverty is dependent on the income level and assets of the people around you.

Absolute Poverty

This type of poverty refers to living in poverty defined by official poverty levels. It is determined independent of comparisons to other people.

Human Capital

Human capital is basically the skills people have. It is an individual's intangible assets of things like their job, money, or home were taken away.

Robin

The segment of the world's population living on less than US$2 a day. Robins walk as their primary mode of transportation, often times sleep on the floor, and primarily cook their meals over open fires.

Drew

The segment of the world that lives on between US$2 to US$8 a day. Drews use bicycles as transportation, own mattresses, and sometimes use gas canisters for cooking in replacement of an open fire.

Taylor

The segment of the world's population that lives on US$8 to US$32 a day. Taylors have running water, transportation (such as a motorbike or a car), have electricity, access to refrigeration, finished at least a high school education, and can afford to go on an occasional vacation.

Cameron

The segment of the world that lives on US$32 a day or more. Camerons have running water at home, at least one car in their driveway, and plenty of diverse, nutritious foods to eat. The Camerons of the world have finished twelve or more years of school. They can travel abroad for vacation and eat out at restaurants. Camerons likely have several bank accounts, access to credit, and retirement accounts.

THE PROMISE OF PRODUCTIVITY

The Agrarian Revolution

The period of human development where approximately 80 percent of the world's population farmed.

The First Industrial Revolution

The period of human development defined by the invention of the steam engine. Steam power helped the agrarian societies industrialize and revolutionize human productivity through technologies like cotton mills, machines, ships, steamboats, trains, wagons, etc.

The Second Industrial Revolution

The period of human development defined by scientific innovations and mass production. Key inventions like electric lighting, gasoline engines, radio, airplanes, chemical fertilizer, and telephones transformed productivity, communication, and subsequently living standards.

The Third Industrial Revolution

The period of human development defined primarily by the advent of digital technology. Technological advancements like semiconductors and the internet expanded the world's scope from analog technologies into a new digital world.

The Fourth Industrial Revolution

A controversial time period of human development defined by rapid technological advancement.

Social Darwinism

This idea argues the theory of "survival of the fittest" should apply to people and corporations. It assumes corporations should be considered people.

A TALE OF TWO NATIONS

Richland

The height of material success for a nation. Represented by military might, market security, established laws, functional legislative processes, functional systems of taxation, a well-educated, mobile, and flexible labor-force, and stable infrastructure among other things. Richland is the epitome of what many people consider a modern-day first world country.

Poorland

Poorland is a nation devoid of all or most of the necessities offered in Richland. Often times Poorland is akin to living at "level one," where needs go unmet, and everyday survival is a gift, not a guarantee.

Extractive Institutions

As defined by Acemoglu and Robinson in Why Nations Fail, extractive institutions are institutions that take away or concentrate people's incentives and opportunities.

Inclusive Institutions

In contrast to extractive institutions, Acemoglu and Robinson also talk about inclusive institutions which are defined as any institution that creates broad-based incentives and opportunities for people by balancing private and social incentives.

Property Rights

Property rights are the rights an individual has to a specific asset, whether tangible or intangible.

HOW YOU GIVE MATTERS

Sympathetic Giving

A common type of giving that is the social equivalent of "a hand-out." The size of the gift is determined based on how much sympathy or pity we feel for the recipient. Ex: giving money to a homeless person on the street.

The Aggravation Principle of Sympathetic Giving

A principle commonly taken by those that live in absolute poverty, where people live their lives under the assumption they would be helped by generous donors.

Expectant Giving

A form of giving treated as a form of exchange.

Charity Theorists

A group of nineteenth century charity workers that practiced in between the religion-based approach to poverty alleviation that dominated at the time and the Social Darwinists of the era.

PART 2

POVERTY MINDSET
Life History Theory
This relates to how organisms allocate resources for survival and reproduction. Within this theory, there are two primary strategies to help explain the trade-off in resource allocation: the fast path and the slow path. For humans, these paths are rooted in the experiences and environments they faced in childhood.

Scarcity
A lack of any good or service.

Scarcity Mindset
Any decision or behavior primarily caused by scarcity.

Poverty Identity
The cumulative social and psychological influences poverty has on a person.

Poverty Trap
The poverty trap is the self-reinforcing cycle that continues to perpetuate poverty.

Aspirations Failure
A failure to aspire to one's own potential.

WHO RUNS THE WORLD?
Submissive Mindset
A harmful mindset mentally imposed on women that encourages self-sabotaging behavior. The mindset stops women from questioning the status quo and encourages behavior that is agreeable and obedient. This behavior is destructive to a woman's sense of self.

Unpaid Work
Common types of routine work often excluded from wage work; for example, routine housework, shopping duties, household and relative care, volunteer work and travel related, etc.

PEOPLE PROBLEMS
Sex Education
Educational programs focused on teaching the essentials of sexuality, human development, contraception use, and fostering positive interactions between people.

Emigration
The act of leaving one's own country to settle permanently in another; moving abroad.

Immigration
The action of coming to live permanently in a foreign country.

CASE STUDY: CHINA
China's Precision Poverty Alleviation Program
The state guided poverty alleviation program in China that focuses on five core tenants to eradicate extreme poverty. The five core tenants are education, ecological compensation, industry, social security, and relocation.

CASE STUDY: LIBERIA
Neocolonialism
Describes the relationship between Liberia and the United States. Though Liberia was never formally colonized, the US has been an indirect colonial ruler of Liberia. In this way, the US has been able to glean some of the benefits of colonialism without needing to manage any of the responsibilities.

The Fourteen-Year War
Liberia's destructive civil war that destabilized the entire
nation and is a core historical factor for why over half of the
nation's population is living in poverty.
Brain Drain
The emigration of highly trained or intelligent people from
a particular country.

PART 3

A HOUSE BUILT ON A ROCK
Money Plus
A five-node approach to solving poverty by shifting away
from the focus of money, and toward a focus on solutions
beyond it.
Big Guys
The UN, IMF, World Bank, foundations, philanthropic orga-
nizations, corporations, and other large funding sources.
The Biz
The NGOs, aid agencies, think tanks, and other similar organizations on the ground doing research and galvanizing local
efforts with their administrative expertise.
People's Champions
Individuals who serve as ambassadors for their
local communities.
Community
According to Raghuram Rajan, a community is the place
where people get capabilities, where they are able to build
a sense of identity and solidarity among others and is the
result of how the people around them influence their life
chances as they develop.

Randomistas

A group of researchers led by the Nobel Prize-winning economist Abhijit Banerjee leading the global charge in changing the general approach toward the world's Camerons helping the world's Robins.

TAKING CARE OF BUSINESS

Career

According to Josh Bersin of Deloitte Consulting, a career is what represents our expertise, our profession, and ultimately our identity.

Automation

Automation, or labor-saving technology is the technology by which a process or procedure is performed with minimal human assistance.

Renaissance Jobs

Roles that combine technical and creative skills with industry experience. Ex: roles like user experience designers and project managers.

Future Jobs Fund

Pilot project in the United Kingdom that ran from October 2009 to March 2011 to create jobs for young and disadvantaged job seekers. It was funded with one billion GBP and was significantly successful, marking a shift away from supply side employment policies toward more inclusive policymaking.

DON'T EAT THE RICH. FEED THEM.

Remittance

A transfer of money, often by a foreign worker, to an individual in their home country.

Leapfrogging
Leapfrogging helps to explain why and how Robins will be able to use twenty-first century tools to solve their nineteenth century problems. It skips over traditionally intermediate stages of development.

Broken Well Problem
A problem relating to the hundreds of thousands of broken wells found all over Africa today. It is a surface level solution to a deeper, structural problem. Further, building wells often isn't sustainable because the target communities are not trained or given the resources to maintain the well.

PART 4

WHAT'S NEXT? YOU DECIDE.
Rawlsian View of Social Welfare
A Rawlsian view of social welfare emphasizes the importance of maximizing living standards of people at the bottom.

Utilitarian View of Social Welfare
A utilitarian view emphasizes the fact every human's life and happiness should be considered equal.

APPENDIX

———

INTRODUCTION

"Accelerating Poverty Reduction in Africa: In Five Charts." World Bank. October 9, 2019. https://www.worldbank.org/en/region/afr/publication/accelerating-poverty-reduction-in-africa-in-five-charts.

"Forbes Billionaires 2020." Forbes. *Forbes Magazine.* n.d. https://www.forbes.com/billionaires/#133a617c251c.

"Goal 1: End Poverty in All Its Forms Everywhere—United Nations Sustainable Development." United Nations. n.d. https://www.un.org/sustainabledevelopment/poverty/.

"Jolliffe, Dean, and Espen Beer Prydz. "Societal Poverty: A Global Measure of Relative Poverty." WDI—Societal Poverty: A global measure of relative poverty. The World Bank. September 11, 2019. http://datatopics.worldbank.org/world-development-indicators/stories/societal-poverty-a-global-measure-of-relative-poverty.html.

"Nguyen, Davis. "Solving Poverty Without a Big Wallet." Filmed May 2017 at UC Davis. TED video. 9:43. https://www.youtube.com/watch?v=5dWFIFfmbok&t=492s

"Simmons, Ann. "US Foreign Aid: A Waste of Money or a Boost to World Stability? Here Are the Facts." *Los Angeles Times.* May 10, 2017. https://www.latimes.com/world/la-fg-global-aid-true-false-20170501-htmlstory.html.

"World Poverty Clock." World Poverty Clock. https://worldpoverty.io/.

CHAPTER ONE: WHERE WE ARE

"Accelerating Poverty Reduction in Africa: In Five Charts." World Bank. October 9, 2019. https://www.worldbank.org/en/region/afr/publication/accelerating-poverty-reduction-in-africa-in-five-charts.

"Goal 1: End Poverty in All Its Forms Everywhere—United Nations Sustainable Development." United Nations. United Nations, n.d. https://www.un.org/sustainabledevelopment/poverty/.

Guidestar.org. Directory of Charities and Nonprofit Organizations. Candid. https://www.guidestar.org/NonprofitDirectory.aspx.

Jolliffe, Dean, and Espen Beer Prydz. "Societal Poverty: A Global Measure of Relative Poverty." WDI—Societal Poverty: A global measure of relative poverty. The World Bank. September 11, 2019. http://datatopics.worldbank.org/world-development-indicators/stories/societal-poverty-a-global-measure-of-relative-poverty.html.

Klein, Ezra. "Anand Giridharadas on the elite charade of changing the world." *The Ezra Klein Show.* Podcast audio, 59:39–59:47, September 4, 2018. https://www.youtube.com/watch?v=FF-GWnZwu98o.

McKeever, Brice. "Brice McKeever." National Center for Charitable Statistics. December 13, 2018. https://nccs.urban.org/publication/nonprofit-sector-brief-2018#the-nonprofit-sector-in-brief-2018-public-charites-giving-and-volunteering.

"Millennium Development Goals (MDGs)." World Health Organization. World Health Organization. June 25, 2015. https://www.who.int/topics/millennium_development_goals/about/en/.

Omer, Sevil. "Fragile States: Helping Children in the Worst of All Worlds." World Vision, August 30, 2017. https://www.worldvision.org/disaster-relief-news-stories/fragile-states-jonathan-papoulidis.

Oxford Poverty & Human Development Initiative (OPHI). "Global Multidimensional Poverty Index." UN Development Programme (UNDP). https://ophi.org.uk/multidimensional-poverty-index/.

Peer, Andrea. "Global Poverty: Facts, FAQs, and How to Help." World Vision. February 27, 2020. https://www.worldvision.org/sponsorship-news-stories/global-poverty-facts.

"United Nations Millennium Development Goals." United Nations. n.d. https://www.un.org/millenniumgoals/poverty.shtml.

World Bank. 2018. *Poverty and Shared Prosperity 2018: Piecing Together the Poverty Puzzle.* Washington, DC: World Bank. License: Creative Commons Attribution CC BY 3.0 IGO

"World Poverty Clock." World Poverty Clock. https://worldpoverty.io/.

CHAPTER TWO: A WAR, A PLAN, AND A NOT-SO-SILVER BULLET

"A Brief History of US Foreign Aid." Council on Foreign Relations. Council on Foreign Relations. World101, n.d. https://world101.cfr.org/global-era-issues/development/brief-history-us-foreign-aid.

Encyclopedia of Russian History. Encyclopedia.com. s.v. "American Relief Administration." April 16, 2020. https://www.encyclopedia.com/history/encyclopedias-almanacs-transcripts-and-maps/american-relief-administration.

Amoros, Raul. "Tracking Billions of Dollars in Foreign Aid in One Map." HowMuch. December 5, 2017. https://howmuch.net/articles/usa-foreign-aid-by-country.

"Calculate the Value of $13 in 1947." Calculate the value of $13 in 1947. How much is it worth today? n.d. https://www.dollartimes.com/inflation/inflation.php?amount=13&year=1947.

"Commission for Relief in Belgium Raises Millions." History of Giving. n.d. https://www.historyofgiving.org/1890-1930/1914-commission-for-relief-in-belgium-raises-millions/.

Dornbusch, Rudiger, Nölling Wilhelm, and P.R.G. Layard. *Postwar Economic Reconstruction and Lessons for the East Today.* Cambridge, MA. The MIT Press, 1993.

History.com Editors. "George C. Marshall." History.com. A&E Television Networks. October 29, 2009. https://www.history.com/topics/world-war-ii/george-c-marshall.

History.com Editors. "Marshall Plan." HISTORY. A&E Television Networks. December 16, 2009. https://www.history.com/topics/world-war-ii/marshall-plan-1.

"History of the Marshall Plan." George C. Marshall Foundation. n.d. https://www.marshallfoundation.org/marshall/the-marshall-plan/history-marshall-plan/.

Ingram, George. "What Every American Should Know about US Foreign Aid." Brookings. Brookings, October 3, 2019. https://www.brookings.edu/opinions/what-every-american-should-know-about-u-s-foreign-aid/.

"Liberia National Debt 2018." countryeconomy.com. October 16, 2019. https://countryeconomy.com/national-debt/liberia.

Miller, Michael Matheson. *Poverty, Inc.* United States: The Action Institute. Amazon. 2014. https://www.povertyinc.org/filmmaker-qa

Moyo, Dambisa. *Dead Aid Why Aid Makes Things Worse and How There Is Another Way for Africa.* London: Penguin, 2010, 82

Pleming, Sue. "US Plans to Cancel $391 Million in Liberia Debt." Reuters. Thomson Reuters, February 13, 2007. https://www. reuters.com/article/us-liberia-usa-debt/u-s-plans-to-cancel-391-million-in-liberia-debt-idUSWAT00695320070213.

Simmons, Ann. "US Foreign Aid: A Waste of Money or a Boost to World Stability? Here Are the Facts." *Los Angeles Times.* November 20, 2017. https://www.latimes.com/world/la-fg-global-aid-true-false-20170501-htmlstory.html.

The Editors of Encyclopaedia Britannica. s.v. "Marshall Plan." January 27, 2020. https://www.britannica.com/event/Marshall-Plan.

"The Truman Doctrine, 1947." US Department of State, n.d. https://history.state.gov/milestones/1945-1952/truman-doctrine.

CHAPTER THREE: WHAT IS POVERTY?

"About Gapminder." Gapminder. https://www.gapminder.org/about-gapminder/.

Bregman, Rutger. *Utopia for Realists.* London: Bloomsbury, 2018.

Brueck, Hilary. "Bill Gates Says He Now Lumps the World into 4 Income Groups—Here's How It Breaks Down." Business Insider. Business Insider, April 5, 2018. https://www. businessinsider.com/bill-gates-doesnt-like-the-term-developing-countries-instead-he-lumps-the-the-world-into-4-income-groups-2018-4?r=US&IR=T.

Cambridge English Dictionary. s.v. "Paternalism." Cambridge University Press. https://dictionary.cambridge.org/us/dictionary/english/paternalism.

"Four Income Levels." Gapminder. https://www.gapminder.org/topics/four-income-levels/.

Hanlon, Joseph, Armando Barrientos, and David Hulme, *Just Give Money to the Poor.* Kumarian Press, 2010.

Ike, Robert and Guthrie. "Tax Evasion: The Main Cause of Global Poverty." Africa at LSE. March 3, 2014. https://blogs.lse.ac.uk/africaatlse/2014/03/07/tax-evasion-the-main-cause-of-global-poverty/.

"Income Level 1." Gapminder. https://www.gapminder.org/fw/income-levels/income-level-1/.

"Income Level 2." Gapminder.https://www.gapminder.org/fw/income-levels/income-level-2/.

"Income Level 3." Gapminder. https://www.gapminder.org/fw/income-levels/income-level-3/.

"Income Level 4." Gapminder.https://www.gapminder.org/fw/income-levels/income-level-4/.

"Information on Developing Countries—Population, Distribution, Growth and Change—National 5 Geography Revision—BBC Bitesize." BBC News. https://www.bbc.co.uk/bitesize/guides/zbswxnb/revision/9.

Ingram, George. "What Every American Should Know about US Foreign Aid." Brookings. Brookings, October 3, 2019. https://www.brookings.edu/opinions/what-every-american-should-know-about-u-s-foreign-aid/.

Mauren, Kris, James F. Fitzgerald, Michael Matheson Miller, Jonathan Witt, Simon Scionka, Tom Small, Magatte Wade, et al. 2015. *Poverty, Inc.*

Oxford Poverty & Human Development Initiative (OPHI). "Global Multidimensional Poverty Index." UN Development Programme (UNDP).

Rodgers, Harrell R. *American Poverty in a New Era of Reform.* London, New York: Routledge, Taylor et Francis Group, 2015.

Rosling, Hans, Ola Rosling, and Rönnlund Anna Rosling. *Factfulness: Ten Reasons Were Wrong about the World—and Why Things Are Better than You Think.* London: Sceptre, 2019.

Simmons, Ann. "US Foreign Aid: A Waste of Money or a Boost to World Stability? Here Are the Facts." *Los Angeles Times.* November 20, 2017. https://www.latimes.com/world/la-fg-global-aid-true-false-20170501-htmlstory.html.

Stiller, Brian, Todd M. Johnson, Karen Stiller, and Mark Hutchinson. *Evangelicals around the World: A Global Handbook for the 21st Century.* Nashville, TN: Thomas Nelson, 2015.

"United Nations Millennium Development Goals." United Nations. United Nations, n.d. https://www.un.org/millenniumgoals/poverty.shtml.

Wheelan, Charles J. *Naked Economics: Undressing the Dismal Science: Fully Revised and Updated.* New York: W.W. Norton & Company, 2019.

CHAPTER FOUR: THE PROMISE OF PRODUCTIVITY: INDUSTRIAL REVOLUTION

CrashCourse. "Coal, Steam, and The Industrial Revolution: Crash Course World History #32." YouTube video. 11:04. August 30, 2012. https://www.youtube.com/watch?v=zhL5DCiz-j5c&list=WL&index=17&t=0s.

CrashCourse. "The Industrial Economy: Crash Course US History #23." YouTube video. 12:31. July 25, 2013. https://www.youtube.com/watch?v=r6tRp-zRUJs&list=WL&index=13&t=0s

CrashCourse. "The Industrial Revolution: Crash Course European History #24." YouTube video. 17:05. November 5, 2019. https://www.youtube.com/watch?v=zjK7PWmRRyg&list=WL&index=18&t=0s

Davis, Nicholas. Thunderbird School of Global Management, and UCL Department of Science. "What Is the Fourth Industrial Revolution?" World Economic Forum. January 19, 2016. https://www.weforum.org/agenda/2016/01/what-is-the-fourth-industrial-revolution/.

Gauthier, Jason. "1870 Fast Facts—History—US Census Bureau." 1870 Fast Facts—History—US Census Bureau. https://www.census.gov/history/www/through_the_decades/fast_facts/1870_fast_facts.html.

"Income Level 2." Gapminder.https://www.gapminder.org/fw/income-levels/income-level-2/.

"Income Level 3." Gapminder. https://www.gapminder.org/fw/income-levels/income-level-3/.

"Industrial Agriculture and Small-Scale Farming." Weltagrarbericht. https://www.globalagriculture.org/report-topics/industrial-agriculture-and-small-scale-farming.html.

Maki, Reid. "10 Basic Facts about Child Labor Globally." Stop Child Labor. Child Labor Coalition, July 16, 2018. http://stopchildlabor.org/?p=4504.

Melani, Lilia. English I. "William MakepeaceThackery–Vanity Fair." (Syllabus, City University of New York, Brooklyn). January 10, 2009. http://academic.brooklyn.cuny.edu/english/melani/novel19c/thackeray/angel.html.

National Archives. "1833 Factory Act." The National Archives. May 23, 2019. https://www.nationalarchives.gov.uk/education/resources/1833-factory-act/.

Portello, Beth, Philippe Diaz, and Martin Sheen. *The end of poverty?* 2010.

Ratcliff, Anna, and Annie Thériault. "World's Billionaires Have More Wealth than 4.6 Billion People." Oxfam International. January 20, 2020. https://www.oxfam.org/en/press-releases/worlds-billionaires-have-more-wealth-46-billion-people.

Schwab, Klaus. *The Fourth Industrial Revolution*. London: Portfolio Penguin, 2017.

Simple History. "The Industrial Revolution (18–19th Century)." YouTube video. 2:37, October 1, 2017. https://www.youtube.com/watch?v=xLhNP0qp38Q&list=WL&index=16&t=0s

The Angel in the House. March 2, 2011. http://academic.brooklyn.cuny.edu/english/melani/novel_19c/thackeray/angel.html.

"The Four Industrial Revolutions." Unit | Salesforce Trailhead. https://trailhead.salesforce.com/en/content/learn/modules/learn-about-the-fourth-industrial-revolution/meet-the-three-industrial-revolutions.

UNCTAD. Technology and Innovation Report 2018: Harnessing Frontier Technologies for Sustainable Development. United Nations publication, Sales No. E.18.II.D.3, New York and Geneva.

Wheelan, Charles J. *Naked Economics: Undressing the Dismal Science: Fully Revised and Updated*. New York: W.W. Norton & Company, 2019.

Williams, Yohuru. "Sound Smart: Child Labor in the Industrial Revolution | History." YouTube Video, 2:12. November 27, 2016. https://www.youtube.com/watch?v=ejc8oDOcN_0&t=8s

CHAPTER FIVE: A TALE OF TWO NATIONS: RICHLAND VERSUS POORLAND

Albertus, Dr. Michael. "Class 8: Property Rights and Development." (lecture, University of Chicago, Chicago, IL, May 2, 2018).

Bregman, Rutger. *Utopia for Realists*. London: Bloomsbury, 2018.

Cotton, Jess. "How to Make a Country Rich." The Book of Life. February 27, 2019. https://www.theschooloflife.com/thebookoflife/how-to-make-a-country-rich/.

"Henley Passport Index 2008 to 2020." Henley Passport Index, n.d. https://www.henleypassportindex.com/passport-index.

Henley & Partners. *Henley Passport Index 2020*. PDF. 2020.

Nagraj, Aarti. "Why Certain Passports Have More Visa-Free Options." *Gulf Business*. November 12, 2016. https://gulfbusiness.com/certain-passports-visa-free-options/.

Rand, Paul, host. "Why Some Nations Prosper and Others Fail, with James Robinson (Ep. 37)." *Big Brains*. Podcast audio. December 2, 2019. https://news.uchicago.edu/big-brains-podcast-why-some-nations-prosper-and-others-fail-james-robinson

"Why Secure Land Rights Matter." World Bank, March 24, 2017. https://www.worldbank.org/en/news/feature/2017/03/24/why-secure-land-rights-matter.

CHAPTER SIX: HOW YOU GIVE MATTERS

Malone, Sean W. "10 Solutions to Intergenerational Poverty: Sean W. Malone." FEE Freeman Article. Foundation for Economic Education, August 29, 2017. https://fee.org/articles/10-solutions-to-intergenerational-poverty/.

Payne, James L. *Overcoming Welfare: Expecting More from the Poor—and from Ourselves.* New York, NY: Basic Books, 1998.

Portello, Beth, Philippe Diaz, and Martin Sheen. *The end of poverty?* 2010.

"US and World Population Clock." Population Clock. US Census Bureau, n.d. https://www.census.gov/popclock/.

CHAPTER SEVEN: POVERTY MINDSET

Akerlof, GA, Kranton, R Economics and identity. *The Quarterly Journal of Economics*, 115(3) (2000): 715–753.

Banker, Sachin, Syon Bhanot, Aishwarya Deshpande. "Poverty Identity and Competitiveness." *Journal of Economic Psychology,* Volume 76, issue C (2020): DOI: 10.1016/j.joep.2019.102214.

Benjamin, DJ, Choi JJ, and Fisher G Religious identity and economic behavior. *Review of Economics and Statistics,* 98(4) (2016): 617-637.

Benjamin, DJ, J.J. Choi, and J.A. Strickland. "Social identity and preferences." *American Economic Review,* 100(4) (2010):1913–1928.

Bertrand, M., S. Mullainathan, and E. Shafir, Am. Econ. Rev. 94 (2004): 419–423.

Bertrand, M., S. Mullainathan, and E. Shafir, J. Public Policy Mark (2006): 25, 8–23.

Bradley, R.H., R.F. Corwyn. "Socioeconomic status and child development." *Annaul Review of Psychology* (2002): 53, 371–399

Carvalho, Leandro, Stephan Meier, and Stephanie W. Wang. "Poverty and Economic Decision-Making: Evidence from Changes in Financial Resources at Payday." *The American Economic Review*, 106(2) (2016): 260–284. doi:10.1257/aer.20140481

Chen Y, Li, SX. Group identity and social preferences. *American Economic Review*, 99(1) (2009): 431–457.

Claro, Susana, David Paunesku, and Carol S. Dweck. "Growth mindset tempers the effects of poverty on academic achievement." *Proceedings of the National Academy of Sciences of the United States of America*, Volume 113, No. 31 (2016): 8664-8668 www.pnas.org/cgi/doi/10.1073/pnas.1608207113

Cohn, A, M.A. Marechal, T Noll. "Bad boys: How criminal identity salience affects rule violation." *The Review of Economic Studies*, 82(4) (2015): 1289-1308.

Collins, D., J. Morduch. "Insufficient Funds." R.M. Blank, M.S. Barr, Eds. New York: Russell Sage Foundation, 2009.

Conger, R.D., M.B. Donnellan. "An interactionist perspective on the socioeconomic context of human development." *Annual Review of Psychology*, (2007): 58, 175–199.

Dalton, Patricio S, Sayantan Ghosal, and Anandi Mani. "Poverty and Aspirations Failure." *The Economic Journal*, 126 (2016): 165–188. Doi: 10.1111/ecoj.12210

Decety, Dr. Jean. "Social influence and decision-making." (lecture, University of Chicago, Chicago, IL, November 5, 2019).

Duflo, Esther. "Lack of Hope and the Persistence of Poverty." (lecture, University of Cambridge, Cambridge, England, 2012).

Duncan, G. J., J. Brooks-Gunn (Eds.). "Consequences of growing up poor." New York, NY: Russell Sage Foundation 1997.

Evans, G.W. "The environment of childhood poverty." *American-Psychologist*, (2004): 59, 77–92.

Evans, Gary, Pilyoung Kim. "Childhood Poverty, Chronic Stress, Self-Regulation, and Coping." *Child Development Perspectives*. Volume 7, No. 1 (2013): 43–48; DOI: 10.1111/cdep.12013

Hoff, E., B. Laursen, and T. Tardif (2002). "Socioeconomic status and parenting." In M. H. Bornstein (Ed.), *Handbook of parenting* (2nd ed., 231–252). Mahwah, NJ: Erlbaum.

Farah, Martha J., Cayce J. Hook, "Trust and the poverty trap." *Proceedings of the National Academy of Sciences of the United States of America*, Volume 114, No. 21 (2017): 5327-5329 URL www.pnas.org/cgi/doi/10.1073/pnas.1704798114

Gandy, Kizzy, Katy King, Pippa Streeter Hurle, Chloe Bustin, and Kate Glazebrook. "Poverty and decision-making: How behavioral science can improve opportunity in the UK." *Joseph Rowntree Foundation Behavioral Insights Team* (2016).

Grant, K. E., Compas, B. E., Stuhlmacher, A. F., Thurm, A. E., McMahon, S. D., and Halpert, J. A. (2003). "Stressors and child and adolescent psychopathology: Moving from markers to mechanisms of risk." *Psychological Bulletin*, 129, 447–466.

Hall, C.C., Zhao J, Shafir E. Self-affirmation among the poor: Cognitive and behavioral implications. *Psychological Science,* (2014): 25(2):619-625.

Horan, PM and P.L. Austin. The social bases of welfare stigma. Social Problems 21(5) (1974):648-657. http://dx.doi.org/10.2307/799640.

Kerbo, H.R. The stigma of welfare and a passive poor. *Sociology & Social Research.* 1976.

Kessler, JB, Milkman KL Identity in charitable giving. *Management Science,* (2016). http://dx.doi.org/10.1287/mnsc.2016.2582.

Kissane, R.J. "What's need got to do with it? Barriers to use of nonprofit social services." *Journal of Sociology & Social Welfare,* (2003): 30:127.

Lybberrt, Travis J, and Bruce Wydick. "Poverty, Aspirations, and the Economics of Hope." *University of Chicago Press,* (2018).

Mani, Anandi, Sendhil Mullainathan, Eldar Shafir, and Jiaying Zhao. "Poverty Impedes Cognitive Function," *Science Magazine*, Volume 341, (2013). http://science.sciencemag.org/content/341/6149/976

Mood, Carina. Jan O. Johnson. "The Social Consequences of Poverty: An Empirical Test on Longitudinal Data," *Social Indicators Research*, (2016). DOI: 10.1007/s11205-015-0983-9.

Rogers-Dillon, R. "The dynamics of welfare stigma." Qualitative Sociology, 18(4) (1995): 439-456, http://dx.doi.org/10.1007/bf02404490.

Sen, A. "Poor, relatively speaking." *Oxford Economic Papers*, (1983): 35, 153–169.

Shah, Anuj K., Sendhil Mullainathan, and Eldar Shafir. "Some Consequences of Having Too Little," *Science Magazine*, Volume 338 (2012). http://science.sciencemag.org/content/338/6107/682

The Mind Tools Content Team, "Cognitive Load Theory," MindTools, 2019. https://www.mindtools.com/pages/article/cognitive-load-theory.htm

World Bank. 2015. "World Development Report 2015: Mind, Society, and Behavior." Washington, DC: World Bank. doi: 10.1596/978-1-4648-0342-0. License: Creative Commons Attribution CC BY 3.0 IGO

CHAPTER EIGHT: WHO RUNS THE WORLD?

Abdul Latif Jameel Poverty Action Lab (J-PAL). "Menstruation as a barrier to education?" June 2011.

Backiny-Yetna, P., Q. Wodon, M. Bussolo and R.E. de Hoyos. "Gender Labor Income Shares and Human Capital Investment in the Republic of Congo. mimeo," World Bank, Washington, DC. 2009.

Banerji, Urvija. "An Indian Village Plants 111 Trees Every Time a Girl Is Born." Atlas Obscura. Atlas Obscura. March 22, 2017. https://www.atlasobscura.com/articles/an-indian-village-plants-111-trees-every-time-a-girl-is-born.

Gates, Bill and Melinda. 2019. "Examining Inequality," GatesFoundation.org. 2019 https://www.gatesfoundation.org/goalkeepers/report/2019-report/#ExaminingInequality

Budowski, M., R. Tillman and M.M. Bergman. "Poverty, Stratification, and Gender in Switzerland." Swiss Journal of Sociology, (2002): 28, 2, 297-317.

Bussolo, M., R.E. De Hoyos, and Q. Wodon. "Could Higher Prices for Export Crops Reduce Women's Bargaining Power and Household Spending on Human Capital in Senegal?" in Bussolo and De Hoyos (eds.). Gender Aspects of the Trade and Poverty Nexus—A Macro-Micro Approach, World Bank, Washington DC.

Buvinic, M. and G.R. Gupta. "Female-Headed Households and Female-Maintained Families: Are They Worth Targeting to

Reduce Poverty in Developing Countries?" Economic Development and Cultural Change, (1997): 45, 2, 259-280.

Diagne, A., M. Zeller, and M. Sharma, "Empirical Measurements of Households' Access to Credit and Credit Constraints in Developing Countries: Methodological Issues and Evidence." IFPRI FCND Discussion Paper No. 90, International Food Policy Research Institute, Washington DC, 2000.

Evans, David, Michael Kremer, Mūthoni Ngatia. "The Impact of Distributing School Uniforms on Children's Education in Kenya." November 2009.

Fafchamps, M., "Ethnicity and Credit in African Manufacturing." *Journal of Development Economics*, 61(1) (2000): 205-35.

"Facts and Figures: Economic Empowerment." n.d. UN Women. https://www.unwomen.org/en/what-we-do/economic-empowerment/facts-and-figures#notes.

Gates, Bill and Melinda. 2020. "Why We Swing for the Fences." Gatesnotes.com. February 10, 2020. https://www.gatesnotes.com/2020-Annual-Letter?WT.mc_id=2020021010000_AL2020_MG-LI_&WT.tsrc=MGLI&linkId=81963272#.

"Globally, Youth Are the Largest Poverty-Stricken Group, Says New UN Report || UN News." United Nations. United Nations. September 20, 2018. https://news.un.org/en/story/2018/09/1019952.

King's College. "Women's Unpaid Care Work Has Been Unmeasured and Undervalued for Too Long." King's College London. January 14, 2020. https://www.kcl.ac.uk/news/womens-unpaid-care-work-has-been-unmeasured-and-undervalued-for-too-long.

King, E., S. Klasen and S. Porter. Women and Development. Copenhagen Consensus 2008 Challenge Paper, Copenhagen, Denmark.

Klasen, Stephan, Tobias Lechtenfeld, Felix Povel. "What about the Women? Female Headship, Poverty and Vulnerability in Thailand and Vietnam." Georg-August-Universität Göttingen, Courant Research Centre, March 2011.

McCarthy, Joe. "Women Are More Likely Than Men to Live in Extreme Poverty: Report." Global Citizen. February 16, 2018. https://www.globalcitizen.org/en/content/women-extreme-poverty-un-report/.

Mehra, R., S. Esim and M. Simms, "Fulfilling the Beijing Commitment: Reducing Poverty, Enhancing Women's economic options." International Center for Research on Women, Washington DC, 2000.

Miguel, Edward, and Michael Kremer. "Primary School Deworming in Kenya: The Abdul Latif Jameel Poverty Action Lab." The Abdul Latif Jameel Poverty Action Lab (J-PAL). https://www.povertyactionlab.org/evaluation/primary-school-deworming-kenya.

Moghadam, V.M. "The feminisation of poverty: notes on a concept and trend." Women's Studies Occasional Paper 2, Illinois State University, 1997.

Nguyen, Trang. "Education and Health Care in Developing Countries." *Education and Health Care in Developing Countries.* Dissertation, Massachusetts Institute of Technology. Dept. of Economics. Massachusetts Institute of Technology, 2008. http://dspace.mit.edu/handle/1721.1/45902?show=full.

Payne, James L. *Overcoming Welfare: Expecting More from the Poor—and from Ourselves.* New York, NY: Basic Books, 1998.

"Plan International UK's Research on Period Poverty and Stigma." Plan International UK. December 20, 2017. https://plan-uk.org/media-centre/plan-international-uks-research-on-period-poverty-and-stigma.

Ratusi, M. and A.V. Swamy. "Explaining Ethnic Differentials in Credit Market Outcomes in Zimbabwe." Economic Development and Cultural Change, (1999): 47, 585–604.

Rodgers, Harrell R. *American Poverty in a New Era of Reform.* London, New York: Routledge, Taylor et Francis Group, 2015.

Rosling, Hans, Ola Rosling, and Rönnlund Anna Rosling. *Factfulness: Ten Reasons Were Wrong about the World—and Why Things Are Better than You Think.* London: Sceptre, 2019, 139

"Second Mile." Second Mile Serving Neighborhoods Strengthening Schools Empowering Homes. Accessed June 3, 2020. https://secondmile.net/pride-for-parents/.

Sigmarsdóttir, Sif. "Once More, Iceland Has Shown It Is the Best Place in the World to Be Female | Sif Sigmarsdóttir." The Guardian. Guardian News and Media. January 5, 2018. https://

www.theguardian.com/commentisfree/2018/jan/05/iceland-female-women-equal-pay-gender-equality.

Storey, D.J. "Racial and Gender Discrimination in the Micro Firms Credit Market? Evidence from Trinidad and Tobago." *Small Business Economics*, 23(5) (2004): 401–22.

Taei, Payman. "Visualizing Women's Unpaid Work Across the Globe (A Special Chart)." Medium. Towards Data Science. March 8, 2019. https://towarddatascience.com/visualizing-womens-unpaid-work-across-the-globe-a-special-chart-9f2595fafaaa.

"The Rana Plaza Accident and Its Aftermath." 2017. The Rana Plaza Accident and Its Aftermath. December 21, 2017. https://www.ilo.org/global/topics/geip/WCMS_614394/lang--en/index.htm#banner.

"This Indian Village Plants 111 Trees When a Girl Is Born." Earth Day. November 18, 2019. https://www.earthday.org/this-indian-village-plants-111-trees-when-a-girl-is-born/.

Villa, Monique. 2017. "Women Own Less than 20% of the World's Land. It's Time to Give Them Equal Property Rights." World Economic Forum. January 11, 2017. https://www.weforum.org/agenda/2017/01/women-own-less-than-20-of-the-worlds-land-its-time-to-give-them-equal-property-rights/.

UNESCO. 2013. *Education Transforms Lives*. Paris, UNESCO

UNESCO. 2018. *Global Education Monitoring Report 2019: Migration, Displacement and Education—Building Bridges, not Walls.* Paris, UNESCO

Welteroth, Elaine. *More Than Enough: Claiming Space for Who You Are (No Matter What They Say).* Random House, 2019, 221.

"What Is Period Poverty?" Bodyform. September 20, 2018. https://www.bodyform.co.uk/our-world/period-poverty/.

World Bank. *World Bank Policy Research Report 2001: Engendering Development through Gender Equality in Rights, Resources, and Voice.* Oxford University Press, New York.

CHAPTER NINE: PEOPLE PROBLEMS

"2019 State of the Nation's Housing Report: Lack of Affordable Housing." Cost of Home, 2019. https://www.habitat.org/costofhome/2019-state-nations-housing-report-lack-affordable-housing.

Bregman, Rutger. *Utopia for Realists.* London: Bloomsbury, 2018.

Camarota, Steven A. "A Record-Setting Decade of Immigration: 2000-2010." Center for Immigration Studies. October 5, 2011. https://cis.org/Report/RecordSetting-Decade-Immigration-20002010

Camarota, Steven A., Karen Zeigler. "Record 44.5 Million Immigrants in 2017: Non-Mexico Latin American, Asian, and African populations grew most." Center for Immigration Studies.

September 15, 2018. https://cis.org/Report/Record-445-Million-Immigrants-2017_

Capps, Kriston. "There's a Big Housing Problem. Here's a Huge Plan to Fix It." CityLab, November 21, 2019. https://www.citylab.com/equity/2019/11/public-housing-homes-for-all-ilhan-omar-green-new-deal/602374/.

Carden, Art. "Are We Serious about Reducing Poverty? Then We Need to Welcome Immigrants." Forbes. *Forbes Magazine*, October 19, 2018. https://www.forbes.com/sites/artcarden/2018/10/19/are-we-serious-about-reducing-poverty-then-we-need-to-welcome-immigrants/#790e006acf25.

Catechism of the Catholic Church. 2nd ed. Vatican City: Vatican Press, 1997. http://www.scborromeo.org/ccc.htm.

Cilluffo, Anthony, and Neil G. Ruiz. "World Population Growth Is Expected to Nearly Stop by 2100." Pew Research Center. Pew Research Center, June 17, 2019. https://www.pewresearch.org/fact-tank/2019/06/17/worlds-population-is-projected-to-nearly-stop-growing-by-the-end-of-the-century/

Gray, Alex. "Here's How Finland Solved Its Homelessness Problem." World Economic Forum, February 13, 2018. https://www.weforum.org/agenda/2018/02/how-finland-solved-homelessness/.

Henley, Jon. "It's a Miracle: Helsinki's Radical Solution to Homelessness." *The Guardian*. Guardian News and Media, June 3, 2019. https://www.theguardian.com/cities/2019/jun/03/its-a-miracle-helsinkis-radical-solution-to-homelessness.

"Housing First Scheme in Finland: Y-Foundation (Y-Säätiö)." The Y Foundation, August 20, 2018. https://ysaatio.fi/en/housing-first-finland.

"Housing First Feasibility Study for Liverpool City Region (2017)." Crisis, November 7, 2017. https://www.crisis.org.uk/ending-homelessness/homelessness-knowledge-hub/housing-models-and-access/housing-first-feasibility-study-for-liverpool-city-region-2017/.

"Information on Developing Countries—Population, Distribution, Growth and Change—National 5 Geography Revision—BBC Bitesize." BBC News. BBC. n.d.

Jay, Meg. *The Defining Decade: What Your Twenties Matter and How to Make the Most of Them Now.* Edinburgh, United Kingdom: Canongate Books Ltd, 2016.

Kurt, Daniel. "Assessing the Pros & Cons of Immigration Reform." Investopedia. Investopedia, May 12, 2020. https://www.investopedia.com/articles/investing/043015/pros-cons-immigration-reform.asp.

Kurzgesagt—In a Nutshell, "Overpopulation—The Human Explosion Explained," Youtube video, 6:39, December 22, 2016.

Mcleod, Saul. "Maslow's Hierarchy of Needs." Simply Psychology. Simply Psychology, March 20, 2020. https://www.simplypsychology.org/maslow.html.

"Myths and Facts About Immigrants and Immigration." Anti-Defamation League. https://www.adl.org/resources/fact-sheets/

myths-and-facts-about-immigrants-and-immigration-en-espanol.

Pritchett, Lant. "Alleviating Global Poverty: Labor Mobility, Direct Assistance, and Economic Growth." CGD Working Paper 479. Washington, DC: Center for Global Development. 2018. https://www.cgdev.org/publication/alleviating-global-poverty-labor-mobility-direct-assistance-and-economic-growth

Rodgers, Harrell R. *American Poverty in a New Era of Reform.* London, New York: Routledge, Taylor et Francis Group, 2015.

Roser, Max. 2014. "Fertility Rate." Our World in Data. February 19, 2014.

Roser, Max, Hannah Ritchie, and Esteban Ortiz-Ospina. "World Population Growth." Our World in Data. May 9, 2013.

Rosling, Hans, Ola Rosling, and Rönnlund Anna Rosling. *Factfulness: Ten Reasons Were Wrong about the World—and Why Things Are Better than You Think.* London: Sceptre, 2019, 95.

Smith, Adam, and Edwin Cannan. *The Wealth of Nations.* Bantam Classic.

The Center for Social Justice, "Prioritizing Growth: The Future of Immigration Policy," August 2019.

"The Number of International Migrants Reaches 272 Million, Continuing an Upward Trend in All World Regions, Says UN | UN DESA Department of Economic and Social Affairs." United Nations. United Nations, September 17, 2019. https://www.

un.org/development/desa/en/news/population/international-migrant-stock-2019.html.

Turner, Terry. "Find Out How This Canadian City Has Eliminated Homelessness." Good News Network, October 7, 2015. https://www.goodnewsnetwork.org/find-out-how-this-canadian-city-has-eliminated-homelessness/#.XewK-JHAqWg. linkedin.

United States Crime Rates 1960–2018. http://www.disastercenter.com/crime/uscrime.htm.

"Very Few Americans See Contraception as Morally Wrong." Pew Research Center's Religion & Public Life Project. May 30, 2020. https://www.pewforum.org/2016/09/28/4-very-few-americans-see-contraception-as-morally-wrong/.

Walmsley, Terrie L., L. Alan Winters, S. Amer Ahmed, and Christopher R. Parsons. "Measuring the Impact of the Movemen of Labour Using a Model of Bilateral Migration Flows," World Bank.

Whitaker, Beth Elise. "Migration within Africa and Beyond." *African Studies Review,* Volume 60, No. 2 (September 2017): 209–220.

Whitaker, Beth Elise, and Jason Giersch. "Political Competition and Attitudes toward Immigration in Africa." Journal of Ethnic and Migration Studies 41 (10) (2015): 1536–57.

"World Population by Year." n.d. Worldometer. Accessed June 3, 2020.

Y-Foundation. "A Home of Your Own." Otava Book Printing Ltd. June 2, 2017.

CHAPTER TEN: CASE STUDY: CHINA

CGTN. "Inside China's 'model town' for poverty alleviation." You-Tube video,6:18, February 26, 2018, https://www.youtube.com/watch?v=EC_lKzAghoQ.

CGTN. "China's War on Poverty: Getting rich by raising camels," YouTube video, 2:15, August 3, 2019. https://www.youtube.com/watch?v=rDv9hhKPwug.

CGTN America. "Sourabh Gupta has more on poverty alleviation in China," YouTube video, 2:34. July 8, 2019. https://www.youtube.com/watch?v=6aJkgaTo-qo. n.d.

Huifeng, He. "China's subsidies lifting rural villages out of poverty, but is Xi Jinping's plan sustainable?" Accessed November 3, 2019. https://www.scmp.com/economy/china-economy/article/3035894/chinas-subsidies-lifting-rural-villages-out-poverty-xi.

Kuhn, Robert Lawrence. China Daily. October 11, 2019. https://www.chinadaily.com.cn/a/201910/11/WS5d9fcc39a310cf3e3556fced.html.

"The Multiple Meanings of Xi's Targeted Poverty Alleviation." *South China Morning Post.* August 5, 2019.

Voices on the Frontline. Directed by Peter Getzels. Performed by Robert Lawrence Kuhn. 2019.

CHAPTER ELEVEN: CASE STUDY: LIBERIA

Africa.com. Liberia. 2019. https://africa.com/heres-what-you-need-to-know-about-liberia/.

Africa, Front Page. Liberia Poverty Rate Stands at 54 Percent—World Bank Report. October 19, 2016. https://frontpageafricaonline.com/news/2016news/liberia-poverty-rate-stands-at-54-percent-world-bank-report/.

Central Bank of Liberia. CBL Concludes National Financial Inclusion Strategy. July 1, 2019. https://www.cbl.org.lr/2press.php?news_id=174&related=7&pg=sp.

CGTN America. "Sourabh Gupta has more on poverty alleviation in China." YouTube video, 2:34. July 8, 2019. https://www.youtube.com/watch?v=6aJkgaTo-qo.

"Country Strategy Paper and Indicative Program." Commission, Government of the Republic of Liberia and the European. 2008–2013.

Dennis, Peter. "A Brief History of Liberia." The International Center for Transitional Justice. 2006.

Development, International Fund for Agricultural. Republic of Liberia: Country Strategic Opportunities Program 2019 (EB 2019/128/R.17). International Fund for Agricultural Development.

Division, United Nations Department of Economic and Social Affairs: Population. Liberia Population. 2020. https://countrymeters.info/en/Liberia.

Fuente, Alejandro De la. "World Bank using Global Monitoring Database." Poverty & Equity Brief, World Bank. 2019.

Group, Liberian Economy. "Liberia's Economic Problems: Long-standing and Widespread Poverty, Unbearably High Foreign exchange rate." November 3, 2019. https://www.theperspective. org/2019/1103201904.php.

Johnson, Obediah. "Only 5% of Liberia's 4.5 Million People Have Access to Electricity." November 26, 2019. https://frontpageafricaonline.com/news/only-5-of-liberias-4-5-million-people-have-access-to-electricity/.

Kaledzi, Isaac. "Liberia: Banknotes in short supply, banks run-out of cash." November 5, 2019. https://africafeeds.com/2019/11/05/liberia-banknotes-in-short-supply-banks-run-out-of-cash/.

Lewis, David. MONROVIA, LIBERIA (1822-). October 8, 2014. https://www.blackpast.org/global-african-history/places-global-african-history/monrovia-liberia-1821/.

Liberia: Mayor Koijee Presents Monrovia's Case at the Ongoing Technical Deep Dive On Climate-Smart Cities. February 20. https://allafrica.com/stories/202002200739.html.

"Liberia: Poverty Reduction Strategy Paper." International Monetary Fund. Washington DC. 2008.

Meisler, Stanley. Liberia. March. 1973. https://www.theatlantic. com/past/docs/issues/73mar/meisler.htm.

Paye-Layleh, Jonathan. Thousands march in Liberia to protest falling economy. January 6, 2020. https://apnews.com/99970d-86827cfb2403893ef735afce94.

Pol, Jurjen van de. "Ex-Liberia Leader Taylor Sentenced 50 Years for War Crime." May 30, 2012. https://www.bloomberg.com/news/articles/2012-05-30/ex-liberia-leader-taylor-sentenced-to-50-years-for-war-crimes.

Republic of Liberia. Pro-Poor Agenda for Prosperity and Development (PAPD). Liberia: UNDP Liberia. 2018.

Shiner, Cindy. Roots of Ex-US Slaves Still Run Deep In Liberia. October 26, 1995. https://www.csmonitor.com/1995/1026/26071.html.

Spatz, Benjamin J. "Liberia, a remarkable African success story, still needs help." September 23, 2013. https://www.csmonitor.com/Commentary/Opinion/2013/0923/Liberia-a-remarkable-African-success-story-still-needs-help.

TheGrio. "Former American slaves played oppressive role in Liberia's past." February 1, 2010. https://thegrio.com/2010/02/01/former-american-slaves-played-oppressive-role-in-liberias-past/.

UNDP. "Inequalities in Human Development in the 21st Century: Briefing note for countries on the 2019 Human Development Report." 2019 Human Development Report. 2019.

Worldometer. Liberia Population (Live). 2020. https://www.worldometers.info/world-population/liberia-population/.

CHAPTER TWELVE: A HOUSE BUILT ON A ROCK

Aizenman, Nurith. "How To Fix Poverty: Why Not Just Give People Money?" August 7, 2017. https://www.npr.org/sections/goatsandsoda/2017/08/07/541609649/how-to-fix-poverty-why-not-just-give-people-money.

Cass, Oren. The Working Hypothesis. 2018. https://www.the-american-interest.com/2018/10/15/the-working-hypothesis/.

Christensen, Clayton, Efosa Ojomo, and Karen Dillion. "Poverty data never tells the whole story." January 22, 2019. https://www.weforum.org/agenda/2019/01/poverty-data-never-tells-the-whole-story/.

Food4Education. n.d. https://food4education.org/#the-issue.

Moyo, Dambisa. "Dead Aid: Why Aid Is Not Working and How There Is a Better Way for Africa." 1st American ed. New York: Farrar, Straus and Giroux, 2009.

Nonprofit, Ventures. 2017. "What Is a Savings Club?" November 30. https://www.venturesnonprofit.org/blog/savings-club/.

Pickert, Reade. Is This Free College Program a Model for the Nation? December 4, 2019. https://www.bloomberg.com/news/articles/2019-12-04/what-free-college-tuition-means-for-tennessee-s-economy.

Rosling, Hans, Ola Rosling, and Rönnlund Anna Rosling. *Factfulness: Ten Reasons Were Wrong about the World—and Why Things Are Better than You Think.* London: Sceptre, 2019, 121.

UChicago. "How the Loss of Community Threatens Society with Raghuram Rajan (Ep. 26)." UChicago Big Brains. Podcast audio, June 3, 2019.

World Bank. Mali: Using Bikes to Get to School and Stay in School. July 25, 2018. https://www.worldbank.org/en/news/feature/2018/07/25/a-bike-for-school-in-mali?cid=ECR_LI_worldbank_EN_EXT.

Yang, Andrew. Move Humanity Forward. 2020. https://movehumanityforward.com/.

CHAPTER THIRTEEN: TAKING CARE OF BUSINESS

Aizenman, Nurith. "How To Fix Poverty: Why Not Just Give People Money?" August 7, 2017. https://www.npr.org/sections/goatsandsoda/2017/08/07/541609649/how-to-fix-poverty-why-not-just-give-people-money.

Cass, Oren. "The Working Hypothesis." 2018. https://www.the-american-interest.com/2018/10/15/the-working-hypothesis/.

Christensen, Clayton, Efosa Ojomo, and Karen Dillion. "Poverty data never tells the whole story." January 22, 2019. https://www.weforum.org/agenda/2019/01/poverty-data-never-tells-the-whole-story/.

Food4Education. n.d. https://food4education.org/#the-issue.

Living on One Dollar. Directed by Zach Ingrasci, Sean Leonard, and Ryan Christofferson Chris Temple. 2013.

Moyo, Dambisa. *Dead Aid: Why Aid Is Not Working and How There Is a Better Way for Africa.* 1st American ed. New York: Farrar, Straus and Giroux, 2009.

Nonprofit, Ventures. What is a Savings Club? November 30, 2017. https://www.venturesnonprofit.org/blog/savings-club/.

Pickert, Reade. Is This Free College Program a Model for the Nation? December 4, 2019. https://www.bloomberg.com/news/articles/2019-12-04/what-free-college-tuition-means-for-tennessee-s-economy.

Rosenberger, Ian. "Why poverty has nothing to do with money." Filmed June 2014 at Grandview Ave. TED video, 19:24.

Simon Torkington. "The jobs of the future—and two skills you need to get them," World Economic Forum. September 2, 2016. www.weforum.org/agenda/2016/09/jobs-of-future-and-skills-you-need/.

UChicago. "How the Loss of Community Threatens Society with Raghuram Rajan (Ep. 26)." UChicago Big Brains. Podcast audio. June 3, 2019.

World Bank. 2018. Mali: Using Bikes to Get to School and Stay in School. July 25. https://www.worldbank.org/en/news/feature/2018/07/25/a-bike-for-school-in-mali?cid=ECR_LI_worldbank_EN_EXT.

Yang, Andrew. 2020. Move Humanity Forward . https://movehumanityforward.com/.

CHAPTER FOURTEEN: DON'T EAT THE RICH. FEED THEM.

Gates, Bill and Melinda. "Why we swing for the fences." February 10, 2020. https://www.gatesnotes.com/2020-Annual-Letter?WT.mc_id=2020021010000_AL2020_MG-LI_&WT.tsrc=MGLI&linkId=81963272#ALChapter1.

Giriyan, Sudhesh. "Outlook 2020: Digital trends that will shape the remittance industry." February 3, 2020. https://www.finextra.com/blogposting/18408/outlook-2020-digital-trends-that-will-shape-the-remittance-industry.

Langevang, Thilde. "Fashioning the future: Entrepreneuring in Africa's emerging fashion industry." Working Paper, Copenhagen: Center for Business and Development Studies: Copenhagen Business School. 2016.

Merriam-Webster.com, Dictionary. s.v. "Charity." https://www.merriam-webster.com/dictionary/charity.

Ojomo, Efosa. 5 Reasons Why These Powerful Innovations Might Be Our Best Shot at Solving Poverty. August 6, 2019. https://www.christenseninstitute.org/blog/5-reasons-why-these-powerful-innovations-might-be-our-best-shot-at-solving-poverty/.

Ojomo, Efosa. "The Poverty Paradox: Why Most Poverty Programs Fail and How to Fix Them." Gaborone. TED video, 15:26. Filmed August 14, 2017.

Rosling, Hans, Ola Rosling, and Rönnlund Anna Rosling. *Factfulness: Ten Reasons Were Wrong about the World—and Why Things Are Better than You Think.* London: Sceptre, 2019.

The Conversation. "We asked Senegalese migrants why they leave home. Here's what they told us." March 19, 2019. https://the-conversation.com/we-asked-senegalese-migrants-why-they-leave-home-heres-what-they-told-us-113760.

World Bank. 2006. "Remittances, Households, and Poverty." Global Economic Prospects, World bank.

CHAPTER FIFTEEN: HELLO, MY NAME IS ROBIN

Hughes, Ailey Kaiser. "Brief: Using Land Policy in Liberia to Improve Life for The Urban Poor." 2020. http://www.focuson-land.com/fola/en/countries/brief-using-land-policy-in-liberia-to-improve-life-for-the-urban-poor/.

Ibukun, Yinka, and Gwen Ackerman. "Africa's Technology Hub Rises in a Congested Lagos Neighborhood." June 11, 2019. https://www.bloomberg.com/news/articles/2019-06-11/afri-ca-s-technology-hub-rises-in-a-congested-lagos-neighbor-hood.

Karmo, Henry. "Liberia: Hike in Tuition Draws Attention of Senator, Poised to Hold Discussion with Education Minister." September 11, 2019. https://frontpageafricaonline.com/news/liberia-hike-in-tuition-draws-attention-of-sena-tor-poised-to-hold-discussion-with-education-minister/.

Smith, Oliver. "15 curious things you might not have known about Liberia." July 26, 2018. https://www.telegraph.co.uk/travel/des-tinations/africa/articles/liberia-facts/#:~:text=Liberia%20is%20171%20years%20old,its%20citizens%20is%2017.9%20years.

Soap, Vermont. "Improving the Productivity and Profitability of Artisanal Soap Making in Liberia." March 26, 2013. https://vermontsoap.com/improving-the-productivity-and-profitability-of-artisanal-soap-making-in-liberia/.

UNICEF. *Basic Education.* 2020. https://www.unicef.org/liberia/basic-education.

World Bank. "World Bank Poverty & Equity and Macroeconomics." Trade & Investment Global Practices Report. 2020.

CHAPTER SIXTEEN: WHAT'S NEXT? YOU DECIDE.

Baicker, Katherine. "Can Economics Save the World?" panel event, Chicago, IL, November 19, 2019.

Bregman, Rutger. *Utopia for Realists.* London: Bloomsbury, 2018.

Hege, Elisabeth, Samien Barchiche, Julien Rochette, Lucien Chabason, and Pierre Barthelemy. "2030 Agenda for Sustainable Development: A first assessment and conditions for success." October 2019. https://www.iddri.org/en/publications-and-events/study/2030-agenda-sustainable-development-first-assessment-and-conditions.

Oxford Poverty & Human Development Initiative (OPHI). "Global Multidimensional Poverty Index." UN Development Programme (UNDP). https://ophi.org.uk/multidimensional-poverty-index/.

Payne, James L. *Overcoming Welfare: Expecting More from the Poor—and from Ourselves.* New York, NY: Basic Books, 1998.

Rosling, Hans, Ola Rosling, and Rönnlund Anna Rosling. *Fact-fulness: Ten Reasons Were Wrong about the World—and Why Things Are Better than You Think*. London: Sceptre, 2019, 189.

Sawe, Benjamin Elisha. "The Most Equal Countries in the World." August 3, 2018. https://www.worldatlas.com/articles/the-most-equal-countries-in-the-world.html.

"World Poverty Clock." World Poverty Clock. https://worldpoverty. io/.

INTERVIEW RESPONSES FOR "HELLO, MY NAME IS ROBIN."

———

The interview responses that inspired the chapter "Hello, My Name Is Robin," in order by question. Some of the responses have been edited for clarity. The names and ages of the interview respondents were not collected to maintain anonymity.

Where do you live?

1. Zayzay community
2. Zayzay community
3. Zayzay community
4. New Georgia Gulf community
5. Chocolate City community
6. Chocolate City community
7. Chocolate City community
8. Chocolate City
9. I live in Lagos, Nigeria.

What is a typical day like for you? (Morning, afternoon, and evening activities)

1. Selling petty goods.
2. Farming and selling petty goods.
3. I don't have a job, but I used to be a community schoolteacher.
4. Due to the coronavirus in Liberia, I don't have a job, but I used to get paid to clean houses and cut grass.
5. Selling goods.
6. Selling fish.
7. I don't have a job now, but I used to be a community schoolteacher.
8. It's like hoping to have a meal and sometimes not getting it.
9. I wake up at 5 a.m. every weekday to prepare for work and leave home at 5:45 a.m. to beat the traffic to work. I work as a cleaner at a law firm from 8 a.m. to 5 p.m. At the close of work, I go through a lot of traffic and get home most days at about 7:30 p.m.

How do you pay for your living expenses?

1. I pay for my expenses through the petty business I am doing.
2. I pay for my expenses through farming and selling petty goods.
3. I pay for my expenses through my salary.
4. I pay for my expenses by cutting my neighbor's yards and cleaning their houses.
5. I pay for my expenses through my business.
6. I pay for my expenses through selling petty goods.
7. I pay for my expenses through my salary.
8. I pay for my living expenses from the meagre salary I earn and a few tips here and there.

Are you renting your home, or do you own it?
1. I am squatting on someone's land.
2. I am squatting on someone's land.
3. I am squatting on someone's land.
4. I am squatting on the Alay (road passing through the community that government not ready to build).
5. I am renting.
6. Renting.
7. Renting.
8. Yes, I am renting.
9. I live in a rented one room apartment.

How many people live with you?
1. I have seven people living with me.
2. I have five people living with me.
3. I have seven people living with me.
4. My wife, two daughters, and myself.
5. I have eight people living with me.
6. I have four people living with me.
7. I have three people living with me.
8. I have six kids living with me.
9. I live with my wife and three children.

If you are sick, how do you handle it?
1. I can go to the government hospital when I am sick because they offer free treatment even though it's not up to standard.
2. I can go to the government hospital when I am sick because they offer free treatment even though it's not up to standard.
3. I do home treatments when I am sick.
4. I buy medication and use it at home.

5. I go to the government hospital when I am sick.
6. I go to the government hospital when I am sick.
7. I go to the government hospital.
8. I go to the government hospital. Sometimes I manage to buy drugs.
9. When we fall sick, we self-medicate with local herbs or buy drugs from our local chemist.

How do you maintain your personal hygiene?
1. I take a bath outside at night or very early in the morning when everybody is still sleeping.
2. I take a bath outside at night or very early in the morning when everybody is still sleeping.
3. I take a bath outside at night or very early in the morning when everybody is still sleeping.
4. I take a bath outside at night or very early in the morning when everybody is still sleeping.
5. I take bath in the bathroom outside.
6. I take a bath outside at nighttime.
7. I take bath outside at nighttime or very early in the morning when everybody is still sleeping.
8. Well, I have a trench toilet. We usually bathe outside and manage to clean everywhere.
9. I keep myself clean by bathing with soap and water.

Are products affordable? (Lotion, soap, shower, etc.)
1. I only use local oil as lotion and locally made soap to take baths.
2. I only use cream as lotion and locally made soap to take baths.
3. I use local oil as lotion and locally made soap to take baths.

4. I use local oil as lotion and locally made soap to take baths.
5. I only use local oil as lotion and locally made soap to take baths.
6. I use cream as lotion and locally made soap to take baths.
7. I use local oil as lotion and locally made soap to take baths.
8. We mostly bathe with iron soap (handmade soap).
9. I keep myself clean by bathing with soap and water.

(If a parent) Do your children go to school?
1. My children are not attending school because I cannot afford to pay their fees.
2. My children are attending government school.
3. My children are attending government school.
4. My children are attending government school.
5. My children are not attending school because I cannot afford to pay their fees.
6. My children are attending government school.
7. My children are attending government school.
8. N/A
9. Yes, my kids go to a local school nearby.

Did you go to school? How long?
1. I did not have the opportunity to go to school.
2. I am a high school graduate.
3. I am a high school graduate.
4. I graduated from sixth grade.
5. I did not have the opportunity to go to school.
6. I am a high school graduate.
7. I am a high school graduate.
8. I am a high school graduate.
9. I only attended primary school for five years.

How do you pay for school fees? How much do you pay?

1. I am not paying fees because my children are not attending school.
2. I pay the fees through my farming and selling. The school fees are 11,000 Liberian dollars.
3. I pay the fees with my salary.
4. Through my daily work and at least 2,000 Liberian dollars at that time (1965).
5. I am not paying fees because my children are not attending school.
6. I pay the fees through my selling.
7. I pay the fees with my salary.
8. I usually pay around 1,600 Liberian dollars for public school.
9. The tuition for my kids is free, but I pay for books and other materials. They are about 15,000 Naira per session.

When you have a problem, who do you go to for help and support? (church, nonprofits, school programs, etc.)

1. My friends and family members are the only people that can help me in times of trouble.
2. I help myself by farming and selling in times of trouble or problems.
3. I help myself through loans in times of trouble or problems.
4. I use credit from my susu with interest.
5. My friends help me in time of problems.
6. I help myself by selling in times of trouble or problems.
7. I help myself through loans in times of trouble or problems.
8. I ask the church to help me. I am a Christian and an active member of the church.
9. I usually ask my employer for help.

Long Term Needs (Goals/Aspirations):

How do you manage your money or plan for big financial goals?

1. My father helps me to keep my money, or I use mobile money.
2. I save my money in the susu.
3. I save my money through mobile money.
4. I save my money in the susu for any big problems.
5. My father helps me to keep my money.
6. I save my money in the susu.
7. I save my money through mobile money.
8. I use my money to buy petty goods like fufu and coconuts that I can sell.
9. I can't plan for big financial goals.

How do you save money?

1. My father helps me to keep my money, or sometimes I use mobile money.
2. I save my money in the susu.
3. I save my money through mobile money.
4. I save my money in the susu.
5. My father helps me to keep my money.
6. I save my money in the susu.
7. I save my money through mobile money.
8. I save my money in the susu.
9. I don't earn enough money to save after expenses.

Do you have any loans or debts?

1. I have no debt or loans.
2. I have no debt or loans.
3. I have no debt or loans.
4. I have loans or debts.

5. I have no debt or loans.
6. I have no debt or loans.
7. I have debts and loans.
8. I have a few debts and loans because I've taken goods and paid back the money in the past.
9. Yes, I have a few debts.

What do you think you can do to improve your life financially in the long-term?
1. I am willing to do business.
2. I am willing to do farming and business.
3. I am willing to do a teaching job.
4. I am willing to do any office job because I can read and write. I am willing to do work that will improve my life.
5. I am willing to do business.
6. I am willing to do business.
7. I am willing to do a teaching job.
8. A good loan or business could help me a lot. Starting a business could improve my life.
9. If I can get a better paying job and a scholarship or sponsorship for my children to attend a better school, it will go a long way in improving my life financially in the long run.

What are you able to do?
1. I am able to sell.
2. I am able to farm and sell.
3. I am able to teach.
4. I am able to work.
5. I am able to sell.

6. I am able to sell fish.
7. I am able to teach.
8. I am able to sell food or dry goods.
9. I am able to learn new skills.

What would be your dream solution to improve your life financially?

1. My dream solution is to have a big business.
2. My dream solution is to have a big business and own a home of my own.
3. My dream solution is to buy land and built house.
4. My dream solution is to save money and pay my daughter's school fees.
5. My dream solution is to have a successful business.
6. My dream solution is to have a big business and own a home of my own.
7. My dream solution is to buy land and build a house.
8. My dream solution is to buy a better business.
9. My dream solution to improve my life financially would be to learn computer or IT-related skills and get a better paying job.

If you were the president of your country, how would you improve things for your community specifically and for your country more broadly?

1. For my community, I would build toilets and bathrooms, install hand pumps, and help to clean. For my country, I would provide free education and free medication.
2. For my community, I would build toilets and bathrooms, hand pumps, and help to clean. For my country, I would provide free education, free medication, agriculture, and security.

3. For my community and my country, I would provide free education, free medication, agriculture, and road networks.
4. For both, I would provide free education and improve the lives of people who cannot afford to help themselves
5. For my community, I would build bathrooms, hand pumps, and help to clean. For my country, I would provide free education and free medication.
6. For both, I would provide free education, free medication, agriculture, and security.
7. For my community and my country, free education, free medication, agriculture, and road network.
8. For both, I would empower every citizen with a business, work opportunities, jobs, and education.
9. If I were the president of my country Nigeria, I would empower the youth by improving the educational sector and making education free. I would make skill acquisition centers where skills can be learned for free and after graduates would be placed in various sectors in the society where they can work to earn a living. The graduates could also gain enough experience to branch off on their own if they wanted to. I would make a stable power supply available to help small-scale industries and entrepreneurs grow their businesses. I would also, through the Central Bank of Nigeria, make low-interest loans accessible for start-up businesses to encourage independence.

Uplift and Empower:
What about your life makes you happy?
1. When my business improves, I am very happy.
2. When I am healthy, I am very happy because good health gives me hope.

3. I get very happy when I hear the word of God and when I get money. .
4. I get very happy when I hear the word of God and when I get money.
5. When my business improves, I get very happy.
6. When I make a lot of money selling fish, I am very happy.
7. I am very happy when I have a job.
8. When I am able to care for my kids and help others in the community, I am very happy.
9. I am happy and grateful to God for good health and a stable mind.

What about your life makes you hopeful for the future?
1. I will be hopeful in life when I own land for myself.
2. I will be hopeful in life when I own a big farm.
3. I will be hopeful in life when I buy land and build my own house.
4. I will be hopeful in life when I buy land and build my own house.
5. I will be hopeful in life when I own land for myself.
6. I will be hopeful in life when I own a big business for myself.
7. I will be hopeful in life when I buy land and build my own house.
8. I will be hopeful in life when I am able to care for myself.
9. I am hopeful for the future because I trust and believe in God to take care of me.

In the future, what do you see yourself doing?
1. I wish to be a very big businesswoman in the future.
2. I wish to own a very big business and a big farm in the future.

3. I wish for my children to have good education.
4. I wish for my children to have good education.
5. I wish to be a very big businesswoman in the future.
6. I wish to own a very big business in the future.
7. I wish for my children to have good education.
8. I wish to own a big business.
9. In the future, I see myself owning my own computer or IT firm and running it successfully.

What is your biggest goal / desire for yourself? For your children?
1. My biggest goal is to have a good partner who will help me and my children stay safe from this hard time.
2. My biggest goal is to improve my life and the lives of my children through education.
3. My biggest goal is to have property.
4. My biggest goal is to have property.
5. My biggest goal is to have a very big business.
6. My biggest goal is to improve my life and the lives of my children through education.
7. My biggest goal is to have property.
8. My biggest goal is to have a better life.
9. My biggest goal is to succeed in life, be financially independent, and give my children the best education at any level they aspire to achieve.

Made in the USA
Columbia, SC
31 August 2020